Everyday, we are bombarded with advertising images of the smiling service worker. The book is written with the aim of focusing beneath the surface of these fairytale images, to seek out and understand the reality of service workers' experience. Within the sociology of work and related literatures, there are an increasing number of empirical studies of different types of service work, but there has been little progress in attempts to theorize the nature of service work, per se. This book fills this gap by bringing together major scholars from the US and UK who use a range of critical perspectives to explore key elements in the organization and experience of contemporary service work. It will make an invaluable secondary text for advanced undergraduates and graduates studying courses/modules such as sociology of work, industrial sociology, social theory and work, organization studies, and organizational theory.

**Marek Korczynski** is Professor of Sociology of Work at Loughborough University. He is the author of *On the Front Line: Organization of Work in the Information Economy* (Cornell University Press, 1999, co-authored with Steve Frenkel, Karen Shire, and May Tam), *Social Theory at Work* (Oxford University Press, 2006, co-edited with Randy Hodson and Paul Edwards) and *Human Resource Management in Service Work* (Palgrave Macmillan, 2002).

**Cameron Lynne Macdonald** is Assistant Professor in the Sociology Department of the University of Wisconsin-Madison. She is the author of *Shadow Mothers: Nannies, Au Pairs, and the Micropolitics of Mothering* (University of California Press, forthcoming) and *Working in the Service Society* (Temple University Press, 1996, co-edited with Carmen Sirianni).

# Service Work

## Critical Perspectives

Edited by
Marek Korczynski and Cameron Lynne Macdonald

Routledge
Taylor & Francis Group
NEW YORK AND LONDON

Learning Resources
Centre

First published 2009
by Routledge
270 Madison Ave, New York, NY 10016

Simultaneously published in the UK
by Routledge
2 Park Square, Milton Park, Abingdon, Oxon OX14 4RN

*Routledge is an imprint of the Taylor & Francis Group, an informa business*

© 2009 Taylor & Francis

Typeset in Minion by
Swales & Willis Ltd, Exeter, Devon
Printed and bound in the United states of America on acid-free paper by
Walsworth Publishing Company, Marceline, MO

*Library of Congress Cataloging in Publication Data*
Service work: critical perspectives / edited by Marek Korczynski and Cameron Lynne Macdonald.
    p. cm.
Includes bibliographical references and index.
ISBN 978-0-415-95317-7 – ISBN 978-0-415-95316-0 – ISBN 978-0-203-89226-8
1. Service industries.   2. Service industries workers.   3. Service industries workers–Labor
unions.   4. Labor unions.   I. Korczynski, Marek.   II. Macdonald, Cameron Lynne.
HD9980.5.S42535 2009
331.7'93–dc22                                                          2008007926

ISBN10: 0–415–95316–2 (hbk)
ISBN10: 0–415–95317–0 (pbk)
ISBN10: 0–203–89226–7 (ebk)

ISBN13: 978–0–415–95316–0 (hbk)
ISBN13: 978–0–415–95317–7 (pbk)
ISBN13: 978–0–203–89226–8 (ebk)

For Sebastian

To Rob

# Contents

# List of Illustrations

**Figures**

**Tables**

# Notes on Contributors

**Alan Bryman** is Professor of Organizational and Social Research, Management Centre, University of Leicester, UK. His main research interests lie in research methodology, leadership, organizational analysis, and Disneyization. He is author or co-author of many books, including: *Quantity and Quality in Social Research* (Routledge, 1988), *Social Research Methods* (OUP, 2001, 2004, 2008), *Business Research Methods* (OUP, 2003, 2007), and *Disneyization of Society* (Sage, 2004). He is co-editor of *The SAGE Encyclopedia of Social Science Research* (Sage, 2004), *Handbook of Data Analysis* (Sage, 2004), and the forthcoming *Handbook of Organizational Research Methods* (Sage, 2008).

**Dorothy Sue Cobble** is a professor at Rutgers University where she teaches labor studies, history, and women's studies. Her books include *Dishing It Out: Waitresses and Their Unions in the Twentieth Century* (1991), which won the Herbert Gutman Book Award; *Women and Unions: Forging a Partnership* (1993); *The Other Women's Movement: Workplace Justice and Social Rights in Modern America* (2004), which won the 2005 Philip Taft Book Prize and other awards; and *The Sex of Class: Women Transforming American Labor* (2007). Her research has been funded by the Charles Warren Center, Harvard University; the Woodrow Wilson Center for International Scholars; the National Endowment for the Humanities; the American Council of Learned Societies and other sources.

**Yiannis Gabriel** is Professor of Organizational Theory at Royal Holloway, University of London. Earlier he held posts at Imperial College and the University of Bath. Yiannis has a degree in Mechanical Engineering from Imperial College London, where he also carried out postgraduate studies in industrial sociology. He has a PhD in Sociology from the University of California, Berkeley. Yiannis is well known for his work into organizational storytelling and narratives, leadership, management learning, the culture and politics of contemporary consumption and organizational psychoanalysis. He has used stories as a way of studying numerous social and organizational phenomena including leader-follower relations, group dynamics and fantasies, nostalgia, insults and apologies. He is the author of *Storytelling in Organizations* and *Organizations in Depth* and five other books. He has been editor of *Management Learning* and associate editor of *Human Relations*. His enduring fascination as a researcher lies in what he describes as the unmanageable qualities of life in and out of organizations.

**Marek Korczynski** is Professor of Sociology of Work at Loughborough University, UK. He is the author of *On the Front Line: Organization of Work in the Information Economy* (Cornell University Press, 1999, co-authored with Steve Frenkel, Karen Shire, and May Tam), *Social Theory at Work* (Oxford University Press, 2006, co-edited with Randy Hodson and Paul Edwards) and *Human Resource Management in Service Work* (Palgrave Macmillan, 2002), which, despite its title, puts forward a sociological analysis of service work and its management. He has edited special issues of: *Gender, Work and Organization* (2005 and 2009), *Journal of Consumer Culture* (2005) and *Human Resource Management Journal* (2005) on the topic of service work. He continues his exploration of the sociology of service work and combines this with research interests on music and work, and on social theory's engagement with work.

**Craig D. Lair** is a graduate of the University of Maryland. His interests include social theory, the sociology of work, and social process of individualization. He is currently working on a book, co-authored with George Ritzer, entitled *The Outsourcing of Everything: Creative Destruction or Destructive Creativity*.

**Cameron Lynne Macdonald** is Assistant Professor at the University of Wisconsin-Madison. She does research on the public/private intersections of caregiving. Her book, *Shadow Mothers: Nannies, Au Pairs, and the Micropolitics of Mothering*, is forthcoming with the University of California Press. She is also the co-editor, with Carmen Sirianni, of the collection, *Working in the Service Society*.

**David Merrill** is a dissertator in the sociology department at the University of Wisconsin-Madison. He has his Master's degree in sociology from the University of Connecticut. In addition to interests in the service sector, he also does work on gender and politics. His dissertation examines the ways in which unpaid caregiving affects civic and political participation. He has published works with Myra Marx Ferree on gender and social movements as well as with Cameron Lynne Macdonald on labor movements among paid caregivers.

**Michael Merrill** is the Dean of the Harry Van Arsdale Jr. Center for Labor Studies at Empire State College SUNY in New York City. He has a PhD in US economic history from Columbia University. His continuing research interests include the origins of commercial society, the transition to capitalism in the US, and the future of trade unionism. His publications include *The Key of Liberty: The Life and Democratic Writings of William Manning, "A Laborer," 1747–1814* (with Sean Wilentz), Harvard University Press (1993); and articles in *William and Mary Quarterly, Labor Studies Journal, Review, Labor History, Radical History Review, New Solutions,* and *Labor's Heritage.*

**Nanette Monin** is Associate Professor at Massey University, New Zealand. Working with the methodologies of narratology and poetics, her text analysis has exposed previously unrecognized social and ethical assumptions in classic management theory texts. She is the author of *Management Theory: A Critical and Reflexive Reading* (Routledge, 2004). She is on the editorial board of *Journal of Management Studies* and *Management and Organizational History.* She has co-edited: *Narratives of Business and Society in New Zealand: Differing Voices,* and *The Global Garage; Home-based Business in New Zealand.*

**Dennis Nickson** is Reader and Deputy Head of Department in the Department of Human Resource Management, University of Strathclyde, UK. He researches and writes in the broad area of human resource management in the service sector, with a particular interest in skills. He has published widely in these areas and is the author of *Human Resource Management for the Hospitality and Tourism Industries.*

**Rhacel Salazar Parreñas** received her PhD from the University of California-Berkeley. Her research focuses upon women, migration and globalization. Her research on migrant Filipina domestic workers has been featured in the *Wall Street Journal, American Prospect,* and was the basis for an award-winning documentary, *The Chain of Love,* by VPRO-TV in the Netherlands. She is the author of *Servants of Globalization* (2001), *Children of Global Migration* (2005), *Engendering Globalization* (in press), and co-editor of *Asian Diasporas* (2007).

**George Ritzer** is Distinguished University Professor at the University of Maryland. Among his awards are Honorary Doctorate from La

Trobe University, Melbourne, Australia; Honorary Patron, University Philosophical Society, Trinity College, Dublin; American Sociological Association's Distinguished Contribution to Teaching Award. Among his books in metatheory are *Sociology: A Multiple Paradigm Science* and *Metatheorzing in Sociology*. In the application of social theory to the social world, his books include *The McDonaldization of Society, Enchanting a Disenchanted World*, and *The Globalization of Nothing*. Sage has published two volumes of his collected works, one in theory and the other in the application of theory to the social world, especially consumption. In the latter area, he is founding editor of the *Journal of Consumer Culture*. He has edited the *Blackwell Companion to Major Social Theorists* and co-edited the *Handbook of Social Theory*. In addition to the *Encyclopedia of Sociology*, he has edited the two-volume *Encyclopedia of Social Theory*. His books have been translated into over twenty languages.

**Janet Sayers** is a Senior Lecturer at Massey University (Auckland, New Zealand). Her main research interest is in contemporary service experiences. Recent research has focused on how and why art (music and the visual arts) is being used by organizations to accentuate experience. She is also interested in how popular culture, especially comedy, comments on customer service experiences, and service workers' experiences. In her spare time she ferries children around to school, hobbies, friends' places and back again, and keeps them company at skate parks.

**Paul Thompson** is Professor of Organizational Analysis and Head of Department of Human Resource Management in the Business School at the University of Strathclyde, UK. Amongst his recent publications are *The Oxford Handbook of Work and Organization*, Oxford University Press (co-edited in 2004 with Stephen Ackroyd, Pam Tolbert and Rose Batt) and *Participation and Democracy at Work*, Palgrave (edited in 2005 with Bill Harley and Jeff Hyman). He has recently become editor of *Work, Employment and Society* (Research Notes and Debates and Controversies sections) as part of the incoming Strathclyde team. Working within traditions of labor process theory and critical realism his research interests focus on skill and work organization, control and resistance, organizational restructuring and changing political economies.

**Chris Warhurst** is Professor of Labor Studies and Co-Director of the Scottish Center for Employment Research at the University of Strathclyde in Glasgow, UK. His research interests focus on labor process and labor market developments and issues. Book publications include *Workplaces of the Future* (Macmillan, 1998), *The Skills that*

*Matter* (Palgrave, 2004) and *Work Less, Live More?* (Palgrave, 2008). He has published articles in journals such as *Sociology, Administrative Science Quarterly, Journal of Organisation Behaviour* and the *Journal of Management Studies.* He has worked in an advisory capacity for the Scottish and Hungarian governments and is currently co-editor of *Work, Employment and Society,* a journal of the British Sociological Association.

# Acknowledgments

The editors, Marek Korczynski and Cameron Lynne Macdonald, would like to thank all the authors who have contributed to this volume. We would also like to thank Barbara Gregory for her good secretarial help. Thanks also to Michael Bickerstaff and Stephen Rutter, our editors at Routledge. For service sector workers everywhere.

# CHAPTER 1

# Critical Perspectives on Service Work

## An Introduction

MAREK KORCZYNSKI AND CAMERON LYNNE MACDONALD

"Have a nice day," says the smiling fast food worker in a McDonald's advert. "Certainly, sir, I can sort that out for you straight away," says a call center worker, positively purring with contentment in a car insurance advert. "If there's anything else you need, just ask," says the smiling nurse to the patient in an advert for private health care.

Everyday, we are bombarded with images of smiling service workers, happy to be able to serve customers. There is also a managerial, quasi-academic, literature which seeks to peddle similar images of happy service workers creating happy customers. Here, we are told about how service work can be organized for a win:win:win scenario for customer, workers and managers. Zemke and Schaaf's discussion of Marriott Hotels captures this nicely (1989, p.118):

> The current Mr. Marriott credits his father with the philosophy of taking care of employees as he wanted them to take care of the customer. "My father knew if he had happy employees, he would have happy customers and that would result in a good bottom line."

In order to study the realm of service work we need to pan beneath the surface of these fairy-tale images of the smiling customer service inter-action. We need theoretical lenses to focus the camera to allow us to see the Disney employee stripped of his dignity and his job for having his hair too long (Van Maanen, 1991), to see the increasingly detailed managerial instructions to employees regarding personal appearance in service jobs (Nickson *et al.*, 2005), to see meter-tall signs saying "Smile" and "Be Friendly" in the staff-only space of a supermarket (Tolich, 1993), to see the tears of pain and resentment among call center employees who have been abused one too many times by customers on a given day (Korczynski, 2003), and to see the resistance among staff who have been told to sell more to customers, but who do not want to force products on customers (Korczynski *et al.*, 2000).

Each of the authors in this book has taken up this challenge and uses a different theoretical lens with which to focus the camera upon the organization and experience of contemporary service work. The book can be thought of as a follow-up to *Working in the Service Society*, published in 1996, and edited by Cameron Lynne Macdonald and Carmen Sirianni. That book featured a series of micro-analyses of different forms of service work, from bank workers to fast food workers and from nannies to waitresses. By bringing those analyses of different service occupations in one place, that book played an important role in placing service work as central to a new sociology of work. The last decade has seen a burgeoning of research in similar areas. For instance, we have seen an explosion of research into the organization of, and experience of call center work, hotel and resort work, and care work of all kinds (Adler and Adler, 2005; Sherman, 2007; Zimmerman *et al.* 2006).

Such a turn to unearth the nature of service jobs, within what after all is a service economy, is very much to be welcomed. However, while the empirical gap in our knowledge of service work is being filled, there is a lingering sense that our *overall theoretical understanding of service work has not advanced in the same way*. Hence, the need for this book. We may have a good deal of empirical research into emotional labor demands made of flight attendants, into control systems in call centers, into peer relations in hospitality jobs, and into the pains and pleasures of care work, but there have been few attempts to develop our theoretical understandings across various types of service work, across service work *per se*. Our primary aim, with this book, is to kick-start work at this theoretical level. And this level is a fundamentally important one. The book brings together authors with different perspectives to offer answers to the key questions: *What types of service jobs do we have? With what implications for workers?* The answers offered at the theoretical level seek to articulate key essential elements in contemporary service work across various types of service occupations. What is *essential* within the nature of contemporary service work, of course, is a contested issue. Different theoretical perspectives tend to highlight different aspects of jobs as capturing the essence of the jobs. While class, control and resistance are the essential aspects of jobs from a Marxist perspective, from a feminist perspective, essential elements in the nature of jobs are the ways in which gender is played out and reproduced. Different perspectives give different ways of looking at different points of focus and lead inevitably to different answers to the same core root question (Korczynski et al., 2006). Such differences are at the very heart of debate, and debate is what we need to take forward further our understanding of service work. If the book provokes such debate, then it will have served its purpose well. Yiannis Gabriel's concluding chapter certainly offers some important pointers on how such a debate may usefully develop.

The rest of this introductory chapter sets out the context for the specific chapters in the book. It does this, first of all, by defining what we mean by service work, and by laying out how service work has historically been neglected within theoretical approaches to the sociology of work, and finally, by raising the critical questions that the chapters that follow will address.

## Service Work and Its Analysis

When attempting to define service work, it is useful to take as a starting point the simple abstraction that all jobs involve work on materials, information or people. Service work can be defined as work that involves working on people. The presence of the service-recipient within the labor process is the central definitional element of service work. Sometimes, such jobs involving direct contact with a service-recipient are labeled front line, or customer-contact, service jobs, and are distinguished from back-of-house, or back-office workers. The latter may work in service organizations but have no direct contact with service-recipients. The main, but not exclusive, focus of the chapters in this book is upon the service jobs involving direct contact with service-recipients. Service work in this sense involves intangibility, perishability (service work cannot be stored), variability (of service recipient expectations and actions), simultaneous production and consumption and inseparability of production from consumption. Scholars have taken one or more these aspects and drawn up sub-categories of service work against them, giving rise to such categories of mass services, service shops and professional services (see Korczynski, 2002). For instance, Leidner (1993) has charted three types of service work against the dimension of inseparability (of the service interaction from the product being sold). First, there are jobs with a weak degree of inseparability such that the service interaction has little bearing on what is sold and consumed. Fast food jobs are good examples here. Second, there are jobs where "a product exists apart from the interaction, but a particular type of experience is an important part of the service. For example . . . airline passengers who buy tickets primarily to get from one place to another are promised friendly service on their journey." Finally, there are jobs where "the interaction is inseparable from the product being sold or delivered – for instance, in psychotherapy . . . or teaching." This book's main focus is on the first two types of service jobs – jobs which are mainly occupied by the "emotional proletariat," to use Macdonald and Merrill's phrase from this volume. Macdonald and Merrill estimate that 29 percent of workers in the US labor force work in the emotional proletariat.

Whyte has pointed out that "when workers and customers meet . . . that relationship adds a new dimension to the pattern of human relations in industry" (1946, p.123). At the very least, then, the worker-service recipient relationship constitutes an aspect unique to the sociology of service work. Within studies of specific service jobs and occupations, the worker-service recipient relationship has been examined in terms of sexualization, of degrees of worker or service-recipient servility, of who controls the interaction, and of degrees of social embeddedness and economic instrumentalism. More profoundly, it has been argued that the addition of this "new dimension to the pattern of human relations" has crucial knock-on effects upon key aspects of work organization, such as the labor process, division of labor, nature of control and forms of authority, and upon the subjective experience of work (Korczynski, 2002). Hochschild's *The Managed Heart* (1983), with its exploration of emotional labor within service occupations, constituted the first important step in this direction. Hochschild alerted us directly to a key unexplored aspect of the service labor process, but also indirectly to how emotional labor demands have important implications for forms of management control and peer relations.

More recently, the emerging literature on aesthetic labor (Warhurst *et al.*, 2003) has also signaled the need to study a previously unexplored part of the labor process that while not unique to service work is likely to be more salient for service work than for work on information and materials. The recognition of the impact of the service-recipient within the labor process upon the wider organization of work has also led some authors to suggest the need to move away from a focus on a management-labor dyad within employment towards to a conceptualization based around a customer-worker-management triangle (Leidner, 1993). Such an approach may necessitate a rethinking of such core sociology of work concepts as conflict, resistance, control and perhaps, by implication, class.

## Service Work and Social Theory: Chapter Outlines

The terrain for social theory's analysis of work, and the neglect of service work within this, was set by Marx, Weber and Durkheim. Readers hoping for a serious consideration of service work in any of the writings of these founding fathers will be disappointed. Each, in his own way, was concerned with the internal logic of work organizations, and with articulating the best way to conceptualize the dyadic relationship between employer and worker. We may forgive their neglect in the sense that their theorizing was primarily informed by the key ruptures in society and in work organizations that occurred during the time of their writing. The rise of the factory system and the development of a civil service bureaucracy stood before Marx and Weber as the two emblematic developments of their time. But, of course, during all this time, forms of service work continued to be key sites of employment.

If social theorists did not turn their eyes to service work, at least some artists did. For instance, we can think of the unsettling picture of the young woman serving behind the bar in Manet's (1882) *Bar at the Folies-Bergère*. And there is Charlie Chaplin's depiction of a singing waiter in his classic *Modern Times* (1936). It has been our historical blinkers that have cast his mocking of factory work as the key motif of this film. Refreshingly, Janet Sayers and Nanette Monin in the second chapter of this book remind us that an important part of the film actually involves Chaplin and his sweetheart involved in service work at the Red Moon Café. Sayers and Monin argue that there is much that is prescient in the scenes at the Red Moon Café. They focus their analysis on the scene in which Chaplin, laughably, has to perform as a singing waiter – just after he has flung off the lyrics to the song that were written on his shirt cuffs. For Sayers and Monin, however, there is nothing laughable in the underlying message that Chaplin is articulating about service work as a commercialization of humanity.

Some of the first theoretical formulations of the implications of the shift to a service-based economy came from George Ritzer and Alan Bryman. Ritzer's McDonaldization hypothesis extended Max Weber's famous theory of rationalization and of the ultimate instrument of rational organization, bureaucracy. He argued that the increasing pervasiveness of rationalization can best be conceptualized in terms of McDonaldization. He sees McDonald's as a clear and easily recognizable manifestation of how far rationalization has gone in contemporary societies. McDonald's epitomizes the process of McDonaldization, but for Ritzer, this process applies to many spheres of life other than just a popular fast food chain. Ritzer defined McDonaldization as encompassing the process of rationalization along four dimensions: efficiency, calculability (or the emphasis on measurement), predictability and control. Wherever there is an emphasis on these four dimensions, the process of McDonaldization can be said to be in motion. At McDonald's the emphasis on these dimensions has been such that a Big Mac is prepared and served in precisely the same way anywhere in the world, accompanied by the compulsory cross-selling garnish, "would you like fries with that?" The fact that the consumer knows exactly what kind of interaction to expect and how to interface with workers in every chain, be it in a fast-food restaurant, a nail salon, or a phone sex service, creates uniform quality for the consumer, economic success for the owner and spiritually deadening interactions for the service worker. Ritzer (1998) has also explicitly argued that McDonaldization can be seen as a dominant force in the service sector of economies. Although the McDonaldization thesis has come under sustained criticism, not least from writers from other critical perspectives (Smart, 1999; Korczynski, 2002; Warhurst *et al.* this volume), it did set an important benchmark in the need for social theory to critically engage with the service economy.

In Chapter 3, Ritzer (with co-author, Craig D. Lair) applies both his McDonaldization thesis and the argument presented in *The Globalization of Nothing* (2004), to understand key trends in the nature of contemporary service work, epitomized by the trend towards outsourced call center work in India. The concept of "nothing" refers to the proliferation of inter-actions, products, and concepts that are centrally conceived and controlled, and therefore devoid of any distinctive content. Ritzer advances this con-cept in opposition to that of "something," that is locally specific, culturally rich, and indigenously controlled social forms. Ritzer, previously, has articulated the concept of "nothing" with reference to consumption. In this chapter, he extends the argument towards service and he centers his analy-sis on the global call center work as an example of a content-free job. Interactions are carefully scripted and the worker is expected to erase all aspects of the local and specific from the customer service interaction to the extent of masking his or her geographic location.

In Chapter 4, we reprint Alan Bryman's 1999 original statement of his thesis of the Disneyization of society. He extends Ritzer's McDonaldiza-tion hypothesis to apply aspects of postmodern theory to consumer culture and the service organizations that organize it. Here the author emphasizes how theming, the dedifferentiation of consumption, merchandising, and the extraction of emotional labor from workers combine to create a dis-tinctly inauthentic and hypercapitalist workplace. As Bryman points out, "the ever-smiling Disney theme park employee has become a stereotype of modern culture." One need only visit the newly-sanitized corporate-branded theme park that is New York's Times Square to see how far Disneyization has penetrated into consumer culture, and thus service interactions.

Chapters 5 and 6 offer a glimpse of what Weber and Marx might have theorized had they lived to see service-based economies. Marek Korczynski explores the contradictions that emerge when bureaucratic principles of efficiency and impersonality are joined with the service organization's need to provide the customer with an enchanting sense of sovereignty. Korczynski argues that service organizations seek to not only create profit by emphasizing efficiency, but also by appealing to customers' sense of service quality, or enchantment. He examines the way in which service work is organized along dual principles of bureaucratization and customer-orientation. Implicitly, service work is organized as a customer-oriented bureaucracy. It is this contradictory structure of the organization of service work that gives rise to the common finding from research that service workers' lived experience of their jobs is a contradictory one. The customer, for instance, is often conceived of as "our friend, the enemy."

Chris Warhurst, Paul Thompson, and Dennis Nickson apply labor process theorizing, originally rooted in Marxist analysis, to service work in Chapter 6. They argue against those who posit service work as the production and consumption of "nothing" and service economies as based predominantly on consumption rather than production. For these authors, claims about qualitative breaks associated with service work, or particular aspects of it, are over-stated and labor process theory offers a vital source of critique of such claims. They point out that service is still focused on the provision and preparation for sale to customers of materiality – beds, burgers and handbags for example. Research within the labor process tradition, from Braverman on, has long had a focus on service work. Indeed, they point out that some of the key developments in the analysis of aesthetic labor and emotional labor within service work have come from research informed by the labor process tradition.

Cameron Lynne Macdonald and David Merrill turn in Chapter 7 from the process of service production to the equally important question, "Who fills what service jobs and why?" Focusing on jobs in the "Emotional Proletariat," they apply theories of intersectionality to explore how and why the emotional proletariat is a gendered ghetto that is simultaneously segmented by ethnicity and social class. Applying feminist theories of intersectionality to discrimination in hiring practices, they demonstrate how the complexities of the service interaction – the implications of customer "preferences" in the service triangle, the investment of the service worker's gendered or ethnic identity as both a selling tool and an inextricable aspect of the service itself – create new and more intractable forms of discrimination in hiring.

Rhacel Salazar Parreñas takes this understanding of gendered service work further in Chapter 8 by pointing to the theoretical significance of the thousands of women who migrate from poor countries to rich ones to provide caring labor. As she points out, the international market in care work leads to an unequal distribution of care resources in the global economy, affecting not only the economies of sending and receiving countries, but also the families left behind by care workers and the lower-tier care workers who care for them. Caring work is after all, women's work, once provided gratis by wives and mothers to their families. This "reproductive labor" now must be replaced in rich countries where women find economic opportunities outside the home and must outsource or replace their housework, childcare and elderly care. Parreñas makes a convincing case for the role of the state in the unequal distribution of care work, not only in migration policies, but in the extent and nature of welfare provisions and the degree to which families must privately contract for care.

Dorothy Sue Cobble and Michael Merrill's chapter on the prospects for service sector unionism brings together aspects of the preceding chapters to indicate both the challenges and opportunities for the labor movement. As they point out, many governments (particularly the US), prevent service-sector organizing by legally forbidding a substantial percentage of service workers from forming unions. Relationships with customers can be an important lever in workers' attempts to mobilize broad support. On the other hand, the extent to which workers identify with their jobs means that workers may privilege self-images as altruistic carers over fair pay and working hours, for example. The extent to which service workers must bring aspects of the self to their work plays both an enabling and an inhibiting role in worker activism. Workers may organize collectively around ethnic, gender and occupational identities, facilitating the creation of non-government organizations and other social support organizations. In this respect her conclusion brings us full circle to classical social theory, offering a vision of occupation-based solidarity that might make Emile Durkheim proud.

In the concluding chapter, Yiannis Gabriel takes up many of themes outlined in the book to look in a new way at the "the tug of war between employees and employers" that has been reconfigured as a customer-worker-management triangle. He focuses particularly on the aspect of care, which he sees as a key dimension in many forms of service work. Care constitutes a key element in the distinctiveness of service work for it cannot be reduced to the enactment of different emotional scripts or resistance to such scripts. Applying psychoanalytic theory, he proposes that care work unleashes certain emotional dynamics that stem from early life experiences that all humans have when, in a state of infantile dependency, they must rely on others for their survival and well-being. This generates a deep ambivalence both for service workers and their customers and this leads to a process of "splitting" to cope with such ambivalence. The psychological process of splitting itself implies a key role for the unleashing of fantasies within service work encounters. He argues that the likelihood of the playing out of fantasies from both customer and worker means that there is a considerable degree of unpredictability and even unmanageability at the service interface. Attempts to theorize this interface must address this unpredictability and unmanageability.

It is apt indeed that the concluding chapter seeks to explore and draw out the importance of ambivalence in service work, for, as these chapter summaries suggest, taken together, the various theoretical perspectives that comprise the critical analysis of service work do not leave us with pat answers. While individual chapters throw up key insights, there appears, on the surface, to be little in the way of shared clear-cut conclusions among the authors. There are three main approaches that can be adopted in the face of such insights presented from multiple critical perspectives. The postmodern approach would be to accept such theoretical ambivalence as reflecting the ambivalence of social reality. Life is a collage and so social theory must also exist as a collage, in which disparate insights from disparate perspectives co-exist. This is the inevitable state of social theory and there is nothing to be gained in seeking to push such forms of knowledge into one frame, or meta-narrative, of contemporary service work. A second approach is to throw one's weight behind one perspective and to construct a case for the superiority of that perspective against others. There is certainly something of this approach within the spirited case put forward by Chris Warhurst and colleagues for labor process theory in this volume. A third approach, that, for us, is likely to be the most fruitful, is to seek to build analytical bridges between some of the perspectives put forward in this volume, to highlight the points of shared understandings that can drive forward a broad critical sociology of service work. Certainly, the approach of intersectionality, that underpins the chapter by Cameron Lynne Macdonald and David Merrill, is embedded in the need for dialogue between analytical approaches. Similarly, the conclusion of Marek Korczynski's chapter on understanding service work through the ideal type of a customer-oriented bureaucracy asks for the productive interplay between critical sociological perspectives. If this volume throws up ambivalence, we invite readers to take up the challenge to develop the critical sociology of service work so that future anthologies on service work can begin to construct synthesis from ambivalence.

## References

Adler, P. and Adler, P. (2005) *Paradise Laborers: Hotel Work in the Global Economy*, Ithaca, NY: ILR Press.

Hochschild, A. (1983) *The Managed Heart*, Berkeley, CA: University of California Press.

Korczynski, M. (2002) *Human Resource Management in Service Work*, Basingstoke: Palgrave Macmillan.

Korczynski, M. (2003) "Communities of coping: Collective emotional labor in service work," *Organization*, 10, 1, 55–79.

Korczynski, M., Shire, K., Frenkel, S. and Tam, M. (2003) "Service work in consumer capitalism: Customers, control and contradictions," *Work, Employment and Society*, 14, 4, 669–87.

Korczynski, M., Hodson, R., and Edwards, P. (2006) "Introduction: Competing, Collaborating and Reinforcing Theories," in M. Korczynski, R. Hodson, and Edwards, P. (eds.), *Social Theory at Work*, Oxford University Press, 1–24.

Leidner, R. (1993) *Fast Food, Fast Talk*, Berkeley, CA: University of California Press.

Macdonald, Cameron L. and Sirianni, C. (eds.) (1996) *Working in the Service Society*, Philadelphia, PA: Temple University Press.

Nickson, D., Warhurst, C. and Dutton, E. (2005) "The importance of attitude and appearance in the service encounter in retail and hospitality," *Managing Service Quality*, 15, 2, 195–208.

Ritzer, G. (1998) *The McDonaldization Thesis*, Thousand Oaks, CA: Pine Forge Press.

Ritzer, G. (2004) *The Globalization of Nothing*, Thousand Oaks, CA: Pine Forge Press.

Sherman, R. (2007) *Class Acts: Service and Inequality in Luxury Hotels*, Berkeley, CA: University of California Press.

Smart, B. (ed.) (1999) *Resisting McDonaldization*, London: Sage.

Tolich, M. (1993) "Alienating and liberating emotions at work," *Journal of Contemporary Ethnography*, 22, 3, 361–81.

Van Maanen, J. (1991) "The smile factory: work at Disneyland," in P. Frost, L. Moore, M. Louis, C. Lundberg, and J. Martin (eds.), *Reframing Organisational Culture*, Newbury Park, CA: Sage.

Warhurst, C., Witz, A. and Nickson, D. (2003) "The labor of aesthetics and the aesthetics of organization," *Organization*, 10, 1, 33–54.

Whyte, W. (1946) "When workers and customer meet," in W. Whyte (ed.), *Industry and Society*, New York: McGraw Hill, 123–47.

Zemke, R. and Schaaf, D. (eds.) (1989) *The Service Edge: 101 Companies that Profit from Customer Care*, New York: NAL Books.

Zimmerman, M.K., Litt, J.S. and Bose, C.E. (eds.) (2006) *Global Dimensions of Gender and Carework*, Stanford, CA: Stanford University Press.

# CHAPTER 2

# Chaplin's *Modern Times*

## *Service Work, Authenticity, and Nonsense at the Red Moon Café*

JANET SAYERS AND NANETTE MONIN

## Introduction

In *Modern Times*, Chaplin's masterpiece about work, he discusses in depth and with much subtlety and humor, the effect of the relentless modernizing machine on the Self. The first factory scene of *Modern Times* is a very powerful allegorical statement about the effect of automation on the individual, but in the Red Moon Café and dance hall which is the final workplace for the Little Tramp, Chaplin also shows a sophisticated understanding of the challenges, ambiguities and contradictions that face the service worker. He shows service workers are even more pervasively controlled than those toiling in the factories.

Chaplin's movie is prescient and still brilliant, and the issues he raises in this film have now been taken up in contemporary critical management literature. These issues include: the management of the body, emotional labor, aesthetic labor, the role of the customer as both co-producer and manager in service work, and the issue of authenticity, amongst others (Abercrombie, 1994; Hochschild, 1983; Korczynski, 2002; Leidner, 1993; Sturdy *et al.*, 2001).

*Modern Times* is famous for its political and social polemic. Chaplin, in middle-age and at the height of his creative powers when this movie was made, was a political man with firmly held humanitarian views. Chaplin was preoccupied during much of the 1930s with the social effects of the Depression and with the rise of nationalism, with unemployment, strikes, political intolerance, and with economic inequalities. He was also very concerned about automation and its effect on workers (Chaplin, 1974; Maland, 1989; McCaffrey, 1971b). Chaplin explored his concerns through his own art form – comedy – and the iconic image of the Tramp being sucked up by and spewed back out of a huge machine has come to symbolize these concerns.

However, the movie is more than political rhetoric about the effects of industrialism and capitalism. What makes the scenes at the Red Moon Café particularly noteworthy is the self-reflexivity that is apparent in Chaplin's comedic method, as he gracefully but tragically sacrifices his own stage persona, the Little Tramp, to the inevitability of technological progress. An early signal of this reflexivity is given when the Tramp is compromised in the machine's bowels. A second look shows Chaplin himself being ground through the wheels of the film industry; rolled through the cogs of a movie projector.

This chapter discusses *Modern Times* in light of contemporary debates regarding service work, because the movie reveals many insights into the debates that currently concern critical scholars, and consequently readers of this book. Our initial analysis of the movie worked with Monin's (2004) critical reading method (Sayers and Monin, 2004). This chapter, based on our initial analysis, is structured as follows: first, we provide some background to the wider themes of the movie, and the comedy of Charlie Chaplin; second, we provide a description of the Red Moon Café setting of the movie and highlight some of its crucial events; third we discuss the movie's narrative in the light of Chaplin's critique of service work; and finally, we allow ourselves to be uplifted by Chaplin's movie and briefly discuss why comedy does matter. We suggest that there is sense in the seemingly nonsensical and heartbreaking solution Chaplin offers – the Nonsense Song.

## The Little Tramp, Chaplin and *Modern Times*

When the Little Tramp is swallowed by the monstrous machine and then spewed back out again, the event evokes the central terrible dilemma for workers in industrial times; the preservation of their essential self, body and soul, in the face of the vast uncaring industrial age. Time was a major theme in *Modern Times*, and modern time is timed to suit the vagaries of production, not the fragile bodies and emotional needs of the ordinary toiling person. Like many recent scholars of service work, Chaplin was concerned with showing the effects of industrialism on the individual: on their emotions (Hochschild, 1983), and even on their souls (Rose, 1990), and the relationship between consumption and the world of work (Du Gay, 1996). So, for example, in the first factory sequence of *Modern Times* we view the Tramp, desperately trying to preserve, in his inimitable fashion, the natural functions of his body. His need to itch, to eat, to swat a fly, to urinate in private, is offered up for our amusement, as the agents of the relentless modernizing machine – his supervisor, his fellow workers, the factory manager, inventors, marketers – all attempt to force him to live in-time with industrialization.

Many unforgettable images pepper the early factory sequences: the supreme significance accorded the clock that begins the movie; the working day for the men as they stream into the factory and clock-in; the herd of white sheep with the one black one; the size of the factory's machines compared to the smallness of the men inside; the Tramp being "eaten" and then spewed back out again; being the guinea pig for a newly invented feeding machine; and even the Tramp clocking out to go to the toilet, but then being confronted with a virtual factory manager watching his every move and then ordering him back to work (Kuriyama, 1992). The message here is that workers do not own any aspect of their lives. The Tramp offers a response to this intense pressure, as he does several times in the movie. He opts to go mad, albeit gracefully, in a chaotic pan-like ballet that completely disrupts the factory. The Tramp's crazy ballet-like dance brings the factory to a standstill.

These first factory scenes make so many powerful statements about industrialization that it is easy to forget the rest of the movie. But the movie is about more than factory work. In addition to working on the assembly line, and as a mechanic's assistant (when the Tramp returns to the factory in the middle of the movie), the Little Tramp tries his hand at other types of work, including as a laborer on the waterfront, a security guard at a department store and a singing waiter at the Red Moon Café. And as well as working, and spending time in other institutions like a mental hospital, and a prison, the Little Tramp falls in love with a kindred spirit also struggling to find her place in the world in the face of vast uncaring opposition, the Gamin, as played by Chaplin's real-life romantic partner, Paulette Goddard. The Gamin is a victim of capitalism through her family's tragedy (her father is shot by police during an unemployment demonstration, and her sisters are taken to an orphanage).

Goddard has a key role in how Chaplin interprets service work, especially when he raises the specter of consumption. The relationship between consumption and production in service work is central, and Chaplin shows throughout the movie that he is aware of the ambiguities and contradictions that face modern subjects when there is inter-dependence between industrial capitalism and conspicuous consumption (the effects of which are also explored by Bauman, 1998; and Korczynski and Ott,

2004). For instance, the Tramp picks up work for a while in a department store as a security guard, where he is meant to be protecting the cathedral to luxury and plenty from theft. The Department store as a retail form evolved to take the mass-produced products of the factory to market (Lancaster, 1995). Prior to his inevitable failure as a security worker (he gets drunks with burglars), the Tramp and the Gamin act out a fantasy of plenty with cake, a luxurious fur coat, children's toys and a comfortable bed. The department store's world of desire is a tipping point for the Tramp. He is usually a simple man with simple needs, and he desperately wants to provide for the Gamin. However, love blinds him to the seductive power of their fantasy. The Tramp, driven by his nature to please, dons some skates from the toy department and a blindfold and performs a show-off ice-dance increasingly close to an unprotected precipice on a mezzanine. This is just one of three major scenes where the seductiveness of consumption is presented in fantasy sequences, as paradises, and which feature the Gamin in a siren-like role, luring the Tramp into spiritual danger, despite her being his muse.

So, we can see that the Tramp's dilemma is that he needs to work, but his nature is to be free. Charlie Chaplin himself in real life is also in a pickle. Chaplin was facing immense pressure at the time this movie was made as the film industry was undergoing radical innovation because of technological progress. *Modern Times* was released almost ten years into the advent of the "talkies," and Chaplin was a magnate of the silent film industry and his greatest invention, the Little Tramp, was a silent film star (see Attenborough (1992) for a film about Chaplin's life); Chaplin was reticent to let him talk on screen (Chaplin, 1964). The Tramp's comedy was innately physical, not verbal, and Chaplin considered he would not translate successfully to the new medium.

Consequently *Modern Times* is not only a social commentary on industrialism and its problems, but a personal treatise on Chaplin's own situation. The movie is both a piece of political rhetoric, but also a personal meditation from a man who spent almost his entire life in service as a performer, and was now facing redundancy.

Chaplin had complete control over all aspects of the production of his movie, but his mental state was often fragile as he suffered from depression. He was a workaholic and a perfectionist at the height of his powers: he was writer and director, he composed the soundtrack, and played the main character (he shared main billing with Paulette Goddard). When he filmed scenes, the process was more akin to writing, redrafting and editing than with modern film-making. He often obsessively re-filmed scenes hundred of times, until he was satisfied. Creation was painful, but commentators have argued that pain was the source of Chaplin's comedy, and that Chaplin knew this, and deliberately called on it to fuel his creative visions. Through comedy Chaplin worked out his "strategy for living" (Stewart, 1976). Comedy was, quite literally, his therapy (Kuriyama, 1992).

For instance, Chaplin's constant use of food gags emanated from a childhood of starvation and deprivation according to both himself and his commentators (Chaplin, 1964; Kuriyama, 1992). He always remembered the fragility of life without enough food, and this gave him a strong sympathetic connection to the victims of industrialization. In *Modern Times* food gags are elevated to an art form. Throughout the movie there are running references to the body's dependency on food and the ways that industrialism has forced this relationship askew. There is an uneasy sense of play around organic and mechanical artifacts, ingested by and entering each other: Chaplin ingesting bolts from the feeding machine; the impaled and fortune-less duck in the Red Moon Café scene; and the Little Tramp himself processed in the belly of the machine. Food is essential to life, is organic, and yet must be "produced" through work and processed by machines to be eaten. Yet, the meaning of food, the fundamental building block of survival and life, is queasily changed in Chaplin's comedy.

Another example of the self-referential aspects of the movie is Chaplin's distrust of authority figures. His family was abandoned by his father, and then the Tramp was put in a workhouse when he was a child as his mother could not feed and care for her two boys. She also suffered mental illness and Chaplin was terrified that he too would succumb to madness (Kuriyama, 1992). The Tramp's experiences with authority in institutions as a child were clearly not pleasant although he avoided discussing this time of his life. Not surprisingly then psychoanalysts have enjoyed deconstructing Chaplin's comedies and their perspectives have fueled readings of *Modern Times* that not only use Marx, but also Freud and Marcuse (Girgus, 1996). Further psychoanalytical readings of *Modern Times* have been concerned with Chaplin's portrayal of women in his movies. Tyler (1985) has argued that Chaplin saw women, authority and technology as synonymous and a close reading of *Modern Times* does attest to a distrust of the psychological power women had over him. Chaplin had intense and troubled relationships with women and these are a matter of public record: he had two expensive divorces with very young women by the time he met Paulette Goddard and he felt immense guilt about his own mother (Kuriyama, 1992).

So, to recap, *Modern Times* can be read in two main ways, as a political and social statement on industrialism and its negative effects on body and mind, and as a personal allegorical statement regarding Chaplin's situation vis-à-vis developments in the film industry. To signal the rest of our discussion, we contend that in the Red Moon Café scene we see the Little Tramp's exploits within industrialism, and Chaplin's self-reflexive meditation on his own situation, converge in a moment of pure authenticity as they join in the perfect but doomed fusion of performer and audience in the "Nonsense Song." Chaplin makes sense by giving us nonsense. And it all makes perfect sense. Why? We answer this question by looking specifically at the Red Moon Café scene, and we start by briefly describing the sequence of events that make up this part of the movie.

### The Red Moon Café Scenes

The second to last main sequence of *Modern Times* takes place in the Red Moon Café, which, from a sign outside, we can see is known for its singing waiters. Paulette Goddard, playing the Gamin, has been transformed from street urchin to smart Café dancer. At the introduction to the Café sequence the camera lingers on a carousel and then switches to a scene of the Gamin, dancing in a wild and carefree pirouette dance in the street outside the café. The carousel, circling to calliope music, and the dipping and dancing of the Gamin are directly juxtaposed. Goddard is dancing in the street, but the value of her movement, aesthetic beauty and playfulness is "discovered" by an entrepreneur, who recognizes her potential. He has his eye on the street, on her, but his back is to his business as he says to his companion "She'd be good at the café." The scene then moves immediately to the Gamin, transformed into costume, dancing to rapturous applause. She is ideally suited to this work, being beautiful, graceful, and in need of a job.

After the scene depicting the success of the Gamin as a working dancer, the next scene shows the Gamin picking up the Tramp as he leaves the police station. In this scene the focus is on the Gamin's transformed appearance. She fusses with her new clothes; she has changed out of the ragged dress she has worn so far. The Tramp immediately notices her new clothes and admires her. The Gamin signals that she has found him a job and convinces both an unsure Café owner and nervous Tramp to have a trial. The Café owner asks if the Tramp can sing, and the Gamin insists he can. This scene is used to build tension towards the Tramp's first utterances on film. The Tramp looks to the camera, and the audience, sharing his concern about his ability to vocalize. He nods towards the audience as the suspense builds towards his first-long awaited vocalizations on film.

Once it is agreed that the Tramp will trial as a waiter, he experiences a new kind of work, different and yet the same, from what he experienced in the factory. The Red Moon Café has a large dance floor with tables around the edges, and a band playing on the podium. It is a fairly plain room, but on the wall there is a wagon wheel that is reminiscent of the clock which introduces the movie. A large chandelier hangs above the dance floor, also carrying through the clock symbol. His boss is the maître de, but he is also bossed about by customers. First the Tramp tangles with a rich citizen's dog. He also has to deal with a complaining customer, and some drunken customers.

The kitchen is a chaotic environment where one man is even sawing wood. At one point the Tramp drills holes in a very large block of cheese, and takes out the cheese, now supposedly Swiss cheese, to a customer. Through most of this kitchen scene the customers can be seen dancing to music through a swinging door.

A difficult customer complains "I've been waiting an hour for roast duck!" The maître de reprimands the Tramp and upset, the Tramp enters the "Out" door from the kitchen to the restaurant, and not the "In" door as he should. He knocks over a fellow worker carrying a large tray of food and chaos ensues in the kitchen. In an echo of the factory scene where the Tramp feeds his supervisor, hopelessly compromised in the machine, the maître de (still berating the Tramp about carving the duck) is called away by another customer – the maître de is as much at the beck and call of the customer as the Little Tramp is himself.

The Tramp attempts to deliver the roast duck to the complaining customer. But he is swept away, again and again, by a crowd of dancers who swirl the struggling Tramp, who is desperately trying to serve the customer, around the dance floor (see Figure 2.1).

The duck he is delivering gets caught on the chandelier so that when the Tramp eventually makes it to the customer's table, he is without duck. Eventually the duck is retrieved, but while the Tramp is still trying to serve the customer, the duck is again taken by a group of drunk football-playing customers – the duck becomes a football in their antics as the Tramp tries to rescue it, but the Tramp has made a hopeless waiter. The owner tells the Tramp he has failed as a waiter, but he gives him one last chance as a singing waiter.

The Tramp is very apprehensive as four singing waiters appear as a prelude to his appearance. The lyrics of the singing waiters can be heard on the movie's soundtrack, saying, "You can hear the darkies singing." In the wings, the Gamin assists the Tramp in his preparation by writing on his cuff the words of the song he is to sing, so he can remember them. After a short practice run, the Tramp strides out onto the dance floor for his première as a singing waiter. He flings out his arms and loses his cuffs. He is left with no words and so he stalls, and then stalls again. The Gamin, from offstage, mouths, "Sing!!" Never mind the words." The Tramp improvises, making up a nonsense song full of gibberish and well-placed Italian-sounding phrases using a popular song tune. His song and dance is a success and he leaves the floor to tumultuous applause, even coming back for an encore. The owner is very pleased and offers him a job, saying "You're great!! I'll give you a steady job." But the Tramp's triumph is

**Figure 2.1** The Tramp being swirled around the dance floor

brief as juvenile officials show up at the club and try to take the Gamin away as an escaped juvenile. The Tramp and the Gamin run off from the café and the authorities (Chaplin, 1936).

### Discussion of Service Work Themes

In the café scene, Chaplin carries through his concerns: with time; authority; the role of language; the dilemma of the individual in the face of massive economic and industrial change; and his own decidedly ambiguous feelings about technology which he both loved and feared in equal measure. The Café sequence is still about the relentless external pressures of modernity on the individual self, but these concerns hone in around the effect of these pressures on the psychology and emotions of the individual engaged in service work. The pressures that the Tramp faces in the café are the exact opposite in nature to himself as a creative free-spirited individual. How is it possible for the Tramp to be true to his own personality, which is expressive but silent, free-spirited and fey, playful and disruptive of authority? When the techniques of his own comedy and craft (the theater, music and dance, the expressive body) are co-opted into the system so decisively and seductively, what is left? In short how can he be authentic in the face of the material world lined up against him, including the techniques of Chaplin's own craft? The following discussion aims to help the reader decipher the happenings so that this battle of wills (between the Self, as represented in the Little Tramp, and industrialism, as represented by the great machine still clanking and whirling on the dance floor) can be perceived.

*Appearances, Emotions and Performance*

The transformation of the Gamin's appearance shows how important appearances and emotions are in this workplace. She has both emotional and aesthetic value in the labor market (as also explored by Hochschild, 1983; and Witz *et al.*, 2003). Her feminine qualities are absorbed by the café/dance hall and she is transformed into a version of her previous fantasy self. Her feminine qualities such as her sexuality, beauty, gorgeous smile, and grace are commodified, much as it has been in a more contemporary example, the airline industry (Hochschild, 1983; Taylor and Tyler, 2000). Indeed, as the entrepreneur noticed, she would ". . . be good at the café." As Hochschild (1983) and others (e.g. Fineman, 2000) have noted in more recent years, employees in many service industries are required to display the correct emotion (surface act) and/or genuinely display (deep act) with an "inside-out" smile in the service engagement. Hochschild argued that by being taught and expected to "act" in their work, service workers are required to invest part of their "true selves" in their work, which is potentially damaging to their psyche as it may result in a loss of Self. When the internal psychological processes of individuals are being manipulated, then their authenticity is at risk. Whole companies manage the emotions of their employees as if they are actors in a stage play required to be the person they are acting (as explored by Van Maanen, 1991 for example). The individual and social consequences of these management practices are still being debated and refined in the academic literature (e.g. as in Bolton and Boyd, 2003). Recently scholars have noted that service workers may actually enjoy the performance aspects of their work, and may even, like the Gamin, find it comes naturally. Goffman (1959) also drawing on a theater metaphor, argues all social interaction is performance, and suggests that presentations are reflections of the expectations of the audience. He makes the point that scripts and props may be used by actors to avoid revealing their true selves to an audience. People can and do develop strategies to enable a sense of control over their own destinies. And yet, identity and a conception of the Self is shaped by the treatment received in the workplace. The workplace is an important place where identity "happens." Although identity is in a state of flux in contemporary times, how one is treated provides the fodder for any person's "strategy for living." If service work is performance, then this does not necessarily leave the service worker completely stage-managed. Chaplin suggests, we think, that the method may also be the answer. He has a few tricks up his sleeve.

Appearances are Chaplin's stock-in-trade: he is well versed in "authentic" and "real" personas and the ambivalences and ambiguities between the real and the unreal. He has spent his entire adult life in the theater and in the fantasy world of the movies, having both his personal and his professional life constructed and criticized by his public. He uses his lifetime of theater experience to set the scene for this workplace as a series of stages within stages.

The Red Moon Café is simply a theater, with a backstage, a front-stage, and wings. There should be no doubt in anyone's mind that work here is performance. Chaplin is in his one true element. The stage analogy, as well as the clock symbol, appears in all the major set pieces. There is a dance floor with tables arranged around it, as if they are around a clock face. There is a raised stage with the musicians upon it, thereby making the set a stage within a stage, within a larger stage (the people watching the movie). On the left is the kitchen, on the right is the dressing room, both clearly representing the back stage areas. In the kitchen theater props are being made by a man sawing wood (why else would he be doing this in a kitchen!). The dressing room features seats and vanity mirrors.

So far this is classic service experience theory, infused with simple theater metaphors (Fitzsimmons and Fitzsimmons, 2006; Grove and Fisk, 1992), although these are rapidly becoming more sophisticated (for example the use of Stanislavski's methods in Grove et al., 2004; Brecht's political theater in Meisiek, 2007; and improvisation in Shaw and Stacey, 2006). To develop the theater analogy Chaplin pays special attention to the characteristics of customers/audiences. First he demonstrates a clear understanding of the authority of the customer in these new work arrangements (as also explored in Keat et al., 1994) which he illustrates throughout this sequence in showing the Tramp lower in the social order than a rich man's dog, a demanding complaining customer, and several drunks. The emotionally belligerent, the emotionally inept/inebriated, and even a dog, are of a higher social order than the Little Tramp as waiter. He is at their beck and call and orders are flying from all quarters.

Everyone is beleaguering the poor Tramp, and telling him what to do, including his co-workers. These co-workers are fully conscripted into the system as they self-manage their own activities (as discussed in Sewell and Wilkinson, 1992), berating each other, as for example in the kitchen scene.

Performance is slavery. Chaplin rams this point home: as the Tramp himself is preparing to become a singing waiter, thereby ruinously compromising his true self, you can hear the singing waiters' mournful dirge about slavery in the background. "You can hear the darkies singing," "all night long" they warn. The Tramp is in peril! If he sings, he is not a silent film icon anymore! If he sings, he has sold-out.

As well as the audience/customers inside the café there are other audiences acting as figures of authority pressuring the Tramp to sing. Less obviously there is the movie audience, and there is the Gamin who is both audience and script-writer for the Tramp's final performance. The movie audience is awaiting the Tramp's first utterances, and they are hungry for this to happen. Chaplin has been savaged by his public before; he knows they are capricious. Like the crowd at a lynching, they are somewhat thirsty for his blood. Chaplin the film-maker gathers in all these different audiences (cinema goers watching the movie, the customers in the Red Moon Café, and the Gamin watching in the wings) for the Tramp's final performance. What's it to be? Capitulation? Postponement?

*The Great Carousel/Machine*

The opening vision of the carousel underpins the Red Moon Café sequence, and it has important antecedents in other scenes in the movie. When the Tramp is accidentally swallowed by the machine in the most-famous factory sequence, basically swallowed by the one that he serves (Stewart, 1976), he goes through the cogwheels to the sound of calliope music, as does the mechanic later on in the movie. The music bears the same relation to the crank and drone of gears and evokes the pounding of horses' hoofs. The carousel is a merry-go-round, a playful toy and a pleasure of childhood, but also a mechanical beast upon which children ride. The carousel is a machine, run by a fan belt, upon which a human being is swung around in circles. The Gamin is shown joyously dancing to the rhythms of the carousel, her body and hands dipping and wheeling in circular motions. The carousel, a machine of pleasure, of movement, is associated with Paulette Goddard dancing, spinning and whirling in the street. Goddard's beauty, which the camera worships throughout the movie in many lingering close-ups, becomes embodied into a machine (Tyler, 1985), and the pleasure of watching this beautiful woman dance is turned into something of value in the labor process. The power of technology, capitalism and aesthetic value are released by the pleasures of a childhood toy, to the sound of music and through the joy of dance.

Chaplin was an accomplished musician and dancer; he wrote the soundtrack to the movie and choreographed the dances. He would have been well aware, as an entertainer, that music and dance would not be sacrosanct from the corrupting influences of capitalism he was attempting to expose. Up to this point in the movie, however, dance has been used by Chaplin to highlight the dilemmas of the Tramp (in the teasing blind-folded ice dance which is used to show the fool-hardiness of conspicuous consumption), or to provide impossible answers (like his mad ballet in the factory). In the café scene as it unfolds, however, Chaplin lets the Tramp become what he himself is – a consummate physical comedian, musician and dancer – using himself and his problems for the entertainment of others. He shows that his craft, including music and dance, can also be used by the great machine. After all, as any musician or dancer knows, music and dance is simply notes and steps in-time.

The central feature of the Red Moon Café sequence is the circular dance floor, and the tables that are arranged around it. The motif of the clock is the central set design feature of this set. The wagon wheel evokes the clock at the beginning of the movie, and this is echoed, as already mentioned, in the chandelier. But the dance floor is also a metaphor for the clock, being circular, with the tables interspersed around it as if they were the clock's numbers. The Tramp is set to tangle with time itself.

The image of the Little Tramp being spun around the dance floor as he desperately tries to reach the complaining and difficult customer waiting for his duck deserves to be at least as famous as his large machine bowel joke. In the Red Café Scene, as he attempts to serve the complaining customer his duck, he is swept away again and again by the dancing customers. Chaplin is moving counter-clockwise with the flow of dancers, but he is also swirling around on his own axis clockwise. He is spinning around like a small internal cog in a much larger clock. Dancers (filmed from above) are round hats and heads; tables are round; the tray which circles above the round heads of the dancers is round; as even the wine bottle and water flask the Tramp carries are round. Dancers circle in a mechanized version of the Gamin's spontaneous carousel dance in the street. All of the above "cogs and wheels" revolve within and around each other. Dancers stop, start and speed up to music just as the machine did when controlled by the pulling of switches and levers. Instead of the relentless evenly spaced precision-timing of the factory machine, a spirited dance provides the timing of the labor process. Feeders (diners) are fodder for the controlling mechanism of music and dance; and the Tramp, as in the factory machine, is fed through its cogs without purpose, preventing him arriving at his destination.

Through all of this swirling and whirling, the duck is never dropped on the floor. The duck is obviously important. Why?

The centerpiece of the slapstick in the café scene is the duck which is decorated in such a way as to evoke a queasy sense of humanness (as does the chicken in the second factory sequence) by the placement of its garnish to look like eyes. The duck's importance is signaled from its first entry into the scene. It is given to the Tramp by the movie audience itself. When Chaplin first receives the duck he comes to the kitchen counter and it is delivered as if the movie screen is the servery. Chaplin appears to be attempting to break down the barrier between the performer and the audience, to create a stronger sympathetic connection between the audience and the Tramp: this scene is Brechtian in its desire to rupture the audience/customer barrier to engage them directly in his dilemma.

The Tramp has a strong sympathetic connection to the duck which has been given to him. The food is as organic and chaotic as is the Tramp himself, but he desperately tries to deliver it and to rescue it from maltreatment. The duck becomes misused as a football: the duck is misplaced and assigned a wrong and degrading role. This also occurs in the earlier factory scene where the chicken replaces the oil funnel the Tramp uses to feed his jammed supervisor. The chicken carcass looks distressingly human, especially when the Tramp pulls off a leg and feeds it to the boss. The Tramp in this scene feeds the supervisor in the same way that the feeding machine miss-feeds him earlier. Roles have been transposed. The Tramp is the feeding machine, the supervisor is compromised in the machine, and the chicken is dead meat. Unsettlingly, the melody of the Nonsense Song can be heard on the soundtrack. In the café scene, the misused duck is shafted upon the chandelier, which symbolizes time. Chaplin the intellectual vaudeville comedian is really cutting loose.

*Language, Authority, and Nonsense*

*Modern Times* is actually a semi-talkie. There is a soundtrack, and voices are used, but the voices are disembodied, technologically mediated and only associated with authority. Chaplin distrusted any disembodied language. For Chaplin the body was everything – it was his mode of communication – but also he could see the pervasive power of technologically-mediated discourse. In the earlier parts of the movie, voice is heard over the radio, through the orders of the boss to increase the rate of production on the factory floor, and on the gramophone as the "mechanical salesman."

Printed words are also recognized as disembodied, and therefore instruments of control intended to curtail the freedoms of the Tramp and the Gamin. During the café scene the action cuts to a scene where truant officers laboriously fill out a warrant for the Gamin's arrest. At another point the Tramp is so flustered by the telling off he receives from the maître de, he mistakenly enters the "Out" door from the kitchen instead of the "In" door, and his confusion results in chaos backstage when he disrupts the flow of work which very much depends, as does the factory-line, on everyone understanding the signs and reading them the same way. The Tramp cannot or will not read the signage in the workplace in the way that is intended. He is an anarchic and mischievous figure, standing outside the conventions of normalizing discourse, while demonstrating his complete mastery of it (Purdie, 1993). By being unable by nature, and unwilling by inclination, to obey, the Tramp de-normalizes what everyone else seems to accept; that these words are not necessarily working in their favor.

The printed word is also featured when the Gamin writes for the Tramp the lyrics for his singing waiter debut on his cuff. Chaplin shows these words being written, just as they are with the arrest warrant. This writing of words is a scripting of his performance. The requirement to speak only certain words in a certain way is fundamental to service management (Cameron, 2000; Leidner, 1993) and since Chaplin's film was made there has been a dramatic increase in scripting practices, ironically stripping social interaction of much of its authenticity (as observed in Ritzer and Stillman, 2001). Chaplin depicts his concern with scripting (he was not one to perform other people's plays), and also shows again his ambiguous feelings about women and authority. But, he loves the Gamin, and so he submits willingly to her despite the dire warnings from the singing waiters going on in the background.

But, of course, the Tramp is too fey a creature to be bound by any figure of authority. He finds his own way and, like a child, accidently (on purpose) flings away the written script in his dramatic introductory flourish, leaving him "wordless" when he is about to demonstrate to the world that he can actually speak. He must improvise to act, and let his true nature spontaneously come forth.

At this point in the movie everything converges: Chaplin's statements about the large political issues he was concerned with; the self-referential aspects of his own position vis-à-vis the technological development of the talkies; his attitudes towards authority; his own intensely personal and self-reflexive techniques of comedy; and his own quest for spiritual and intellectual freedom and happiness. To survive in the new era the Little Tramp must speak, but he cannot if he is to remain authentic. Chaplin must give in to the inevitability of talkies to survive himself, but he must preserve the integrity of his creative vision.

And so, the Tramp hangs wordless before his various audiences, and hushes them with a subtle but distinctive hand gesture, which is characteristic of his attempts to ward off authority figures. He gathers himself to act, building up the anticipation, and everyone is drawn together. Then the Tramp unleashes himself in a pure and genuine moment that does not diminish over time or with repeated viewings.

In a sublime moment of comedy, Chaplin commits a very courageous act, and sacrifices the Tramp rather than see him whimper and limp into a medium he is not suited for. To an extent Chaplin gives the baying audience what they want. The Tramp utters his first (and last) words on screen. But, as he dangles his song in front of his audiences' faces, he snatches it away at the last minute. What he utters is complete nonsense in a "beautifully doomed last move" (Stewart, 1976). He sings nonsense, but it is not exactly nonsense, because everyone should be able to understand the story he is telling, especially considering his celebrity; it is the story of a rich, foolish older man, flirting with a pretty young fortune-seeker, and their brief relationship.

The Tramp, channeling Chaplin, provides pure vaudeville physical comedy. This is what Chaplin is: a physical showman and comedian, a gifted musician, and a graceful dancer. He shows through his voice-less art everything that needs to be said. He takes the parts of man and woman, and provides us with their motivation, their emotions, and illustrates their story with props, costumes, and even a car, all with his body and face. He tells their entire story, showing her flirtatiousness, his foolishness, the seduction, and their eventual farewell. He reveals the essential self of both the Tramp and himself. The Tramp is Chaplin, and Chaplin, unlike the voices of authority trying to push him into restraining social mores; doesn't actually take himself too seriously. He sings nonsense during this unveiling, and his routine is so perfectly pitched that the release of laughter still reverberates seventy years later.

Which begs the question; why does nonsense matter? Specifically, why does it matter vis-à-vis understanding service work? To answer this, we propose that humor and comedy provide a way into critique that is not fully appreciated in critical management studies. Specifically *Modern Times* illustrates the potential power of humor to undo a master narrative.

Chaplin himself has argued that:

> . . . through humor we see in what seems rational, the irrational; in what seems important, the unimportant. It also heightens our sense of survival and preserves our sanity. Because of humor we are less overwhelmed by the vicissitudes of life. It activates our sense of proportion and reveals to us that in an over-statement of serious lurks the absurd.
>
> (Chaplin, 1964, p. 227)

One of humor's functions is to overturn master narratives and in so doing it provides an escape of sorts from the logic which builds expectations of familiar outcomes. Consequently humor sometimes sparks a furious response because it collapses the assumed conceptual foundations of modernity, and coherence of the rational world of systems (political, economic and social). These systems are generally solemn and self-important as power takes itself very seriously indeed and expects obeisance.

Chaplin provides a master class in how to undermine these conceptual foundations, using nonsense, the perfect comic vehicle to break a meta-narrative. Pure comedy is often said to provide reassurance at the expense of truth, such as with safety-valve theories of humor (as discussed in Collinson, 2002). But real masters of the form bend the rules. Kuriyama has argued that the subtlest and greatest comedy, the product of artistic maturity, is remorselessly impure and double-edged. Impure comedy frustrates the audience's comic expectations and insidiously acknowledges "the destructive power of the very forces it promises to contain" (p. 29).

Chaplin's comedy stands out because of: his themes which he believed in passionately and had an intense and prolonged intellectual engagement with; his empathy for the vulnerable in society which fueled his humanitarianism; and his willingness to take everything so personally. He was an artist, and he engaged himself body and soul to bring his vision to the screen. He used his art form to communicate this vision without compromising it: by seeing, undoing, and then re-describing, thereby twisting the meta-narrative, and himself, into a different shape.

In the last scene to the movie Chaplin cheers up a sad Gamin, and they walk off into the sunset hand in hand, both determined to make the most of their lot (as unemployed vagrants). They have both had a taste of success but it has come to nothing. But for the first time the Little Tramp has someone with whom to walk into the sunset.

## Conclusion

What the can we learn from *Modern Times*? And is there anything more to say about service work than what Chaplin said in 1936?

We hope we have demonstrated that *Modern Times* is not irrelevant in this day-and-age. There is surprisingly little Chaplin didn't appear to understand about critical perspectives on service work. In fact, it may be time to reboot *Modern Times* on our computers because as a comedian that did not need language, his movie reaches across national and language boundaries just at a time when we need it. Without words he has "discussed" the same themes we consume ourselves with now: authenticity, emotional labor, aesthetic labor, and the colonization of service workers' souls (or not).

We entered *Modern Times* intrigued by previous insights (e.g. Korczynski, 2002), interested in understanding contemporary service work, and comedy as a form of critical distancing that we could use in our critiques of management texts. Chaplin provided a master class for us in critical distancing, and we have exited our analysis affected and enlightened by his revelations. *Modern Times* provides a model for political/ethical critique that turns what could be a remote intellectual exercise into a vehicle for engagement. This is what art can offer critical management scholars; a pedagogical tool and a method for critique. An audience is more easily persuaded by emotional (versus rational) capture, and art can do this. The rhetorical power of *Modern Times* lies in the Little Tramp's charm and unique view of the world; we identify with his vulnerability, childlike spontaneity and seeming (but always failed) attempts to "fit in." Captured, we are then drawn into a nonsensical world (the one the Little Tramp inhabits) which actually makes more sense than the meta-narratives we are used to.

When we watch *Modern Times* we watch a very serious comedy about the psychic and physical pain wrought by industrialization. To accentuate this most obvious message of the film, Chaplin's greatest symbol – the innocent, child-like, charming but fundamentally anarchic Little Tramp, beloved by millions – is ground through and destroyed by the processes of technological industrialization. His response is to use this source of pain to expel out into the world a profoundly inspired commentary on the human condition through the gibberish of the Nonsense Song. At the same time he has given us a commentary on service work which highlights its central dilemmas, and which remain as relevant today as when he "discussed" them on screen for the enjoyment of his 1936 audience. His one Achilles heel is his portrayal of women, which perhaps says more about Charlie Chaplin than it does about women and work. But we prefer to accept what he has offered rather than berate him academically for being a man of his times, and showing his human fallibilities so honestly.

The Little Tramp is a man-child who faced the world in a unique way. Whether he was battling a bully, or spreading butter sadly on his pancakes, Chaplin's silent clown wove a tragic/comic spell. The Nonsense Song was a transformative and purely authentic moment for the Little Tramp as he improvises using the raw material of his craft, exposing Charlie Chaplin the entertainer, completely human, intensely vulnerable, but still acting up to make everyone laugh. As the Tramp finally became who he really was – as he finally found his place in the world and danced and broke into a gay, charming song – he gave us his last real moment as the Little Tramp (McCaffrey, 1971a). The Little Tramp is to die. The Tramp is not a talking icon and he cannot survive in the age of the talkies. Chaplin knew this (Chaplin, 1964). This is the Little Tramp's swan song, his little death on screen.

Is it possible to have a gentle and loving suicide? For the Tramp's self-immolation on the public stage is surely this; softly mocking Chaplin himself (his public persona as a lover of very young women) and his audience whilst showcasing his power as a physical comedian and his ambivalence about the power of disembodied language. This final swan-song is both understated and poignant, and yet the Nonsense Song is an incandescent and translucent moment. It is the moment just before death, when the soul of the Little Tramp flies out with his words, leaving the world a few grams lighter.

## Note

We are grateful to *Modern Times* Charlie Chaplin © Roy Export Company Establishment for permitting reproduction of the still.

# References

Abercrombie, N. (1994) "Authority and consumer society," in R. Keat, N. Whiteley, and N. Abercrombie (eds.), *The Authority of the Consumer*, London: Routledge, 43–57.

Attenborough, R. (Director) (1992) *Chaplin*, U.S.A.: Artisan Entertainment.

Bauman, Z. (1998) *Work, Consumerism and the New Poor*, Buckingham: Open University Press.

Bolton, S.C. and Boyd, C. (2003) "Trolley dolly or skilled emotion manager? Moving on from Hochschild's 'Managed Heart'," *Work, Employment and Society*, 17, 2, 289–308.

Cameron, D. (2000) "Styling the worker: gender and the commodification of language in the globalized service economy," *Journal of Sociolinguistics*, 4, 3, 323–47.

Chaplin, C. (Director) (1936) *Modern Times*, "The Chaplin Collection" (includes a special features disk), New South Wales: Roy Export Company Establishment.

Chaplin, C. (1964) *My Auto-Biography*, London: The Bodley Head.

Chaplin, C. (1974) *My Life in Pictures*, London: The Bodley Head.

Collinson, D.L. (2002) "Managing humor," *Journal of Management Studies*, 39, 3, 269–88.

Du Gay, P. (1996) *Consumption and Identity at Work*, London: Sage.

Fineman, S. (ed.) (2000) *Emotion in Organizations*, London: Sage.

Fitzsimmons, J. and Fitzsimmons, M. (2006) *Service Management: Operations, Strategy, Information Technology* (5th edn.), Sydney: McGraw-Hill/Irwin.

Girgus, S.B. (1996) "The moral and psychological dilemma of 'Modern Times': Love, play, and civilization in Chaplin's last silent classic," *Thalia: Studies in Literary Humor*, 16, 1/2, 3–15.

Goffman, E. (1959) *The Presentation of Self in Everyday Life*, London: Penguin.

Grove, S. and Fisk, R. (1992) "The service experience as theatre," *Advances in Consumer Research*, 19, 455–61.

Grove, S., Fisk, R. and Laforge, M. (2004) "Developing impression management skills of the service worker: an application of Stanislavsky's principles in a service context," *The Service Industries Journal*, 24, 2, 1–14.

Hochschild, A. (1983) *The Managed Heart: Commercialization of Human Feeling*, Berkeley, CA: University of California Press.

Keat, R., Whiteley, N. and Abercrombie, A. (eds.) (1994) *The Authority of the Consumer*, London: Routledge.

Korczynski, M. (2002) *Human Resource Management in Service Work*, London: Palgrave.

Korczynski, M. and Ott, U. (2004) "When production and consumption meet: cultural contradictions and the enchanting myth of customer sovereignty," *Journal of Management Studies*, 41, 4, 575–99.

Kuriyama, C.B. (1992) "Chaplin's impure comedy: The art of survival," *Film Quarterly*, 45 (Spring), 26–9.

Lancaster, W. (1995) *The Department Store: A Social History*, London: Leicester University Press.

Leidner, R. (1993) *Fast Food, Fast Talk: Service Work and the Routinization of Everyday Life*, Los Angeles: University of California Press.

McCaffrey, D. (1971a) "An evaluation of Chaplin's silent comedy films, 1916–36," in D. McCaffrey (ed.), *Focus on Chaplin* 82–95, London: Prentice-Hall International Inc.

McCaffrey, D. (1971b) *Focus on Chaplin*, Englewood Cliffs, NJ: Prentice-Hall.

Maland, C.J. (1989) *Chaplin and American Culture: The Evolution of a Star Image*, Princeton: Princeton University Press.

Meisiek, S. (2007) "Dissonances, awareness and aesthetization: Theatre in a home care organization," in P. Guillet de Monthoux, C. Gustafsson, and S.E. Sjöstrand, (eds.), *Aesthetic Leadership: Managing Fields of Flow in Art and Business*, London: Palgrave Macmillan.

Monin, N. (2004) *Management Theory: A Critical and Reflexive Reading*, London and New York: Routledge.

Purdie, S. (1993) *Comedy: The Mastery of Discourse*, Toronto: University of Toronto Press.

Ritzer, G. and Stillman, T. (2001) "From person-to system-oriented service," in A. Sturdy,

I. Grugulis and H. Willmott (eds.), *Customer Service: Empowerment and Entrapment*, New York: Routledge, 102–16.

Rose, N. (1990) *Governing the Soul: The Shaping of the Private Self*, London: Routledge.

Sayers, J. and Monin, N. (2004, 7–0 September) "Comedy, pain and nonsense at the Red Moon Café: the little tramp's death by service work in '*Modern Times*'." Paper presented at the 2nd Art of Management Conference, Paris.

Sewell, G. and Wilkinson, B. (1992) "Someone to watch over me: surveillance, discipline and the just-in-time labor process," *Sociology*, 26, 2, 271–89.

Shaw, P. and Stacey, R. (2006) *Experiencing Risk, Spontaneity and Improvisation in Organizational Change*, London: Routledge.

Stewart, G. (1976) "Modern hard times: Chaplin and the cinema of self-reflection," *Critical Inquiry*, 3 (Winter), 295–314.

Sturdy, A., Grugulis, I. and Willmott, H. (eds.) (2001) *Customer Service: Empowerment and Entrapment*, New York: Palgrave.

Taylor, S. and Tyler, M. (2000) "Emotional labor and sexual difference in the airline industry," *Work, Employment and Society*, 14, 1, 77–95.

Tyler, P. (1985) *Chaplin: The Last of the Clowns*, London: Garland Publishing.

Van Maanen, J. (1991) "The smile factory: work at Disneyland," in P.J. Frost, L. Moore, C.C. Lundberg, and J. Martin (eds.), *Reframing Organizational Culture*, London: Sage, 58–76.

Witz, A., Warhurst, C. and Nickson, D. (2003) "The labor of aesthetics and the aesthetics of organization," *Organization*, 10, 1, 33–54.

# CHAPTER 3

# The Globalization of Nothing and the Outsourcing of Service Work

GEORGE RITZER AND CRAIG D. LAIR

## Introduction

In this chapter we apply the concept of "nothing" (Ritzer, 2004a) to service work that is increasingly being off-shored and outsourced across the globe. On the one hand, this is an extension of the concept of nothingness from its initial application to consumption and consumer environments to service work (and ultimately to work in general). In this, we explore how service work can be defined in terms of nothingness. On the other hand, since service work is increasingly taking place within a global context, a phenomenon due in part at least to its off-shoring and outsourcing, we explore whether the globalization of service work is simultaneously a process of the "globalization of nothing" or, alternatively, a process that moves "something" around the globe. And though these issues are explored in an array of geographical and service work environments, in this chapter we focus on service work that is being off-shored and outsourced from the U.S. to India with particular emphasis on the call center industry. Does the off-shoring and outsourcing of such service work involve the globalization of nothing? This is the question to be explored in this chapter.

We explore three sets of conceptual problems in our discussion. The first outlines the basic conception of nothing and its counterpart, something. We also outline two aspects of globalization – grobalization and glocalization – and show how these concepts are related to, but not

31

synonymous with, nothing and something. Then we show how something/ nothing can be applied to service work. In the second section, we outline how service work is becoming increasingly global in nature and how the global nature of service work is driven, in part at least, by the processes of off-shoring and outsourcing. If this is the case, and if the something/ nothing distinction can be applied to service work, then is the globalization of service work, brought about via outsourcing and off-shoring, a process of the globalization of nothing? This question is answered in the third section. As will be seen, though there is the potential for the globalization of service work to involve something, this potential has not been fulfilled in practice. To date, most of the outsourcing and off-shoring of service work has contributed to the globalization of nothing, often in unique ways. We end by exploring what the future of the outsourcing and off-shoring of service work holds for the U.S., India, and a number of other countries as well.

## Appling the Concept of Nothing to Service Work

### The Something of Nothing

In *The Globalization of Nothing*, Ritzer (2004a) has argued not only "that we are witnessing a general historical trend in the direction of more and more nothing," but also that "nothing is increasingly becoming a global phenomenon" (Ritzer 2004a: 4 and 2 respectively). But what is this nothing that is sweeping the globe? Nothing can be defined as "a *social form that is generally centrally conceived and controlled, and is comparatively devoid of distinctive substantive content*" (ibid. 3). That is, these are generic forms that lack uniqueness or individual attributes. In contrast to nothing is *something* or "*a social form that is generally indigenously conceived and controlled, and is comparatively rich in distinctive substantive content*" (ibid. 7). That is, something is a unique and individual form that cannot easily be replicated. For example, a local restaurant that tailors its menu to locally and seasonally available products cannot easily be transplanted to another location without the local content (i.e. the "something") that defines this restaurant being changed in the process (e.g. a restaurant in Maryland that defines its "something" around its fresh crab cakes would be difficult to transplant to the landlocked farmlands of Iowa without its "something" being, if not lost, then at least changed, in the process).

Contrast this situation to a chain of fast food restaurants, a social form that is characterized by a high degree of nothingness: since fast food restaurants impose a highly uniform look and menu selection upon their franchises, any one restaurant in a fast food chain could be easily replaced any other one from anywhere in the world with no major changes needing to be made and little being lost in the process. In fact, fast food restaurants are almost a paradigmatic example of nothing. For one, since they are franchises, virtually by definition they are centrally conceived. For example, the McDonald's corporate office conceptualizes almost all of the aspects of a franchise's business (e.g. their look, location, menu, ingredients, food preparation techniques, etc.). As such, there is little to no innovation on the part of local franchises in terms of how its business will be run or organized.

Control is vested in the central offices and not the local franchises. In part, this control stems from the centralized planning, organization, and conceptualization that the central office imposes on its franchises. However, the central office has a number of other means to control local franchises as well. For example, it monitors its local franchises to make sure they are in-line with corporate standards and if the local franchise is found to be neglectful of these standards, this could lead to the loss of the franchise.

Third, fast food restaurants lack distinctive content. The whole idea of fast food restaurant chains is premised on the idea that they are virtual clones of each other and are thus highly indistinguishable. This uniform indistinguishably can be seen along multiple dimensions where nothingness is manifest. This includes place (i.e. fast food restaurants are *non-places* where their physical space is largely lacking in any distinctive features and/or local geographic ties), people (i.e. fast food restaurants turn its employees into *non-people*, or people who generally lack distinctive content/personalities because of how their actions and behaviors are structured by the organization), things (i.e. fast food restaurants produce *non-things* or uniform products that largely lack specific ties to place or time such as regional or seasonal food), and services (i.e. fast food restaurants provide *non-services* or generally uniform and unvarying services most often provided by non-people). For these reasons, fast food restaurants are a paradigmatic example of nothingness. Of course, it must also be kept in mind that "nothing is nothing." That is, no social form is completely lacking in terms of content, local control, and/or local ties. In other words, everything possesses at least some bit of something. Nevertheless, fast food restaurants are excellent examples of the definition of nothingness offered above.

The contrast between nothing and something is not, however, meant necessarily to imply a judgment about either of these forms or of the increasing global presence of nothing: something is not always good and nothing is not always bad. Nevertheless, nothingness can be linked to certain social pathologies. Treating people and places as if they lack distinctive content and are highly interchangeable tends to dehumanize the former and disenchant the latter. This being said, the general argument put forward about nothing and its global dispersion is meant to be descriptive in nature – to describe an unfolding social trend. In particular, it is to show

how a specific social force – grobalization – and its various sub-processes, are acting to aid the transfer of nothingness globally.

## The Grobal and the Glocal

Grobalization (Ritzer 2004a) was a concept developed to counterbalance the predominance of the concept of glocalization (and the related terms of hybridization and creolization) found in the globalization literature. As developed by Robertson (1994), glocalization was intended to emphasize how, through globalization, there has been the integration of global and local elements that has produced new, heterogeneous, and/or hybrid social forms. An example would be the increasing hybridization of food: Mexican, Italian, and Chinese food in the U.S. become hybrid forms (e.g. Mexican-American, Italian-American, and Chinese-American) where, in each case, these foods are not reducible to the products of any one country or any one culture. Rather, they represent a new, hybrid form of food (Husted, 2001). His idea has been used to highlight the possibilities of the new heterogeneous identities, cultures, and products and services that globalization makes possible.

Grobalization, in contrast, was developed to emphasize "the imperialistic ambitions of nations, corporations, organizations, and the like and their desire, indeed need, to *impose* themselves on various geographic areas" (Ritzer, 2004a, p. 73 – emphasis added). Fueled by their need to *grow* profits, power, and/or global control, grobal structures act to deliver not new, hybrid or heterogeneous social forms, but rather to spread homogeneous and uniform social products throughout the global marketplace. Thus, American fast food chains are highly grobal in nature because they, by and large, offer the same uniform, American-inspired menu the world-over. Although they often add in a few local (but still McDonaldized) menu items, for the most part these chains are not seeking to create glocal cuisine with their menu options, rather, their goal is to deliver a standard product to new, untapped markets. Thus, while glocalization emphasizes the possibilities of heterogeneity and hybridity, grobalization emphasizes a countervailing drive toward ever greater homogeneity and uniformity.

Seen in this light, it should not be surprising that certain elective affinities exist between glocalization/grobalization and something/nothing. That is, processes of glocalization tend to produce something, while processes of grobalization tend to produce nothing. This is not to say that this is always the case (there are cases of the glocalization of nothing and the grobalization of something), just that something and glocalization, and nothing and grobalization generally tend to go together under globalization. But why is there this elective affinity between these processes, especially between nothing and grobalization?

The answer is simple: since nothing is a relatively content-less form and thus does not base its identity on specific cultural nuances, it is easier to export to a global market. This also serves to facilitate its consumption in the global marketplace since, by not being overly tied to the specific content of local culture; it can more easily be received in various locales all across the globe. This helps to explain why Hollywood continues to produce more action-packed, violence-filled R-rated movies than it does family-friendly G and PG-rated movies, despite the fact that the latter make more money domestically than do the former. Since violence and action are not culturally-specific phenomena (e.g. the thrill of a car chase is not something that can only be appreciated by one specific culture) these types of movies are easily exportable and thus are easy to bring to an international audience. In contrast, family-friendly American movies often play on the cultural nuances of this society, and although they earn more in the domestic market, they are not easily exportable to other cultures and tend not to do well in the global marketplace (Media Awareness Network n.d.). Thus, in this case there is a huge financial incentive to produce run-of-the-mill, standard format, indistinct action movies (i.e. nothing), as opposed to smart, nuanced, and culturally sensitive films (i.e. something).

However, the linkage between financial considerations and grobalization is not limited to the film industry. Rather, the process of grobalization in general is fueled, in part at least, by this financial motive as capitalism and the drive to maximize profits pushes products into the global market place. However, in order to be easily transported and received, these products have to be largely lacking in distinctiveness. As such, capitalism tends to push nothing into the global marketplace thereby linking the process of globalization with the process of grobalization. But capitalism is not the sole driver of grobalization. In fact, grobalization is fueled by other processes – including McDonaldization and Americanization – each of which acts in its own way to contribute to the production and global dissemination of nothing.

McDonaldization is the theory of how the rational principles upon which the McDonald's fast-food franchise empire is founded (i.e. *efficiency, calculability, predictability,* and *control,* particularly through the *substitution of nonhuman for human technology)* are coming to dominate more and more sectors of American society as well as of the rest of the world (Ritzer, 2004b, p.1). McDonaldization contributes to the production of nothing because rationality, when applied to goods and services, tends to strip them of their content as *systems* (e.g. of production and distribution) are emphasized at the expense of *substance* (Bryman, 2006; Ram, 2006). In contrast, Americanization contributes to the production of nothing not only because America has been the inventor of most of the empty forms that are paradigmatic of nothingness (e.g. shopping malls and franchised fast food restaurants), but also because America has been the number one global exporter of these forms. Thus, grobalization's affinity with nothingness is aided by these sub-processes which are intimately involved in the production and distribution of nothing on a world-wide scale.

In contrast, glocalization and something lack the power-base to perpetuate themselves on a global scale. Thus, while glocalization and something can be powerful forces, their power is overwhelmingly confined to their local environment. And though the development of something is perhaps the most natural of things, to the extent that globalization takes on the form of grobalization, something is threatened by the spread of nothing. It is for this and the above reasons that it has been argued that we are in the midst of a historical trend heading decisively in the direction of nothingness (Ritzer, 2004a). This is not to say that grobalization washes the world clean of something, or that processes of glocalization are nonexistent. Rather it is to say that despite these reserves and even resurgences of something and glocalization, there is a general trend toward nothingness fueled in large part by the processes of grobalization.

This prediction, as outlined in *The Globalization of Nothing*, was largely confined to the realm of consumption. That is, it is based on evidence from, and analysis of, the world of consumer goods and consumer settings. As such, it did not address the issue of to what extent the something/nothing distinction can be applied to the other side of economic life: work. Here we would like to argue that this distinction between something and nothing can easily be extended to encompass the world of work and can be used to assess to what degree certain jobs are characterized by nothing or something. Indeed, this extension is quite natural given that the context for much of the initial analysis of nothing were in sites of consumption, largely non-places, where workers, employed as non-persons to perform non-services, were also present. Already, many issues relevant to the service work industry, in particular, were addressed (e.g. the issue of a service versus a non-service) even if this was not the explicit focus of *The Globalization of Nothing*. However, the full range of issues to be explored, and the full potential of the something/nothing dichotomy, when applied to service work, has yet to be realized. Here we turn the lens of the something/nothing (and grobal/glocal) distinction in the direction of service work in an attempt to fulfill this potential.

*Something, Nothing, and Service Work*

The application of "nothing" and "something" to the service work industry is an important extension of this concept especially since many service work jobs can be seen as being characterized by a high degree of nothingness. Thus, in contrast to the high hopes of some "post-industrial" theorists (e.g. Bell, 1999 [1973]) that new technologies would eliminate the drudgery of manual work and replace routinely performed tasks with skill and knowledge-intensive service-based jobs, the development of a service-based economy has actually acted to create a host of service jobs that are just as, if not more, routinized and rationalized as any manufacturing job. For example, almost the entirety of jobs in McDonaldized settings, what Ritzer (1998) calls "McJobs," fall along these lines. These jobs are also defined by a high degree of nothingness as a worker's actions, and often interactions with customers, are, to the degree possible, controlled and decided in advance by the corporation. The result of this is that the distinctive traits of individual workers or skills that they have that are not in-line with the system already established are squeezed out: from the corporation's point of view, ideally all that is left is what *it* has determined is the best manner of operation for its employees, and is something that is uniformly applied the world over. For example, employees of Disney World who play one of Disney's characters (e.g. Snow White or Cinderella) are to check the vicissitudes of their life at the door and to (literally) step into the shoes of a character that has already been defined. In this case, it is the employee's job to conform to this already defined identity as the character is not to be tailored to the individual cast member.

The Disney character, however, is just one of the many McJobs that can be seen as being characterized by a high degree of nothingness. Others, to name but a few, include (not surprisingly) fast food workers, insurance agents, phone sex operators, and many retail/customer service workers (see Ritzer 2006 for an overview of many of these McJobs). However, there is one particular example of a McJob characterized by a high degree of nothingness that is of special relevance to this chapter: call center work.

As Cameron (2000) has found, many call centers script how their employees are to interact with customers (this is also the case in other McJobs, for example, those in fast food restaurants). However, call centers seek not only to control *what* their workers say, but also *how* they say it. That is, they seek to control not only the *script* of the employee, but also the *style* of his/her speech. Thus, call center employees are encouraged to "smile" over the phone and make the customers feel as if the employee has been waiting for their calls all day (ibid., 334; see also Hochschild's (1983) work on emotional labor). As such, an employee's own speech patterns and tones of speech are not supposed to be evident in their interactions with customers. Instead, all that is to be left is a generic script delivered in a uniformly happy manner. As will be seen, this is a particularly important issue when, because of the possible negative reaction of some American clients to having to interact with a non-American service worker, call center workers in countries such as India not only have to pattern their speech in terms of corporate norms (e.g. using scripts and "smiling" over the phone), but also in terms of cultural patterns (e.g. adopting American names, speech patterns and/or accents).

Issues like these raise an interesting question in regard to an increasing trend in service work: with the high levels of nothingness found in service work, would not the outsourcing and off-shoring of service work be a process of the globalization of nothing? This is the central question this chapter seeks to answer. However, the answer is not as straightforward as the question. In part, this is due to the claim by outsourcing and off-shoring advocates that by accessing high-quality labor pools overseas, businesses are able to acquire and engage the distinctive talents of these workers. That is, far from erasing or eliminating what is distinctive about these workers, it is claimed that these distinctive attributes are celebrated, promoted, and employed through this work. If one reads the idea of glocalization broadly, this could be seen as an example of this concept (i.e. the local talents are combined in a productive manner with broader global economic forces).

Similarly, it could be argued that these jobs, far from being defined by nothing, are actually something (i.e. they have distinctive content) and that workers are able to employ their "something" (i.e. individual talents) in these occupations. As will be seen below, these claims are mostly just that, claims. Nevertheless, globalization does open the possibilities of the emergence of something in the service work environment and this needs to be explored in the context of increasingly globalized service work. However, before dealing with these issues, it is first important to outline how service work is increasingly being globalized and how this increasingly global nature of service work is the product of two trends that have recently come to affect the service work industry: off-shoring and outsourcing.

## The Globalization of Service Work: Outsourcing and Off-shoring

Aided by advances in information and communication technologies that allow for the near-instantaneous transfer of information from one part of the globe to another, as well as the more general process of globalization and the increasingly global flows of people, goods, and finances, more and more service work is becoming global in nature. That is, it is increasingly possible for service providers and service recipients to be separated by hundreds, if not thousands, of miles. Of course, this is not a universal development: some forms of service work such as the care work that Parreñas discusses in this volume require that service provider and client be in close geographical proximity to one another in order to be effective. However, this does not mean that these forms of work are untouched by processes of globalization. As Parreñas shows, in cases where jobs are not part of a global flow (i.e. in cases where forms of work are relatively immobile), the workers who fill them often are part of that flow so that, as a result of international migration, care on the local level is provided by a pool of global labor.

That being said, our focus will be on two developments that, while initially manifesting themselves in the manufacturing sector, are increasingly allowing many forms of service work to move globally: outsourcing and off-shoring. Though these are terms that are often employed, they are used in many different literatures, often in multiple and even contradictory, manners. Thus, it is important to specify exactly what is meant by each term in order to avoid any confusion.

In general, *outsourcing* refers to the transfer of activities once done within one entity to another, outside entity. For example, companies such as General Electric and Citigroup have transferred the development of some of their software applications back-office work, formerly done in-house, to the third-party companies of Infosys Technologies and Wipro (Rai 2004). In this example, the outsourcing involves a transfer of activities from a company in one country to a company in another county (both Infosys Technologies and Wipro are Indian owned and operated), though, this does not necessarily have to be the case for outsourcing to occur. That is, activities transferred from one party to another in any location, be it foreign or domestic, is an example of outsourcing.

However, a number of more specific terms have been used in some literatures to clarify exactly where certain activities are being transferred. For example, when outsourcing occurs within a home country, this is sometimes referred to as *domestic outsourcing*. In contrast, when the transfer of activities is from one country to another, especially across oceans, this is commonly referred to as *off-shore outsourcing* (this is also the type of outsourcing that people fear will lead to a loss of jobs in their home country).

However, *off-shoring*, as distinct from offshore outsourcing, refers to instances where "a multinational company moves or expands some [or all] of its operations and jobs to overseas locations" (Hira and Hira, 2005, p.201). In other words, while off-shoring involves the transferring of activities to non-domestic locations, this transfer takes place within a single corporate structure. That is, there is no third-party involved in this transfer of activities. Thus, off-shoring occurs when companies such as Ford expand their operations outside the U.S. since all of these activities take place under Ford's corporate umbrella.

As can be seen, off-shoring and outsourcing are not the same thing. However, as corporate strategies, they share the same primary motivation: to take advantage of lower labor costs available in places outside of their home territory. Moreover, in many respects, it was the practice of off-shoring that gave rise to the recent upsurge in outsourcing. At first many manufacturing firms, especially in the auto industry, sought to take advantage of the lower labor costs in some foreign countries by moving their operations there. However, over time, many of these same firms realized that even lower costs could be realized if these operations were not only moved, but were fully externalized with the result that these would become things that the company would buy instead of make itself (e.g. buying parts produced by a third-party instead of manufacturing the parts itself).

While the revolutions of off-shoring and outsourcing were initially concentrated in the manufacturing sectors of industrialized countries, it was not until a "new wave" of outsourcing (Bardhan and Kroll, 2003, p.1) that began to affect white collar, service sector jobs in the 1990s, and accelerating through the first part of this century, that much public attention, and indeed much public concern, began to be devoted to these issues. As Rajan (cited in Farrell *et al.*, 2005, p.5) puts it specifically in terms of outsourcing:

> It is hardly the size of the [outsourcing] phenomenon that accounts for the uproar [over it]. More important, I think, is concern about how big this trend could become and the fact that it is affecting a segment of the workforce that hitherto was never really subject to this kind of competition, namely service workers.

Indeed, many service jobs have, or potentially could be, outsourced to countries around the globe. The McKinsey Institute has calculated that in 2005, 565,000 service jobs were being outsourced and estimated that by 2008 the number will grow to 1.2 million (ibid., p.7).

However, the potential to outsource service jobs depends in large part on the nature of the work. As Bardhan and Kroll (2003, p.4) note, the characteristics of jobs likely to be outsourced globally are those with no face-to-face contact with the customer; with high information content; where the work process is telecommutable or Internet enabled; where a high wage differential exists between similar jobs in different countries; where there are low setup barriers; and where there is a low social networking requirement. The McKinsey Institute has confirmed this characterization in its estimates of the potential to outsource service jobs in different segments of the service sector: they predict that the lowest-levels of outsourcing will be in the retail and health care segments where face-to-face contact is an essential part of the work process, while packaged software and IT services, work that does not necessarily need to involve face-to-face contact with a customer and can be done over the Internet, have the greatest potential to be outsourced (Farrell *et al.* 2005, p.8).

One industry that readily realized the potential to outsource work that is not anchored in face-to-face contact with its customers is that of call center work. Since contact between employee and customer is made phone-to-phone in this industry, this work can take place anywhere there is a phone line thus making it easy to establish operations nearly anywhere on the globe. Also, in this type of work, there are low setup costs involved (office space and phone lines are relatively cheap) and the networking involved is, for the most part, supplied by the contracting company (i.e. either their customers call the call center's employees, or the employees call both actual and potential customers from a list given to them by the contracting party). Given these characteristics, it is not surprising that a great deal of outsourcing has taken place in this industry.

Moreover, given the particular characteristics of India (e.g. relatively low-wages, a high proficiency of English in the population, suitable technical infrastructure, and a highly skilled labor pool), it is not surprising that this country has been the major recipient of both off-shored and outsourced call center jobs: India is the current leader in the "global customer contact industry" (Elmoudden, n.d., p. 5). As Taylor and Bain (2003, p.7) point out, in terms of absolute figures the number of call center workers in India remains relatively small. However, there is the potential that the early "trickle" of companies moving their operations to India could easily become a "flood" if the promises of high-quality, low-cost labor prove to be true. As of 2004 there were 120,000 people in India employed in the call center industry (Research and Markets, p.2004), but this number needs to be seen as part of a rapid upswing in employment in the industry. In 2000, this industry employed only 8,600 workers but it is expected to employ 270,000 by 2008 (Nascomm cited by www.bpoindia.org). Similar growth is seen in the number of call centers in India: while in 2005 there were over 200, the number is also expected to rise to nearly 500 by 2009 (Datamonitor cited in *Computer Business Review*, 2005).

However, call center work is only one of many service sector jobs that have been, or are being, outsourced globally. While the headlines were once dominated by the outsourcing of IT tasks, the current trend in outsourcing is moving more in the direction of business-process outsourcing (BPO), or the outsourcing of non-core, yet necessary, business operations (*The Economist*, 2005). This includes such services as finance and accounting, human resources, and design and engineering. However, the outsourcing of service work has moved into other areas including the creation of innovations in software processing that earn (U.S.) patents (Rai, 2003), the handling of e-loans (Rai, 2004a), creating software architecture of early blueprints for programs (Lohr, 2004), financial reporting (Steinberg, 2004), the preparation of tax returns, medical transcription (Drezner, 2004), the reading and interpreting of medical test results (e.g. X-rays, CAT scans, MRIs) (Pollack, 2003), and even U.S.-based legal work (Bellman and Koppel, 2005). Though some of these examples might be surprising, all of this work generally conforms to Bardhan and Kroll's (2003) characterization of jobs that are easily outsourced due to their high-information content which, through various information technologies, can easily be transported around the globe with a simple click of a button.

The innovative use of technology is further pushing the envelope of outsourcing to areas of work that have traditionally required the co-presence of both the worker and the customer. For example, some businesses are replacing receptionists with TV-screens that broadcast the image of a receptionist located in a "remote" location (i.e. a location that could potentially be anywhere in the world) who can, through the high-speed transfer of video images, meet, greet, and direct clients where to go. The same is true "[i]n San Jose [where] the concierge in the lobby of the Westin Hotel, Anna, shows up to work each day on a plasma screen, even though she is physically located 60 miles away. She could very easily be in another country" (*RealComm Advisory*, 2004). At the same time, McDonald's is experimenting with the use of remote call centers to handle drive-thru orders (CBS News 2005). Thus, the person taking someone's Big Mac order in LA might be located in North Dakota or, in time, another country altogether. As these examples show, companies are seeking to find ways of outsourcing service work normally considered to be resistant to outsourcing.

This situation raises a crucial question: why are companies not only outsourcing service work, but taking such elaborate steps to outsource work that does not generally lend itself to outsourcing? Two reasons are given for their decision to outsource. The first is financial considerations; all else being equal, by moving service work from high-cost locations to lower-cost ones, businesses can reduce their operating expenses and labor costs and thereby increase their profits. In some cases, labor costs for white-collar jobs can be as little as one-tenth the cost in low-wage nations such as India as in the U.S (Baily and Farrell, 2004, p.1). In the case of computer programmers, while U.S. average salaries range between $60,000 and $80,000, comparable salaries in India are between $5,880 and $11,000 (*CIO* cited in Bardhan and Kroll, 2003). Similarly, the average salary in the U.S. of call center work, including benefits and bonuses, is $46,000 per year compared to $6,000 in India and $7,300 in the Philippines. Given these cost differentials, it is not surprising that the McKinsey Institute has found that lower labor costs is the greatest motivation in the decision to outsource for most of the segments of service sector they surveyed (Farrell *et al.*, 2005, p.9).

Proponents of outsourcing also cite another rationale for outsourcing service work: outsourcing service work can increase its quality and customer satisfaction (this is something that Brady [2003] sees as "a hidden benefit of globalization"). For example, McDonald's experiment with outsourcing drive-thru order takers is justified by the fact that it could "allow McDonald's employees [in the store] to focus on delivering better customer service" (CBS News, 2005). Similarly, in the case of call center work that is outsourced, "those manning the phones . . . overseas often provide better customer service than their American counterparts" (Brady, 2003). One reason for this increased service lies in the perception of, and desire for, call center work between the U.S. and developing countries which can be measured in terms of the interest for these jobs in the respective countries: Patrick Hamlin, CEO of Livebridge Inc, a customer service company located in Portland Oregon, reports that for every position posted in the U.S. his company receives about four applications; in India, the number is eighty (ibid.). Moreover, in India almost all call center workers are college educated (Cutting Edge Information cited in ibid.).

Of course, lower cost and higher quality workers and services are not mutually exclusive motivations:

> The logic behind going global with [i.e. outsourcing] accounting, data entry and customer-service tasks is compelling. While call center workers in the U.S. can make in the high $30,000 range or more a year,[1] their Indian counterparts might earn $4,000, or up to $7,000 for a management-level post. Including other expenses, total cost savings of 30% to 40% are possible in moving back-office tasks overseas. *What's more, the quality of the work can surpass expectations.* While clerical and call center jobs in the U.S. often are seen as mediocre-paying dead-ends, the same work is a relatively high-paying, high-status job in a developing country. *That can translate into better-educated, more-motivated employees halfway around the globe.*
>
> (Aron and Singh, 2002 – emphasis added)

An argument could be made that the desire for better quality and customer service in the global outsourcing and off-shoring of service work utilizes the skills of local workers in a manner that would not be possible without this global dimension of business. If this were the case, then it could be argued that a process of glocalization, as opposed to grobalization, was taking place. And, if the distinctive talents of this local population are used in a meaningful way (e.g. if they were employed to perform non-routine services), then the global outsourcing and off-shoring of service work would help to contribute to the production of something. As will be seen, however, these promises of outsourcing and off-shoring have remained largely empty. That is, the reality is that the motivating force in the global transfer of service work jobs has been decidedly grobal in nature: i.e. it has been driven primarily by the desire of businesses to cut costs and impose their way of doing things. Moreover, although many of the jobs that are being off-shored and/or outsourced are initially defined by a high-degree of nothingness, when they are transferred overseas new and different forms of nothingness can be seen as arising in this process. And though there is the potential that the outsourcing of higher-level service work could contribute to the production of something (e.g. research and development departments working in an international context), this potential has, for the most part, remained unfulfilled. Why and how this is so in the case of service work is seen in the next section.

## The Outsourcing of Service Work and the Global Dispersion of Nothingness

To see how the global outsourcing and off-shoring of service work largely involves grobalization and facilitates nothingness, we can trace how the outsourcing/off-shoring of this work is bound up with three of the main producers of nothingness – capitalism, McDonaldization, and Americanization.

### Capitalism: Bottom Line Motivation

On the one hand, businesses are very interested in the local characteristics of the places to which they move, or plan to move, their service operations. For example, India is a prime source of outsourcing U.S.-based legal work because its legal system, like the U.S. system, is rooted in English common law. Similarly, India and other countries where English, if not the primary language, is at least prominent in the culture and educational system, are attractive to U.S. businesses because communication is allowed to take place between service providers and customers. Also, local pools of talented and/or high-skilled workers are very attractive to firms looking to outsource their operations overseas. Thus, India is a prime location for outsourcing IT work in part because its higher education system produces large numbers of high-skilled workers in such fields as computer engineering and other high-skilled occupations. However, the local factor that businesses most care about in looking to move their operations is the local economy and the cost of labor.

In short, India and other countries are so attractive to U.S. businesses looking to move their operations because they can get qualified, if not overly qualified, labor at costs dramatically less than what is found in the U.S. If this were not the case, it would seem that there are a number of different courses a company could pursue particularly if it was trying to increase the quality of its services *without* moving its operations overseas. For example, a business could simply hire better educated, more qualified workers locally; this would seem a logistically more convenient solution than hiring people from across the globe. And, if workers were not initially overly motivated to work in such settings, companies could do what organizations always do in attempting to attract scarce resources: use incentives (e.g. increased pay, better benefit plans) to lure higher-level workers. Perhaps organizations could also ease some of the restrictions they have on workers so as to give them space to display their individual talents/abilities (i.e. give them expanded room to display their "something"). All of these seem fairly simple solutions as opposed to moving entire divisions of companies overseas or contracting with a third-party located half a world away.

As we have seen, companies are not doing this and the reason is that while these businesses want quality in their services, they want the quality at a *value*. That is, it is not quality or the local characteristics so much that motivates these moves overseas, but instead the value (i.e. lower-cost) of the quality that can be purchased in other countries. For example, if programmers in India were paid double what American programmers were paid, one can rest assured that the amount of IT work outsourced by the U.S. to India would decline dramatically (and we could even see the outsourcing of computer work from India to the U.S.). Thus, the motivation that stands behind the bulk of the outsourcing and off-shoring of service work is decidedly grobal in nature – it is to increase a corporation's profits. And to the extent that local elements are considered important in the decision of if, or where, to move a business's operations, this consideration is made not in terms of the local population but rather in terms of the business's goals.

It is, however, possible that grobal intentions could lead to glocal outcomes. That is, even if the desire of businesses were purely bottom line in nature, this could facilitate the creation of something-filled and glocalized jobs. As we will see below, this potential has not been actualized in practice as the work that is outsourced/off-shored is either highly McDonaldized to begin with, and thus characterized by a high degree of nothingness, or is McDonaldized in the transfer, thus reducing much of the somethingness of these jobs to nothing.

*McDonaldization: McJobs go Global*

Though popular attention tends to focus on the loss of high-skilled, high-paying jobs (i.e. jobs with "something" to them), most of the service work that has been outsourced globally and/or off-shored, at least thus far, tends to be highly routine and repetitive. Thus, even if an occupation encompasses a full range of tasks, from work that involves a great degree of discretion and thought on the part of the individual, to work that is highly repetitive and requires minimal thought on the part of the worker, it is the latter that is most likely to be outsourced globally. For example, though legal work is increasingly being outsourced to places such as India, it "is likely to hit low-level work typically performed by legal assistants, paralegals and possibly even junior lawyers who cut their teeth on rote assignments" such as legal research and the reviewing of documents, not the higher-end, more complicated legal tasks such as arguing a case or offering legal advice (Crawford 2004). Similarly, tax preparation, though a professional occupation, involves a large amount of routine work that can easily be outsourced. Thus, big companies such as "Ernst & Young LLC [are] sending some simple tax-return processing work to India, and a handful of U.S. companies have sprung up to help smaller accounting firms do the same" (Wessel, 2004). Even medical work that is outsourced such as radiology is confined to the more routine aspects of this work: says Supratim Sarkar, a company spokesman for Wipro, an Indian based company that is receiving outsourced radiological work from some U.S. hospitals, "They [the radiologists in India] do not do full reads, they do not pass medical judgment." Instead, the Indian radiologist only sends a preliminary report back to the United States. Teleradiology Solutions, another Indian-based radiological firm, uses Indian doctors who are neither U.S. licensed nor board certified. Nevertheless, these workers can receive an image from the U.S., review it, make a preliminary diagnosis, and fax this back to the U.S. usually within 30 minutes (Tanner, 2004). These are jobs, however, that though repetitive, are at the higher end of the service work spectrum. What about lower level service work jobs that, as a whole, tend to more be more routine and repetitive from the start?

The example of call center work in India is here again instructive: in a preliminary study of the difference in managerial strategies employed in house, outsourced (to the U.S.), and off-shore outsourced call centers (to India), Batt *et al.* (2005) have found data that suggests that "transactions that are simple and codifable" are the jobs that are most likely to be outsourced offshore, while more complex service interactions are most likely to be kept in-house (Batt *et al.*, 2005, p.26). This would seem to suggest that even at the lower end of the service sector, the jobs that are most likely to be outsourced and/or off-shored are those that are the most repetitive and routine.

However, this study had another important finding as well:

despite relying on a more educated and full-time work force, the Indian centers have work systems that are more tightly constrained and standardized than those found among U.S. subcontractors. With the exception of reliance on scripts, which is higher in the U.S. outsourced centers, Indian managers report substantially lower levels of discretion over handling customer requests and use of problem solving groups.

(ibid., 20)

In other words,

[d]espite the fact that off-shore centers in India hire workers with relatively high levels of education and offer considerable initial training, the high levels of process standardization do not let employees

use their human capital [i.e. their distinct abilities] in ways that can improve operational performance.

(ibid., 25)

In short, the somethingness of these workers is prevented from trickling into the nothingness of this job.

Thus, overall there is little indication that the outsourcing or off-shoring of service work involves a substantial proportion of something. In fact, the situation seems to be quite the opposite: what is being outsourced and off-shored most often are non-jobs or the parts of jobs that are the most lacking in terms of distinctive content. And even when there is a pool of workers with the skills and abilities to contribute something to these jobs, the somethingless nature of these jobs prevents this from happening. However, it is not only that nothing is being dispersed globally by the outsourcing and off-shoring of service work jobs, it is also the case that new and different forms of nothingness are also being created as a result of the transfer of service work overseas.

*Americanization, Nothingness, and Indian Culture*

It is true that aside from the cost differential of the wages between the two countries, the particulars of a locale are sometimes influential in the decision to transfer service work especially when these particularities closely resemble the characteristics of the exporting nation (e.g. similar legal structures or a common language). However, even in cases where these relatively similar characteristics are present, many firms actively try to strip away any remnants of local flavor that remain because some Americans are hostile to the idea of interacting with a foreign service worker. Again, call center work is particularly indicative here for though these workers may speak English, they often have a local/non-Americanized accent. As a result, call centers, especially in India, are taking great pains to *prevent* their locality being transparent to American callers, and to allow American customers to have the illusion that they are interacting with someone from their home country. In part this is done by not allowing workers to disclose their locations. However, more elaborate attempts at this include teaching Indian workers aspects of American culture (e.g. American holidays and films) as well as colloquial American phrases. But many Indian firms also require that workers go through "accent neutralization" courses which attempt to stamp out the "mother tongue influence" of the local language(s) (McKay, 2004; Mirchandani, 2003). Though arguably this would lead to better service interactions for American customers not disposed to interacting with foreign service workers, this raises a series of concerns for the workers, their identities, and their local culture: "The call center industry is extracting a sliver of Indians who are actively de-Indianizing themselves and adopting Western names and identities, accent, and culture" (Pal, 2004). Indeed, this situation has led some (e.g. McMillin [2006]) to wonder if these workers, by insourcing American culture and speech are, at the same time, outsourcing their identities.

In short, the cultural identities of these workers, as well as their language, are reduced to nothing in this type of work. It could be argued that this reduction to nothingness is endemic to any type of call center work given that, as Cameron (2000) has shown, even call centers that are in-house operations regulate what and how their workers speak. There is an important difference in this situation however. As Cameron notes, the stylizing (i.e. how workers speak) that is imposed upon these workers is not that of a national or international language, rather, it is a corporate norm (op. cit., p.324). In this regard, any leveling of local culture to nothingness would be predominately intranational in nature. In the case of outsourced and off-shored call center work in India, however, the reduction of local culture to nothingness is international in nature: i.e. Indian culture is made to conform to American standards.

But the making of Indian life conform to American standards extends beyond language. For example, in order to take phone calls from Americans call center workers must work the overnight hours (e.g. from 10 p.m. to 6 a.m.) (Lal, 2003; McKay, 2004). Thus, it is not only the speech of these workers that is made to conform to American standards, it is also their temporality. Mirchandani (2003, p.11), refers to this as a process of the "colonization of time" where the Western clock is exported around the world and used as the global standard. This situation is largely the reverse from the example of radiological work mentioned above. In the latter case, outsourcing the reading of X-rays and such to India can occur in such a manner that the work conducted in India is performed not only during their daylight hours, but also in the overnight hours of the U.S. In terms of time, this situation can be seen as being mutually beneficial to both parties: Indian doctors are receiving work they otherwise would not have in hours roughly considered to be normal working day, while U.S. doctors are freed from working overnight shifts. For call center workers, though they are receiving work they may not otherwise have, they are receiving it on temporal terms not of their own: their time is thus American time in more than one sense.

It is for these and the above reasons that we can indeed say that the outsourcing and off-shoring of service work, though not universally so, has, to date, been largely a process of the grobalization of nothing.

## Conclusion

Though the outsourcing and off-shoring of service work have the potential to transfer something around the globe in glocalized developments, to date what has been globalized have been routine and largely repetitive service sector jobs. In other words, what we have seen has been the globalization of nothing fueled overwhelmingly by processes of grobalization. And though true for a number of service sector jobs that are now being off-shored and outsourced globally (e.g. radiology, legal work, accounting) this has been particularly so for the call center industry in India. However, as we have seen in the case of this industry, it is not just that jobs with a high degree of nothingness are being off-shored and outsourced (thus dispersing them globally). It is also that in some cases the potential something that these "foreign" workers could contribute to the service interaction is not allowed to develop: the dictates of the non-job do not allow this. Moreover, though corporations do seek out places to outsource and offshore their work based on their local characteristics, and particularly the prevailing labor costs in the area, in many cases these same corporations attempt to eliminate any local flavor these workers might have by having them conform to non-local standards. As such, it is the case that, despite the potential to be otherwise, the global outsourcing and off-shoring of service work is contributing to the globalization of nothing not only in the sense of moving non-jobs around the globe, but also in some cases intensifying the nothingness of these jobs in ways not found when these jobs are confined to domestic markets.

Many works have been critical of globalization and its negative effects. Our work shows a trend similar to that described in Klein's (2002) analysis of outsourcing practices involving more manual types of work (e.g. the assembly of electronic goods and the stitching of clothes). Although outsourcing theoretically involves only the *transfer* of work from one source to another, the nature of this work often changes in the process. The result is a job that is not only quantitatively different than before as companies outsource to places where labor costs are cheaper, but also one that is qualitatively different as well. In Klein's (ibid., p.218) case, this means that formerly "company-owned manufacturing turned – somewhere over the Pacific – into 'orders' to be placed with 'third-party contractors'" who offer little of the benefits or job security associated with these jobs before they moved. In our case, this means that many forms of service work, though initially defined by a high degree of nothingness, see the degree of nothingness associated with job content increase as a result of outsourcing. This is the case in spite of the fact that the workers in India are on average better educated and more (if not over-) qualified for this type of work than their American counterparts. Such workers could easily handle work that is more something than nothing, but they are rarely given the opportunity given the nature of the occupations being outsourced.

This is an ironic development since the promise of outsourcing and off-shoring is, in part at least, that the skills and abilities of highly-educated and well-trained workers from the world-over could be harnessed and used to the benefit of all. However, as we have seen, the nature of outsourcing and off-shoring, at least as they are practiced today, often prevents much of this talent from manifesting itself. This, of course, need not be the case and outsourcing and off-shoring could live up to their potential. However, what exactly it is that will make this change possible is a question that remains unanswered.

## Note

1   The salary levels for U.S. call center workers cited here are lower than those cited on the previous page. Please note, however, that the salary figures listed on the previous page include benefits and bonuses, while the figures here do not.

## References

Aron, R. and Singh, J. (2002) "The rush to send back – office business overseas," (web page). Available at http://knowledge.wharton.upenn.edu/100902_ss.html.
Baily, M. and Farrell, D. (2004) *Exploding the Myths About Off-shoring*, New York: McKinsey Global Institute.
Bardhan, A.D. and Kroll, C.A. (2003) *The New Wave of Outsourcing*, Paper 1103 Berkeley, CA: Fisher Center for Real Estate and Urban Economics.
Batt, R., Doellgast, V. and Kwon, H. (2005). *Service Management and Employment Systems in U.S. and Indian Call Centers*, CAHRA Working Paper 05–12.
Bell, D. (1999) [1973] *The Coming of Post-Industrial Society*, New York: Basic Books.
Bellman, E. and Koppel, N. (2005) "Legal services enter outsourcing domain," *The Wall Street Journal*, pp. B1ff.
Bpo India.org. (n.d.) "knowledgeBase" (webpage). Available at http://www.bpoindia.org/knowledgeBase/#.
Brady, D. (2003). "All the world's a call center: Outsourcing doesn't just save cash. It can lift quality," *Business Week*, 43.
Bryman, A. (2006) "Global implications of McDonaldization and Disneyization," in G. Ritzer (ed.), *McDonaldization: The Reader*, 2nd edn., Thousand Oaks, CA: Pine Forge Press, pp. 319–24.
Cameron, D. (2000) "Styling the worker: gender and the commodification of language in the globalized service economy," *Journal of Sociolingistics*, 4, 3, 323–47.
CBS News. (2005) "Outsourcing drive thru?" (webpage). Available at http://www.cbsnews.com/stories/2005/03/11/national/main679730.shtml.
Computer Business Review Online. (2005) "Outsourcing services: India calling" (webpage). Available at http://www.cbronline.com/article_researchwire.asp?guid=6A466E5E-70A3-4D72-A9E5-AFEDEDD19B57.
Crawford, K. (2004) "Outsourcing the lawyers: add attorney to the growing list of white-collar jobs being shipped overseas. How far will it go?" *CNNMoney.Com*.
Drezner, D. (2004) "The outsourcing bogeyman," *Foreign Affairs* 83 (3, May/June): 22–34.
Economist, The (2005) " 'Time to bring it back home?' Outsourcing," *The Economist* 63.
Elmoudden, S. "A review of global gendering in offshore call centers: the case of India and the Philippines," Working Paper, University of Colorado at Boulder.
Farrell, D., Laboissiere, M., Pascal, R., Rosenfeld, J., De Segundo, C. and Sturze, S. (2005) *The Emerging Global Labor Market: Part I – The Demand for Off-shore Talent in Services*, New York: McKinsey Global Institute.
Hayes, F. (2003) "Outsourcing angst," *Computerworld*.
Hayes, W.M. (2003) "Outsourcing call center pays off for Delta," *InformationWeek*.

Hira, R. and Hira, A. (2005) *Outsourcing America: What's Behind Our National Crisis and How We Can Reclaim American Jobs*, New York: AMACOM.

Hochschild, A.R. (1983) *The Managed Heart: Commercialization of Human Feeling*, Berkeley, CA: University of California Press.

Husted, B.W. (2001) *Cultural Balkanization and Hybridization in an Era of Globalization: Implications for International Business Research*, 81–95, Northampton, MA: Elgar Publishing.

Klein, N. (2002) *No Logo*, New York: Picador.

Lal, P. (2003) "1-800-Call-center: India as the world's receptionist," *PopMatters*.

Lohr, S. (2004) "Evidence of high-skill work going abroad," *The New York Times*, C2.

McKay, J. 23 Mar (2004) "All day, all night, the phone calls come in," *Pittsburg Post-Gazette*.

McMillin, D. 2006. "Outsourcing identities: call centers and cultural transformation in India," *Economic and Political Weekly* (January 21): 235–41.

Media Awareness Network. n.d. "The business of media violence" (webpage). Available at http://www.media-awareness.ca/english/issues/violence/ business_media_violence.cfm?RenderForPrint=1.

Mirchandani, K. (2003) "Making Americans: transnational call centre work in India," Unpublished Paper.

Pal, A. (2004) "Indian by day, American by night," *The Progressive*, August.

Pollack, A. (2003) "Who's reading your x-ray?" *The New York Times*, 3, 1ff.

Rai, S. (2003) "In India, a high-tech outpost for U.S. patents," *The New York Times*, C4ff.

Rai, S. (2004a) "Financial firms hasten their move to outsourcing." *The New York Times*, W1.

Rai, S. (2004b) "An industry in India cheers Bush's victory," *The New York Times*.

Ram, Uri. (2006) "Glocommodification: how the global consumes the local – McDonalds in Israel," in G. Ritzer (ed.), *McDonaldization: The Reader*, 2nd edn., Thousand Oaks, CA: Pine Forge Press, pp.325–34.

Realcomm Advisory (2004) "Receptionists outsourced to India?" (webpage). Available at http://www.realcomm.com/advisory.asp?aid=124.

Research and Markets. (2004) *Outsourcing Call Centers To India*.

Ritzer, G. (1998) *The McDonaldization Thesis: Explorations and Extensions*, London: Sage Publications.

Ritzer, G. (2004a) *The Globalization of Nothing*, Thousand Oaks, CA: Pine Forge Press.

Ritzer, G. (2004b) *The McDonaldization of Society: Revised New Century Edition*, Thousand Oaks, CA: Pine Forge Press.

Ritzer, G. (ed.) (2006) *McDonaldization: The Reader*, Thousand Oaks, CA: Pine Forge Press.

Robertson, Roland (1994) "Globalisation or glocalisation?" *International Communication*, 1, 33–52.

Steinberg, J. (2004) "Media talk; Reuters takes outsourcing to a new level with journalists," *The New York Times*, C6.

Tanner, L. (2004) "U.S. doctors turn to outsourcing to help diagnose ills," *The Seattle Times*.

Taylor, P. and Bain, P. (2003) *Call Centres in Scotland and Outsourced Competition from India*, Stirling: Scotecon.

Taylor, P. and Bain, P. (2005) " 'India calling to the far away towns': The call centre labour process and globalization," *Work, Employment and Society*, 19, 2, 261–82.

Wessel, D. (2004) "The future of jobs," *Wall Street Journal*, April 2.

# CHAPTER 4

# The Disneyization of Society

ALAN BRYMAN[1]

Ritzer's (1993) concept of McDonaldization represents a stimulating and important attempt to address large-scale issues concerning social change and the nature of modernity and to link these topics to some minutiae of everyday life. Ritzer is at pains to point out that McDonald's is merely a symbol of McDonaldization though it has undoubtedly been a major force behind the process. McDonaldization refers to "the process by which *the principles* of the fast-food restaurant are coming to dominate more and more sectors of American society as well as the rest of the world" (Ritzer, 1993, p.3, emphasis added). This means that McDonaldization is not simply about the spread of McDonald's restaurants or of restaurants explicitly modeled on them; nor is it a process that can be specifically attributed to McDonald's alone, since the restaurants incorporate practices that were formulated long before the McDonald brothers started their first restaurant, such as scientific management, Fordism, and bureaucracy.

The purpose of this chapter is to propose that a similar case can be made for a process that I will call "Disneyization," by which I mean:

the process by which *the principles* of the Disney theme parks are coming to dominate more and more sectors of American society as well as the rest of the world.

My view of Disneyization is meant to parallel Ritzer's notion of McDonaldization: it is meant to draw attention to the spread of principles exemplified by the Disney theme parks. Of course, the Disney theme parks are sites of McDonaldization too. A number of Ritzer's (1993) illustrations of the four dimensions of McDonaldization – efficiency, calculability, predictability, and control – are drawn from Disney parks and from theme parks that appear to have been influenced by them. There are, moreover, numerous parallels between McDonald's restaurants and the Disney parks (Bryman, 1995, p.123; King, 1983). Bryman (1995) has addressed the question of whether the Disney theme parks can be regarded as McDonaldized institutions in the context of a discussion of the "McDisney theme park." While he found that the model of McDonaldization applied broadly, he was less convinced that it applied well to the calculability dimension. Even if Disney parks could be regarded unambiguously as sites of McDonaldization, it is not at all certain that this would capture their significance. Indeed, the notion of Disneyization has been coined in order to reflect and build upon the suggestion that there is more to the parks than their being McDonaldized institutions. Further, we may well find that the McDonald's fast-food restaurants will be bearers of Disneyization, in much the same way that Disney theme parks are bearers of McDonaldization.

There are at least two terms that seem to be extremely similar to Disneyization. The first is "Disneyfication." It has been used by one of Walt Disney's biographers to refer to

> that shameless process by which everything the Studio later touched, no matter how unique the vision of the original from which the Studio worked, was reduced to the limited terms Disney and his people could understand. Magic, mystery, individuality . . . were consistently destroyed when a literary work passed through this machine that had been taught there was only one correct way to draw.
>
> (Schickel, 1986, p.225)

For Schickel, then, Disneyfication referred to the often criticized way in which Walt Disney, his co-workers and their successors put an original work through a Disney mincer to emerge with a distorted version of it. The outcome of the process was and is instantly recognizable as a Disney product. This is a view that has been voiced by many critics over the years (Sayers, 1965), and as soon as a new Disney feature film is released, it occasions a nearly automatic criticism for its perversion of stories and contexts.

Warren (1994) writes about the Disneyfication of the metropolis and as such is concerned with the way in which the Disney parks have been taken to represent "a whole approach to urban planning" (1994, p.90). Disneyfication is not explicitly defined, but can be inferred from the components of the Disney city. First, it is a social order which is controlled by an all-powerful organization. Second, we find a breach between production and consumption which is achieved "through the visual removal of all hint of production and the blanketing of consumption with layers of fantasy so that residents are blinkered from seeing the actual labor processes that condition and define their lives" (1994, p.92). Thirdly, it is only residents' capacity to consume that is viewed as in any sense significant or important. Haas (1995) also writes about Disneyfication but in the context of the gangster novel in the form of the Disney version of E.L. Doctorow's novel, *Billy Bathgate*, which was filmed by Touchstone Pictures, a division of Disney. For Haas, the novel underwent Disneyfication in the sense that the Disney version of the story was "sanitized" and "clean and civilized" (1995, pp.74, 79). Disneyfication is also evident in the themes of patriarchy and innocence that are overlaid on Doctorow's story. These notions of Disneyfication are illuminating but are meant to have limited domains of application: literary works and urban planning. The notion of Disneyization being presented here is meant to have a broader frame of reference in a manner that is parallel to McDonaldization.

A second term that borders Disneyization is Ritzer and Liska's (1997) notion of "McDisneyization." The concept is not defined, but it is clear that it represents a fusion of the principles of McDonaldization and distinctively Disney-like characteristics, though the latter are not outlined in a formal manner. However, the analytic slant of the term is largely upon the "Mc" part of the process because the significance of Disney seems to lie mainly in being an agent of McDonaldization in relation to tourism. For example, the authors suggest that:

> While McDonald's itself has not been without influence in the tourist industry, it is Disney and its phenomenal success that has been most responsible for bringing the principles of McDonaldization . . . to the tourist industry.
>
> (Ritzer and Liska, 1997, p.98)

While Ritzer and Liska's analysis is instructive, the present exercise will emphasize the Disneyesque elements.

Various writers have also produced motifs which have affinities with Disneyization. Wasko (1996) writes about the "Disney Universe." The use of this term is meant to denote the near-universality and hence global reach of the company and its products and the fact that it "has created a self-contained universe which presents consistently recognizable values through recurring characters and familiar repetitive themes" (Wasko, 1996, p.349). Thus, Wasko notes that the classic Disney Universe, as revealed primarily in the feature films, comprises: escape and fantasy; innocence; romance and happiness; sexual stereotypes; individualism; and the reinvention of folk tales. Yet another kindred term is Rojek's (1993) discussion of "Disney culture," by which he means a moral order imbued by an image of leisure as "rational recreation."

These various conceptualizations and discussions of Disney parks and the company's other products suggest that various writers have been seeking to assess their broader salience and significance. With the possible exception of Ritzer and Liska's (1997) notion of McDisneyization, the writers have tended to emphasize the ideological underpinnings of Disney phenomena and have been only tangentially concerned with the wider proliferation of these features. Also, as has been suggested, the treatments of Disneyfication have tended to have limited domains of application. The present discussion will seek to build upon these fruitful beginnings by emphasizing the principles associated with the Disney parks which have spread increasingly beyond their gates. As far as possible, an attempt will be made not to stumble into McDonaldization territory, so that the distinctiveness of Disneyization can be retained. This distinctiveness will be further investigated in the conclusion where the contrasting theoretical roots of McDonaldization and Disneyization (in Weber's concept of rationalization and consumer culture respectively) will be explored.

In the following account of Disneyization, four dimensions will be outlined. In each case, the meaning of the dimension and its operation in the context of the Disney parks will be outlined, its diffusion beyond the realms of the Disney parks will be indicated, and aspects of any of the dimensions which precede the opening of the first Disney theme park (Disneyland in California) in 1955 will be explored. The overall aim is to identify large-scale changes that are discernible in economy and culture that can be found in, and are symbolized by, the Disney parks. As with Ritzer's (1993) treatment of McDonald's in relation to McDonaldization, it is not suggested that the Disney parks *caused* these trends, though the parks' success may have hastened the assimilation of Disneyization.

The four trends are:

1 theming
2 dedifferentiation of consumption
3 merchandising
4 emotional labor

This list is probably not exhaustive, any more than McDonaldization's four dimensions can be so regarded. They are meant to be considered as four major trends which are discernible in and have implications for (late) modernity.

## Theming

Theming represents the most obvious dimension of Disneyization. More and more areas of economic life are becoming themed. There is now a veritable themed restaurant industry, which draws on such well-known and accessible cultural themes as rock and other kinds of music, sport, Hollywood and the film industry more generally, and geography and history (Beardsworth and Bryman, 1999). These themes find their expression in chains of themed restaurants, like Hard Rock Café, Planet Hollywood, All Sports Café, Harley-Davidson Café, Rainforest Café, Fashion Café, as well as one-off themed eating establishments. Diners are surrounded by sounds and sights that are constitutive of the themed environment, but which are incidental to the act of eating as such, though they are major reasons for such restaurants being sought out. In Britain, themed pubs are increasingly prominent and popular, while in the USA, bars themed on British pubs are big business too. Hotels are increasingly being themed and it is no coincidence that two of the more successful themed restaurant brands – Hard Rock Café and Planet Hollywood – are being deployed for such a purpose. Ritzer and Liska (1997) suggest that cruise ships are increasingly becoming themed. In Las Vegas, virtually every new hotel on the "strip" is heavily themed. The famous strip now contains such themes as Ancient Rome (Caesar's), Ancient Egypt (Luxor), ye olde England (Excalibur), the movies (MGM Grand), city life (New York New York), turn-of-the-century high life on the Mediterranean (Monte Carlo), the sea (Treasure Island), and so on. It seems quite likely that this penchant for themed hotels will proliferate though possibly not with the exotic façades that adorn the Las Vegas establishments. Certainly, the theming of hotel rooms as in the Madonna Inn near San Luis Obispo, California, and in the Fantasy Hotel in West Edmonton Mall (see below) seems to be becoming increasingly prominent (Eco, 1986; Hopkins, 1990).

Shopping in malls is increasingly being accomplished in themed environments. Mall of America in Minneapolis and West Edmonton Mall in Edmonton, Alberta exemplify this feature. Cohn, quoting it would seem from a publicity leaflet about Mall of America, notes that:

> South Avenue was "chic sophisticated . . . cosmopolitan shopping and flair"; North Garden "lushly landscaped . . . a park-like setting with gazebos, trellises and natural skylights"; West Market "reminiscent of a European railway station"; and East Broadway a honky tonk, all neon and chrome.
>
> (Cohn, 1996, p. 4.1, ellipses in original)

Cohn also notes that the Muzac changes according to which land one is in. In West Edmonton Mall, one encounters arcades modeled on the boulevards of Paris and on Bourbon Street in New Orleans along with the conventional juxtapositions of North American malls. Similarly, the MetroCentre in Gateshead contains themed shopping areas like the Mediterranean Village (Cheney, 1990). Adjacent to Caesar's in Las Vegas is a small mall (though soon to be greatly expanded) called the Forum Shops where the shops and restaurants, which include a Planet Hollywood, are surrounded by signs of Ancient Rome.

Gottdiener (1997) suggests that airports are increasingly becoming themed environments. It must also not be forgotten that many amusement parks have also been themed, so that one tends to hear much more about theme parks than about amusement parks. Even Knott's Berry Farm, which is close to but predates Disneyland, has taken on the trappings of a theme park with the familiar layout of themed "lands." In spite of Gallic horror at the arrival of Euro Disneyland (now Disneyland Paris) in 1992, Parc Asterix is not only a theme park constructed around the well-known cartoon characters, but also comprises themed lands. There is, then, evidence of a growing use of theming, to the extent that Gottdiener (1997) writes about "the theming of America." But what was the thinking behind the theming of Disneyland?

Accounts of the founding of Disneyland agree that Walt Disney hit upon the principles of theming as a device for differentiating his vision from the tawdry and grimy amusement parks to which he had taken his daughters. He noticed that many parents were like him in that they only frequented these parks to appease their children. He felt that it should be possible to create an environment which adults would be just as keen to visit as children. In fact, he was more than successful in this regard, because the ratio of adults to children visiting the parks has been estimated as 4:1. For Walt Disney and his successors, theming was a mechanism to achieve the goals of appealing to adults as much as children and of distinguishing Disneyland from amusement parks. It is well known that Disneyland was conceived as a celebration of America's past and as a paean to progress, or as Walt Disney put it: "the older generation can recapture the nostalgia of days gone by, and the younger generation can savor the challenge of the future" (in Mosley, 1985, p.221). The former element allowed Walt Disney to lace many of the attractions and environments with heavy doses of nostalgia that he felt would have a direct appeal to adults. Main Street USA, the thoroughfare to the attractions, exemplifies this sentiment with its unashamed harking back to turn-of-the-century middle America with which many American adults could associate themselves. Similarly, Frontierland recalls the era of the Wild West but in a very cinematic mold and was designed to provide therefore a set of images to which adults could easily relate. Moreover, the very process of theming was central to this product differentiation strategy, since most amusement parks were loose assemblages of rides of various degrees of thrill.

Theming accomplished at least two things in this connection. First, it established coherence to the various rides and attractions in Disneyland and the environments in which they were located. Second, in the design of rides and attractions, the accent was placed on their theming rather than on the thrill factor, which was the emphasis in traditional amusement parks. Indeed, Walt Disney initially did not plan for roller coaster rides in order to set his park apart from the amusement parks he loathed so much. Gradually, such rides have been incorporated as a result of pressure from younger visitors who found Disney fare too tame. However, when such rides were built they were in heavily themed form, for example, Big Thunder Mountain Railroad (themed on prospecting in the Wild West), Space Mountain (space travel) and Splash Mountain (*Song of the South*). By establishing coherence to rides and by placing an emphasis on the theme rather than on thrills, Walt Disney was able to differentiate Disneyland from the traditional amusement parks that he so disliked. Much of this is captured in the Euro Disneyland share prospectus which was issued in October 1989. The prospectus outlines the "Disney theme park concept":

> Rather than presenting a random collection of roller coasters, merry-go-rounds and Ferris wheels in a carnival atmosphere, these parks are divided into distinct areas called "lands" in which a selected theme . . . is presented through architecture, landscaping, costuming, music, live entertainment, attractions, merchandise and food and beverage. Within a particular land, intrusions and distractions from the theme are minimized so that the visitor becomes immersed in its atmosphere. (p. 13)

But it would be a mistake to think of Disneyland as the progenitor of theming. It may have (and almost certainly has) acted as a high profile spur to a realization of the significance and possibilities of theming, but its basic principles can be discerned in a number of forerunners. Two types of precursor stand out. One is amusement parks which had incorporated elementary theming features at an early stage. Coney Island's Luna Park and Dreamland Park provide examples of this, in that attractions were clothed in exotic and sometimes erotic motifs (Kasson, 1978). A second type of forerunner is the exposition which acted as a means of displaying modernity's wares by suffusing them with a sense of continuing scientific and technological progress and with utopianism. A number of writers have drawn attention to the continuities between the Disney theme parks and expositions and world's fairs (Findlay, 1992; Nelson, 1986). Marlin (1994) has suggested that the Chicago Railroad Fair of 1948 was a particular inspiration for Disneyland. The fair was designed to celebrate the centenary of the first train to enter the city. It showcased many futuristic trains and an even greater number of trains of the past. It therefore combined the celebration of the past with visions of the future which would be a feature of Disneyland. Furthermore, the rolling stock was surrounded by carefully recreated models and settings. According to Marlin these included: a model dude ranch; a mechanical representation of Yellowstone Park's Old

Faithful geyser; and a French Quarter, Indian Quarter and an area modeled on the beaches of Florida's Gulf Coast. There were also numerous shows including re-enactments of historical events. Marlin argues that what was significant was not the originality of these ideas, many of which could be seen in the Century of Progress Exposition in Chicago in 1933; instead, the significance lay in the "coherence and concentration of the experience" (1994, p.105). It was this aspect of the fair, in particular, that she regards as a major inspiration for the form that Disneyland assumed. Disneyland's originality lies in the combination of the transformation of themed *attractions* into one of themed environments with the transformation of the world's fair/exposition concept into a *permanent* site.

## Dedifferentiation of Consumption

The term "dedifferentiation of consumption" denotes simply the general trend whereby the forms of consumption associated with different institutional spheres become interlocked with each other and increasingly difficult to distinguish. For one thing, there has been a tendency for the distinction between shopping and theme parks to be elided. Walt Disney realized at a very early stage that Disneyland had great potential as a vehicle for selling food and various goods. Main Street USA typified this in that its main purpose is not to house attractions but to act as a context for shopping. As Eco puts it: "The Main Street façades are presented to us as toy houses and invite us to enter them, but their interior is always a disguised supermarket, where you buy obsessively, believing that you are still playing" (1986, p.43). Nowadays, the Disney theme parks are full of shops and restaurants to the extent that many writers argue that their main purpose increasingly is precisely the selling of a variety of goods and food. With many attractions, visitors are forced to go through a shop containing relevant merchandise in order to exit (e.g. a shop containing Star Wars merchandise as one leaves the Star Tours ride in the two American Disney parks and Disneyland Paris). In the EPCOT Center, a Disney World theme park which opened in 1982, there is an area called World Showcase which comprises representations of different nations. But one of the main ways in which the nations and their nationhood is revealed is through eating and shopping. Indeed, the buildings which iconically represent some of the countries do not contain attractions at all (e.g. Britain, Italy), or perhaps contain little more than a film about the country concerned (e.g. Canada, France). However, each "country" has at least one restaurant (some, like France, Mexico and China, have two) and at least one shop. It is not surprising, therefore, for many commentators EPCOT and indeed the other parks are often portrayed as vehicles for selling goods and food. Thus, the Euro Disneyland share prospectus presented as one of the main management techniques associated with "the Disney theme park concept" the fact that "Disney has learned to optimize the mix of merchandise in stores within its theme parks, which consequently are highly profitable and achieve some of the highest sales per square meter for retail stores in the United States" (p. 13). If we add hotels into this equation, the case for dedifferentiation in the parks is even more compelling. At Disney World the number of hotels has grown enormously since Michael Eisner took the helm at the Walt Disney Company in 1984. In addition to being themed (see previous section), there has been a clear attempt to ratchet up the number of guests staying in its hotels by emphasizing their advantages over non-Disney ones. For example, Disney guests are able to enter the parks earlier and can therefore get to the main attractions before the arrival of hordes of tourists. They are also able to secure tables for the sought after restaurants (especially the EPCOT ethnic ones) from their hotels rather than having to take a chance on their availability when they turn up at the parks. Also, for some time now Disney has been offering its hotel guests inclusive length-of-stay passes to the parks. It is striking that it was recognized during the days when Euro Disneyland's financial troubles were common knowledge that one of the reasons for its problems was not the number of visitors to the parks but the fact that they were not spending as much on food, souvenirs and Disney hotels as had been predicted (Bryman, 1995, p.77). Thus, we see in the Disney parks a tendency for shopping, eating, hotel accommodation and theme park visiting to become inextricably interwoven. Any distinctions are further undermined by the fact that Disney have created what is essentially a mall in the center in Disney World (Disney Village, formerly called Disney Marketplace) and have announced that they will be developing a mall adjacent to Disneyland Park (Finch, 1997).

In some very large shopping malls, the opposite has happened, though this too represents further evidence of the dedifferentiation of consumption: the mall designers have built theme parks and other leisure facilities. This extends well beyond the eateries and cinemas that are standard mall fare. At Mall of America is a seven acre theme park called Knott's Camp Snoopy, which features 23 rides. There is no entrance fee and visitors pay for each ride. In the first six months of operation, the park took more than 4 million rides (Spellmeyer, 1993). Early research showed that the average visitor spends 3.1 hours in the mall which includes a half-hour visit to Camp Snoopy, but since then the average visit to the mall has been calculated as 2.6 hours (Cohn, 1996). As is well known, West Edmonton Mall has similarly incorporated a giant water park and theme park attractions in "Fantasyland." One of Ghermezian brothers who own and operate the company that was responsible for the Mall's design was apparently very influenced by the Disney theme parks (Hopkins, 1990: 9–10). The

MetroCentre similarly contains "an enormous fantasy kingdom of fairground rides" (Urry, 1990, p.149). The rationale for this hybridization of consumption and theme park attractions is well summed up by the mall developer, Bill Dawson, who is quoted as saying: "the more needs you fulfill, the longer people stay" (in Crawford, 1992, p.15). Moreover, in broadening the range of facilities on offer, the mall transforms itself from a local amenity to a tourist attraction and at least one investment analyst predicts that the trend towards injecting amusements into malls will continue (Barber, 1995, p.132). Further illustrations of dedifferentiation of consumption include the way in which many airport terminals are being turned into mini-malls (Hamilton and Harlow, 1995) and such simple manifestations as the tendency for many museums and heritage attractions to force visitors to exit through a shop. Moreover, hotels and casinos using the Hard Rock Café and Planet Hollywood brands are being built in different locations. McDonald's is frequently involved in a form of dedifferentiation of consumption when it links its fare with Disney cartoon characters and films. It also attached itself to the opening of the Segaworld theme park in September 1996 by offering free burgers to visitors.

Las Vegas is possibly a better illustration than the Disney theme parks of Disneyization in the form of dedifferentiation. For a start, the hotels mentioned in the previous section could equally be described, and probably more accurately, as casinos. Each houses a massive casino, although they could equally be described as casinos with hotels attached. But in recent years, dedifferentiation has proceeded apace in Las Vegas. You may enter the forum shops at Caesar's on the moving walkway but the only exit is to walk through the casino. More than this, in order to attract families and a wider range of clientele (Grossman, 1993), the casino/hotels have either built theme parks (e.g. MGM Grand, Circus Circus) or have incorporated theme park attractions (e.g. Luxor, Stratosphere, New York New York, Treasure Island, Excalibur). In the process, conventional distinctions between casinos, hotels, restaurants, shopping, and theme parks collapse. Crawford has written that "malls routinely entertain, while theme parks function as disguised marketplace" (1992, p.16), but current trends imply that even this comment does not capture the extent of dedifferentiation.

## Merchandising

In this discussion, I will use the term "merchandising" simply to refer to the promotion of goods in the form of or bearing copyright images and logos, including such products made under license. This is a realm in which Disney have been pre-eminent. Walt Disney's first animated star was arguably not Mickey Mouse, but Oswald the Lucky Rabbit, around which he and his studio had created a popular series of shorts in 1927. When he tried to negotiate a better financial deal over these shorts, Walt found that it was not he but the distributor that owned the rights to them. As a result, the studio had no rights to Oswald's name and therefore to the small range of merchandise that had begun to appear bearing the character's name and image. Thereafter, he zealously guarded his rights in this regard. A major factor may well have been the revenue-producing capability of merchandise bearing Oswald's image, including a pop-up puppet, stencil set, celluloid figures and posters (Tumbusch, 1989: 28).

Merchandising and licensing proliferated, however, in the wake of Mickey's arrival in November 1928 (deCordova, 1994). A year later, Walt Disney Productions was transformed into four mini-companies, one of which dealt with merchandising and licensing. Deals were handled through first of all by George Borgfeldt and in 1934 onwards by the flamboyant Kay Kamen. Walt Disney certainly did not create the idea of merchandising or even of merchandising animated cartoons characters. Felix the Cat was the subject of a large range of merchandise in the mid-1920s (Canemaker, 1991). What Walt Disney did realize was its immense profitability. In the years after Mickey's arrival, the company did not make large sums from its cartoons, because Walt Disney's incessant quest for improvements in the quality of animation cut deeply into the studio's profits. To a very large extent, he was able to finance expensive technical innovation and his unyielding insistence on quality by using profits from merchandise. Klein (1993) has suggested that about half of the studio's profits were attributable to merchandise (see also, Merritt and Kaufman, 1992, p.144). Indeed, some writers have suggested that in later years, the design of cartoon characters, in particular their "cuteness," was at least in part motivated by a consideration of their capacity to be turned into merchandise (Bryman, 1995; Forgacs, 1992). It may also account for the changes in Mickey's increasingly less rodent-like appearance over the years (Gould, 1979).

The Disney theme parks have two points of significance in relation to merchandising as a component of Disneyization. First, and most obviously, they provide sites for the selling of the vast array of Disney merchandise that has accumulated over the years: from pens to clothing, from books to sweets and from watches to plush toys. Sales from merchandise are a major contributor to profits from the parks. The parks are carefully designed to maximize the opportunity for and inclination of guests to purchase merchandise. Second, they provide their own merchandise. This occurs in a number of ways, including: tee-shirts with the name of the park on them; EPCOT clothing or souvenirs with a suitably attired cartoon character on them, such as a "French" Mickey purchased in the France pavilion or a sporty Goofy purchased in the Wonders of Life pavilion; merchandise deriving from characters specifically associated with the parks, such as Figment (a character in the Journey into Imagination ride in EPCOT); and a petrified Mickey looking out from the top of the Twilight Zone Tower of Terror (a Disney-MGM Studios attraction) emblazoned on clothing. Thus, while the merchandising of Disney creations predates the first Disney park by nearly thirty years, the parks exemplify this aspect of Disneyization by virtue of their substantial promotion of a host of items. Indeed, Davis (1996) suggests that theme parks have become major vehicles for merchandising and that this at least in part accounts for the growing tendency for media conglomerates to buy or build them. Davis writes somewhat more generally about the "cross-promotion" of goods, which itself can be seen as a principle of Disneyization, but as she observes, merchandising is central to the appeal of cross-promotion: "Licensed images and . . . merchandise are at the heart of the matter, and the potential of the theme park industry to sell and support licensed products is central to synergy" (1996, p.407). Fjellman, similarly, refers to the merchandise associated with Disney films as being part of "an endless round of self-referential co-advertisements" (1992, p.157).

Over the years, it has become increasingly apparent that more money can be made from feature films through merchandising and licensing than from box office receipts as such. While hugely successful merchandise bonanzas like those associated with *Star Wars*, *Jurassic Park* and *The Lion King* are by no means typical; they represent the tip of a lucrative iceberg. Like many movies, television series also often form the basis for successful lines of merchandise and indeed it has sometimes been suggested that they are devised with merchandise and licensing potential very much in mind. There are no guarantees, however. If a movie flops, like *Judge Dredd*, even though based on a popular comic book character and having superficial merchandise potential, the products will either not be developed or will not move out of stores. Also, the merchandising of even fairly successful films like *Flintstones* and *Casper* can be disappointing (Pereira, 1995). Certainly, Disney seems to have been very disappointed with the merchandise sales associated with *Dick Tracy*, produced by Touchstone Pictures (Grover, 1991, p.261). Even so, the potential for merchandising in relation to movies is reckoned to be huge and is an important element in what Wasko *et al.* (1993) refer to as "the commercialization of US films" and more generally in "the commodification of culture" (1993, p.271). The potential of merchandising lies behind the tremendous growth in studio stores, like those associated with Disney and Warner Brothers, a market into which MGM, Sony and others are moving. Moreover, there has been a trend in recent years for licensing firms buying up the rights to merchandising of a variety of traditional characters, including Thomas the Tank Engine, Noddy and other Enid Blyton characters, *Marvel* comic characters, and Sooty (Alberge, 1996; Fox, 1996; Lee, 1996).

But it would be a mistake, of course, to view merchandising purely in terms of the movies and cartoon characters. The new themed restaurant chains all follow the lead of Hard Rock Café of developing extensive lines of merchandise, including the ubiquitous tee-shirt which simultaneously informs where wearers have been on their holidays and acts literally as a walking advertisement for the chain. You do not necessarily have to eat in the establishment in order to purchase the items. Very often, if not invariably, you can enter the shop area without needing to eat the food. In the case of the Rainforest Café chain, the shopping area is often as big as many restaurants; this contrasts somewhat with the small booths in Hard Rock Café, All Star Sports and Planet Hollywood restaurants. Professional sport has succumbed to the attractions of merchandising and in Britain major clubs and events can be the focus for successful merchandising (Longmore, 1996; Truss, 1996). Kuper, for example, has written that Manchester United Football Club "tripled its turnover to £60m over the last five years, largely thanks to merchandising" (1996, p.2). While British universities have lagged behind their North American counterparts, it appears that they too have realized the potential of what one news reporter appropriately refers to as "Disney-style merchandising" (Swanton, 1997, p.vi).

## Emotional Labor

Ritzer (1993) was somewhat silent about the nature of work under McDonaldization, but it is clear from his view that since it incorporates Scientific management and Fordism the work tends to be dehumanizing and alienating. More recently, Ritzer (1998) has written about "McJobs," that is, jobs specifically connected to the McDonaldization of society, and links his reflections with insights from labor process theory (Braverman, 1974). While he finds the insights of this theory instructive, he notes that there is more to these jobs than their being "simply the deskilled jobs of our industrial past in new settings" (Ritzer, 1998, p.63). McJobs have a number of new characteristics including "many distinctive aspects of the control of these workers" (1998, p.63). In particular, Ritzer draws attention to the scripting of interaction in service work. Not only does this process result in "new depths in . . . deskilling" (1998, p.64) but also it entails control of the self through emotional labor, which has been defined as the "act of expressing socially desired emotions during service transactions" (Ashforth and Humphrey, 1993, pp.88–9). Drawing on the work of Hochschild (1983) on airline attendants and Leidner (1993) on insurance salespersons at Combined Insurance in the USA, he notes that in addition to interaction with clients being controlled, the organization seeks to control "how they view themselves and how they feel" (1998, p.64). This is revealed in the insistence that workers exhibit cheerfulness and friendliness towards customers as part of the service encounter. There is some uncertainty about how far emotional labor is associated with McJobs. Leidner (1993) conducted research on work in a McDonald's outlet (where presumably one finds the archetypal McJob) and argued that the kind of emotional labor discerned by Hochschild could be found among counter workers. Such a finding would be consistent with Reiter's research on Burger King which "urges employees to be pleasant, cheerful, smiling, and courteous at all times" and to "show obvious pride in their work" (1996, p.136). However, Ritzer (1998) argues that emotional labor is not a feature of McDonaldized organizations, because they are mainly interested in workers' overt behavior rather than with how they feel about themselves.

There is some disagreement, then, about how far emotional labor accompanies McDonaldization, but there is no doubt that many aspects of this form of control are spreading, as the work of the authors cited in the previous paragraph suggests (for reviews of much of the evidence for this trend, see Ashforth and Humphrey, 1993; Wharton and Erickson, 1993). But emotional labor is in many ways exemplified by the Disney theme parks. The behavior of Disney theme park employees is controlled in a number of ways and control through scripted interactions and encouraging emotional labor is one of the key elements (Bryman, 1995, pp.107–13). The friendliness and helpfulness of Disney theme park employees is renowned and is one of the things that visitors often comment on as something that they liked (Sorkin, 1992, p.228). Moreover, anyone with even a passing knowledge of the parks *expects* this kind of behavior. The ever-smiling Disney theme park employee has become a stereotype of modern culture. Their demeanor coupled with the distinctive Disney language is designed among other things to convey the impression that the employees are having fun too and therefore not engaging in real work. In one instance, at least, the diffusion of emotional labor from the Disney theme parks was very direct: Findlay (1992) maintains that the city of Anaheim's stadium and convention center, built in the mid-1960s, consciously adopted a Disney-style approach to handling customers. He quotes a local newspaper article as saying that at both organizations could be found "an attractive and smiling staff" who had been tutored in a "Disneyland vocabulary" (1992, p.101).

It was not quite that way at the beginning, however. In Disneyland's very early days, Walt Disney was appalled by the behavior of some of the park's staff toward visitors. The staff, many of whom had been hired by lessees, lacked training and were gruff and unhelpful towards visitors. The only employees who exhibited the kind of behavior Walt wanted were the attraction operators who had been trained by the company itself. According to Randy Bright, a Disney Imagineer: "What Walt really wanted were employees with a ready smile and a knack for dealing pleasantly with large numbers of people" (1987, p.111). The Disney University was created precisely in order to inculcate the necessary training and was responsible for a new vocabulary. According to the founder of the Disneyland University, one of the central elements of the early training approach was to inculcate the principle that "[i]n addition to a 'friendly smile', we sold the importance of 'friendly phrases' " (France, 1991, p.22). Since then Disney has developed seminars which introduce executives from a variety of organizations to its distinctive approach to human resource management (Blocklyn, 1988; Eisman, 1993) and has publicized this approach more generally (e.g. Johnson, 1991). These seminars may have been instrumental in the further diffusion of this aspect of Disneyization. Moreover, a number of management texts have emphasized this ingredient of the success of the Disney theme parks (e.g. Connellan, 1996; Peters and Waterman, 1982; Zemke, 1989).

Needless to say, the manifestations of emotional labor are sometimes repudiated and behavior that is inconsistent with Disney principles of how hosts and hostesses should act is exhibited, as a number of commentators have observed (e.g. Koenig, 1994; Sutton, 1992; Van Maanen and Kunda, 1989). However, to concentrate on these features is to miss the point: as Van Maanen and Kunda (1989) observe, there is an almost remarkable acceptance among Disney staff of the emotional requirements of the job. Moreover, the very fact that these emotional requirements sometimes occasion considerable resentment among hosts or hostesses (Project on Disney, 1995) is a reflection of the demands of emotional labor just as it was for Hochschild's (1983) airline attendants. Even among some former Disney hosts or hostesses who have had adverse employment experiences, there seems to be a certain ambivalence that combines a certain degree of admiration with a recognition that the job was not for them (Zibart, 1997).

## Conclusion

In this chapter, I have sought to position the concept of Disneyization in two different ways and senses. On the one hand, I have employed a term that has been used much less often than "Disneyfication" which now has a number of connotations, some of which are pejorative. By adopting a term with less conceptual baggage, it is possible to outline its features in a more untrammeled manner. Second, I have had in mind a kind of analogue to Ritzer's (1993) influential concept of McDonaldization. In other words, like McDonaldization, Disneyization is depicted as a large-scale social process which is made up of a number of analytically separate components. Many institutions may be described as *both* McDonaldized and Disneyized, thereby perhaps warranting being referred to as McDisneyized, following Ritzer and Liska (1997). Shopping malls and theme parks are prominent examples. However, Disneyization and McDonaldization may sometimes overlap with respect to certain institutions but they are distinctively different processes. What is more, as this chapter has suggested, institutions may be McDonaldized but not Disneyized or Disneyized but not McDonaldized or may even be Disneyized in some respects and McDonaldized in others. The Disney theme park itself may be an example of this last pattern. Bryman (1995) has argued that it displays characteristics of three of the four dimensions of McDonaldization and is obviously a Disneyized institution.

McDonaldization and Disneyization can be depicted as having contrasting intellectual traditions. Ritzer positions McDonaldization in relation to the classical concern in social theory with rationalization exhibited by Weber and others, whereas the intellectual heritage of Disneyization is much closer to recent more theoretical concerns about consumerism. This contrast could be taken to imply that they are grounded in different images of society. Ritzer (1993, pp.156–8) has unambiguously located McDonaldization in relation to modernity, but as he also observes "consumption . . . is often considered the hallmark of postmodern society" (1998, p.9). This raises the consideration of whether the grounding of Disneyization in consumerism and the consumer society implies a quite distinctive intellectual heritage from McDonaldization and equally a different vision of the nature of the society in which each flourishes? Disneyization can be depicted as having points of affinity with many of the attributes of a consumer culture identified by writers like Baudrillard (1970/1998), Bauman (1998), Featherstone (1991) and Jameson (1991) who emphasize the sign value of goods and their connectedness to notions of life style and individuals' personal identity projects. There are different aspects to this current of thought, not the least of which is that it encapsulates both the propensity of people to respond to goods and services in terms of sign value and the conscious manipulation of signs by the suppliers of goods and services. These features can be discerned in relation to Disneyization in the growing use of theming devices and in the deployment of copyright images in merchandising coupled with the individual's preparedness to respond to them. The dedifferentiation of consumption is also relevant here as it is to do with the ways in which people are encouraged to get on with their consumption projects while actually giving the impression that they are doing something else. Emotional labor serves to convey a sense that the employee is not engaged in work, so that the consumer is not reminded of the world of work and can get on with the happy task of buying, eating, gambling and so on. The smiling, helpful demeanor may also encourage spending in its own right.

The identification of Disneyization with theories of consumer culture seems to imply that whereas McDonaldization is a modern phenomenon,

Disneyization is a post-modern one. However, one has to be cautious about such simple connections, not least because Ritzer's (1998) more recent writing on McDonaldization displays a greater preparedness to associate it with postmodern themes and writings. Certainly, there are many features in Disneyization that are frequently associated with post-modernity: the proliferation of signs, dedifferentiation of institutional spheres, depthlessness, cultivated nostalgia, and the problematization of authenticity and reality. However, it is important not to fall headlong into an immediate association with postmodernity: as Beardsworth and Bryman observe in relation to themed restaurants, for consumers to enjoy the experiences associated with trends like Disneyization ". . . they must know that their feet remain firmly planted on modern ground in order to be sure of the reassuring securities of modernity: punctuality, physical safety, comfort, reliability, hygiene, etc." (1999). On the other hand, Disneyization and the consumer culture in which it is embedded (and which it cultivates) appear to betoken a sea change of considerable proportions. On that basis, Disneyization would seem to be inconsistent with McDonaldization. In fact, as has been suggested above, they represent contrasting trends which co-exist. My purpose here has been to suggest that the growing interest in McDonaldization and its spheres of application (e.g. Hartley, 1995; Parker and Jary, 1995; Prichard and Willmott, 1997; Smart, in press) should not obscure the significance of other trends and that the apparently all-encompassing tone of the notion of the McDonaldization of society should not blind us to aspects of the modern world that do not appear to be readily subsumed by it. Disneyization is one of the "other trends" that needs to be considered in tandem with McDonaldization while it also represents an attempt to capture certain features of the modern world with which McDonaldization does not readily deal.

McDonaldization and Disneyization also differ is that the precursors to the former – scientific management, Fordism, and bureaucracy – have been underway for a century or longer. It has been possible to point to a number of precursors to Disneyization, but in most cases its chief impact has been felt in much more recent years. Further, Disneyization is almost certainly nowhere near as extensive as McDonaldization – at the moment. McDonald's itself gave a huge boost to the spread of McDonaldization, but whereas fast-food restaurants can crop up all over the place, Disney-style theme parks cannot. Thus, while the lessons of the Disney theme parks are widely emulated (selling and theming strategies, use of emotional labor), the fact that they are less prevalent and prominent almost certainly means that their lessons diffuse more slowly. None the less, the pace of diffusion of the four dimensions of Disneyization seems to be increasing (e.g. Gottdiener, 1997, pp.1–4), so that its significance may well be similarly accelerating.

In the end, the crucial question is whether the concept of Disneyization is useful. Many writers have found the idea of McDonaldization helpful as a capsule statement about the nature of social change and of modernity and as a reference point for discussing these changes. It has been used as a reference point for discussions of specific institutional spheres (for example, Bryman, 1995; Hartley, 1995; Smart, in press). It is in a similar context and with similar purposes in mind that the concept of Disneyization has been proposed. However, in the case of Disneyization there is one further purpose. The term "Disneyfication" has been deployed in a variety of ways with a variety of meanings to a variety of objects. Clearly, writers have felt that "Disney" signifies something meaningful in terms of its effects, but the general approach to writing about Disneyfication lacks coherence and has rather pejorative overtones. I have been concerned in this chapter to provide a specific set of denotations for the term "Disneyization" and in large part to avoid the disparaging tone of much previous writing.

## Note

1 This is a reprint from *Sociological Review* (1999), 47, 1, 25–47. Thanks to Blackwell for granting permission.

## References

Alberge, D. (1996) "Enid Blyton's family sells Noddy and Big Ears," *The Times*, January 24, 3.

Ashforth, B.E. and Humphrey, R.H. (1993) "Emotional labor in service roles: the influence of identity," *Academy of Management Journal*, 18, 88–115.

Barber, B.R. (1995) *Jihad vs. McWorld*, New York: Ballantine.

Baudrillard, J. (1970/1998) *The Consumer Society: Myths and Structures*, London: Sage.

Bauman, Z. (1998) *Work, Consumerism and the New Poor*, Buckingham: Open University Press.

Beardsworth, A. and Bryman, A. (1999) "Late modernity and the dynamics of quasification: the case of the themed restaurant," *Sociological Review*, 47.

Braverman, H. (1974) *Labor and Monopoly Capitalism*, New York: Monthly Review Press.

Bright, R. (1987) *Disneyland: Inside Story*, New York: Abrams.

Bryman, A. (1995) *Disney and his Worlds*, London: Routledge.

Canemaker, J. (1991) *Felix: the Twisted Tale of the World's Most Famous Cat*, New York: Pantheon.

Chaney, D. (1990) "Subtopia in Gateshead: the MetroCentre as a cultural form," *Theory, Culture and Society*, 7, 49–68.

Cohn, N. (1996) "Talking shop," *Sunday Times* (Travel section) 21 January: 1.

Connellan, T. (1996) *Inside the Magic Kingdom: Seven Keys to Disney's Success*. Austin, TX: Bard.

Crawford, M. (1992) "The world in a shopping mall," in *Variations on a Theme Park: The New American City and the End of Public Space*, M. Sorkin (ed.), New York: Noonday, 3–30.

Davis, S.G. (1996) "The theme park: global industry and cultural form," *Media, Culture and Society*, 18, 399–422.

De Cordova, R. (1994) "The Mickey in Macy's window: childhood, consumerism, and Disney animation," in *Disney Discourse*, E. Smoodin (ed.), New York: Routledge, 203–13.

Eco, U. (1986) *Travels in Hyperreality*, London: Pan.

Eisman, R. (1993) "Disney magic," *Incentive*, September: 45–56.

Featherstone, M. (1991) *Consumer Culture and Postmodernism*, London: Sage.

Finch, J. (1997) "Cash-starved Euro Disney turns shopping mall developer," *Guardian* 26 August, 15.

Findlay, J.M. (1992) *Magic Lands: Western Cityscapes and American Culture After 1940*, Berkeley, CA: University of California Press.

Fjellman, S.M. (1992) *Vinyl Leaves: Walt Disney World and America*, Boulder, CO: Westview Press.

Forgacs, D. (1992) "Disney animation and the business of childhood," *Screen*, 33, 361–74.

Fox, N. (1996) "Cartoon heroes are drawn into a money machine," *Sunday Times (Business section)* February, 4: 9.

France, V.A. (1991) *Window on Main Street*, Nashua, NH: Laughter Publications.

Gottdiener, M. (1997) *The Theming of America: Dreams, Visions and Commercial Spaces*, Boulder, CO: Westview Press.

Gould, S.J. (1979) "Mickey Mouse meets Konrad Lorenz," *Natural History*, 88, 30–6.

Grossman, C.L. (1993) "Vegas deals new hand of family fun," *USA Today (International Edition)*, 11 August: 5A.

Grover, R. (1991) *The Disney Touch: How a Daring Management Team Revived an Entertainment Empire*, Homewood, IL: Irwin.

Haas, R. (1995) "Disney goes Dutch: Billy Bathgate and the Disneyfication of the gangster genre," in E. Bell, L. Haas, and L. Sells (eds.), *From Mouse to Mermaid: The Politics of Film, Gender and Culture*, Bloomington, IN: Indiana University Press, 72–85.

Hamilton, K. and Harlow, J. (1995) "Retailers fly in to exploit airport shopping boom," *Sunday Times (Business section)*, 14 May, 2.

Hartley, D. (1995) "The McDonaldization of higher education: food for thought," *Oxford Review of Education*, 21, 409–23.

Hochschild, A. (1983) *The Managed Heart*, Berkeley, CA: University of California Press.

Hopkins, J.S.P. (1990) "West Edmonton Mall: landscape of myths and elsewhereness," *Canadian Geographer*, 34, 2–17.

Jameson, F. (1991) *Postmodernism, or, the Cultural Logic of Late Capitalism*, London: Verso.

Johnson, R. (1991) "A strategy for service – Disney style," *Journal of Business Strategy*, 12, 38–43.

Kasson, J.F. (1978) *Amusing the Million: Coney Island at the Turn of the Century*, New York: Hill & Wang.

King, M.J. (1983) "McDonald's and Disney," in M. Fishwick (ed.), *Ronald Revisited: The World of Ronald McDonald*, Bowling Green, OH: Bowling Green University Popular Press, 106–19.

Klein, N.M. (1993) *Seven Minutes: The Life and Death of the American Animated Cartoon*, London: Verso.

Koenig, D. (1994) *Mouse Tales: A Behind-the-Ears Look at Disneyland*, Irvine, CA: Bonaventure Press.

Kuper, A. (1996) "Dutch football looks to its future – and sees custard," *Financial Times*, March 16, 2.

Lee, A. (1996) "Sooty goes hand in glove with Japanese for £1.2," *The Times*, May 24, 10.

Leidner, R. (1993) *Fast Food, Fast Talk*, Berkeley, CA: University of California Press.

Longmore, A. (1996) "Roll up, roll up and sell the game," *The Times*, 22 May, 46.

Marlin, K.A. (1994) *As Seen on TV: The Visual Culture of Everyday Life in the 1950s*, Cambridge, MA: Harvard University Press.

Merritt, R. and Kaufman, J.B. (1992) *Walt in Wonderland: The Silent Films of Walt Disney*, Perdenone: Edizioni Biblioteca dell'Imagine.

Mosley, L. (1985) *The Real Walt Disney*, London: Grafton.

Nelson, S. (1986) "Walt Disney's EPCOT and the world's fair performance tradition," *Drama Review*, 30, 106–46.

Parker, M. and Jary, D. (1995) "The McUniversity: organization, management and academic subjectivity," *Organization*, 2, 319–38.

Pereira, J. (1995) "Toy sellers wish that Pocahontas were a lion," *Wall Street Journal*, July 24, B1.

Peters, T. and Waterman, R. (1982) *In Search of Excellence: Lessons from America's Best-Run Companies*, New York: Harper & Row.

Prichard, C. and Willmott, H. (1997) "Just how managed is the McUniversity?" *Organization Studies*, 18, 287–316.

Project on Disney (1995) *Inside the Mouse: Work and Play at Disney World*, Durham, NC: Duke University Press.

Reiter, E. (1996) *Making Fast Food: From the Frying Pan into the Fryer*, 2nd edition, Montreal & Kingston: McGill-Queen's University Press.

Ritzer, G. (1993) *The McDonaldization of Society*, Thousand Oaks, CA: Pine Forge.

Ritzer, G. (1998) *The McDonaldization Thesis*, London: Sage.

Ritzer, G. and Liska, A. (1997) " 'McDisneyization' and 'Post-tourism': complementary perspectives on contemporary tourism," in C. Rojek and J. Urry (eds.), *Touring Cultures: Transformations of Travel and Theory*, London: Routledge, 96–109.

Rojek, C. (1993) "Disney culture," *Leisure Studies*, 12, 121–35.

Sayers, F.C. (1965) "Walt Disney accused," *Horn Book*, December, 602–11.

Schickel, R. (1986) *The Disney Version: the Life, Times, Art and Commerce of Walt Disney*, revised edition, London: Pavilion.

Smart, B. (ed.) (in press) *Resisting McDonaldization*, London: Sage.

Smith, J.L. and Byrne, C. (1997) "Greeks put Disney's Hercules on trial," *Sunday Telegraph*, August 31: 6.

Sorkin, M. (1992) "See you in Disneyland," in M. Sorkin (ed.), *Variations on a Theme Park: The New American City and the End of Public Space*, New York: Noonday, 205–302.

Spellmeyer, A.W. (1993) "Mall of America: confounding the sceptics," *Urban Land*, 52, 43–6, 81–3.

Sutton, R.I. (1992) "Feelings about a Disneyland visit: photography and the reconstruction of bygone emotions," *Journal of Management Inquiry*, 1, 278–87.

Swanton, O. (1997) "Pocahontas, eat your heart out," *Guardian* (Higher Education Section), February 25, vi.

Truss, L. (1996) "Memorabilia fails the taste test," *The Times*, 20 December, 38.

Tumbusch, T. (1989) *Tomart's Illustrated Disneyana Catalog and Price Guide*, Radnor, PA: Wallace-Homestead.

Urry, J. (1990) *The Tourist Gaze: Leisure and Travel in Contemporary Societies*, London: Sage.

Van Maanen, J. and Kunda, G. (1989) " 'Real feelings': emotional expression and organizational culture," *Research in Organizational Behavior*, 11, 43–103.

Warren, S. (1994) "Disneyfication of the metropolis: popular resistance in Seattle," *Journal of Urban Affairs*, 16, 89–107.

Wasko, J. (1996) "Understanding the Disney Universe," in J. Curran and M. Gurevitch (eds.), *Mass Media and Society*, 2nd edition, London: Arnold, 348–68.

Wasko, J., Phillips, M., and Purdie, C. (1993) "Hollywood meets Madison Avenue: the commercialization of US films," *Media, Culture and Society*, 15, 271–93.

Wharton, A.S. and Erickson, R.J. (1993) "Managing emotions on the job and at home: understanding the consequences of multiple emotional roles," *Academy of Management Journal*, 18, 457–86.

Zemke, R. (1989) *The Service Edge: 101 Companies That Profit from Customer Care*, New York: New American Library.

Zibart, E. (1997) *The Unofficial Disney Companion*, New York: Macmillan.

# CHAPTER 5

# Understanding the Contradictory Lived Experience of Service Work

## The Customer-Oriented Bureaucracy

MAREK KORCZYNSKI

In this chapter, I lay out how a body of research has shown the existence of deep-seated contradictions within the lived experience of front line service work.[1] This research shows that for many contemporary service workers there are simultaneously pleasures and pains within their experiences of work. There are both tensions and spaces in their work lives. I then present the model of a customer-oriented bureaucracy as a lens through which to understand the contradictory nature of contemporary service work. The final section of the chapter considers the uses and limitations of the customer-oriented bureaucracy as an analytical tool.

### Introduction – The Contradictory Lived Experience of Service Work

There is now a substantial body of research into service work which shows the existence of deep contradictions within the lived experience of service workers. In this section, I briefly lay out some of the key points of contradictions uncovered within this research, focusing particularly on the relations between workers and service-recipients (customers, from hereon). I then show how this research has also shown the existence of simultaneous tensions and spaces within the experience of service work.

In one of the finest studies of service work, Benson (1986) shows how workers in a department store had a deeply contradictory relationship with customers. On the one hand, relations with customers could be a key arena of satisfaction for these workers. On the other hand, customers could be a key source of dissatisfaction – humiliation, and pain. In the memorable phrase of the department workers themselves, customers were experienced as "our friend, the enemy." Customers can be a key source of satisfaction and pleasure for service workers in a number of ways. One of the most important of these is the way in which customer-service worker relationships can become socially embedded, such that both participants step outside of (and thus implicitly resist) the narrow economic instrumentality of a customer-worker relationship. It is easy to think of this occurring in a romanticized view of past times. Indeed, Studs Terkel captures the ideal of socially embedded worker-customer interactions well. In his collection of conversations with American people in *American Dreams: Lost and Found* (1999), he describes Gaynell Begley:

> She is behind the counter at the store. There is a steady stream of customers; small children, old people, husky young men off the road repair gang . . . She addresses each by name. There are constant soft, jocular exchanges. "A transaction here is not entirely economic. It's a matter of friendship and socializin'" for a minute. That's as important to me as getting "that quarter".

Far from being lost to the past, forms of socially embedded relationships and encounters with customers continue to provide an important source of satisfaction for service workers. For instance, consider the following from Anna, a call center worker interviewed by Bolton and Houlihan (2007, p.254):

> Sometimes with the customer, when it's going how I like it, and when it is "quality" calls, I can honestly say that I enjoy it, I really do. I can say I feel like I've done something form, and they'll tell me that. When they call me by my name and they are happy and the customers will laugh at a joke that I make, and I can have a conversation with them. . . . Because I do enjoy speaking to people. . . . That's what I do like about the job. . . . That's brilliant.

It is highly relevant that when asked in their own words about the satisfaction from helping customers, workers tend to use the language of helping people, mothers, kids, rather than *customers*. Williams (1987, p.106) reports a survey of Australian flight attendants which shows that the most important reasons for becoming a flight attendant was "working with people." She notes that,

> this was emphasized again in interviews as positive aspect of the job.

"I enjoy flying because I meet people – caring for people – to do something for someone. Doing extra if someone is ill gives me satisfaction." "Helping mothers with a baby and the 'thank you' means more to you than the travel". Another said: "Little kids traveling on their own, you get pleasure out of doing that sort of thing."

When asked for particular examples of satisfying incidents front line workers tend to talk of "this old man," or "this nice woman." In other words, they are relating to the service recipient primarily as socially embedded people, rather than as customers. Even at McDonalds, there can be a not insignificant degree of social embeddedness in the service encounter. Leidner (1993, p.230) writes on the basis of her ethnographic study of two service firms, "many of the encounters between workers and customers at McDonald's and between agents and prospects of Combined Insurance were experienced by both parties as real social exchanges." Further, a key satisfaction for workers from customers comes from having "regulars" with whom it is enjoyable to interact (Tolich, 1993). As Hodson and Sullivan (1997, p.280) put it:

> Many service workers prize their regular customers because they have the opportunity to build a personal relationship with the customer. In this case, a genuine relationship may replace the struggle to control the relationship.

As Bolton and Houlihan (2005) acutely argue, we need to be able to bring the humanity back into the analysis of service work (also see Lopez, 2006 and O'Donohue and Turley, 2006) – to be able to see the skillfully humane at work.

At the same time, a consistent finding in research into the experience of service work is that customers also represent an important source of dissatisfaction and pain for service workers. For instance, Korczynski and Bishop (2008) outline cases of unemployment benefits staff working in constant fear of being sworn at, threatened, or even physically assaulted. One male worker expressed the deep effects that customer abuse and the threat of customer abuse can have on staff:

> it only needs one nasty incident and you can really shake people's self confidence, and from personal experience I never feel comfortable, you can feel the adrenalin rise straight away and you immediately think where's this gonna end? Can I cope with that abuse today which is often personal, you know. They make it personal, they'll comment about your thighs or your shape or whatever and there will be bad language and you think, can I really cope with that today, do I deserve it. And of course you don't. (p.151)

Notably, Stein's (2007) review of research concludes that to an important degree the worker-customer relationship has the potential to be experienced as "toxic" – with the feelings of toxicity from customers spreading rapidly among front line staff. At its worst, the situation becomes managed as normal and everyday by supervisors and manager.

> A trainer told workers who were upset by angry students' rebukes to "think of yourself as a trash can. Take everyone's little bits of anger all day, put it inside you and at the end of the day, just pour it in the dumpster on your way out of the door." Not surprisingly, workers found this advice offensive.
>
> (Eaton, 1996, p.296)

Not only does research shows customers as a source of pleasure, and as a source of pain, it also shows that these happen simultaneously in many service workplaces. Tolich's (1993, p.368) ethnographic study of a supermarket concludes that, "grocery clerks simultaneously viewed their customers as sources of stress and satisfaction." Williams (1987, pp.106–7) reports that a survey of Australian flight attendants showed while "working with people" was the dominant reason for taking on the job, "passenger attitude" was the second most important source of job dissatisfaction. The motif of service workers regarding customers as "our friend, the enemy" is one with wide applicability in the contemporary service economy.

Indeed, the picture of service workers' contradictory relations with customers needs to be nested within a picture of wider contradictions in the experience of service work. Much research shows the existence of *simultaneous spaces and tensions within the experience of service work.* Again, Benson's (1986, p.6) study brings this out well:

> when managers and customers exerted unified pressure on the saleswomen, her life could be difficult indeed; but when she could play one off against the other she could create new space for herself on the job.

If caught between the pressures from customers and management, the service work can be experienced as tension-ridden. As one store worker interviewed by Weatherly and Tansik (1992, p.5) put it:

> I'm damned if I do; damned if I don't. You just can't win. Either [the boss] is mad at me, or the customer is. If I don't get my work done, [the boss] is going to yell at me. But if I don't help the customers, they get pissed at me.

Most commonly, this tension is experienced as a tension between quality and quantity targets. For instance, much research into call center work shows that many workers feel torn between a desire to give quality calls to customers and the management targets to deliver a large (and specified) number of calls per day (Deery and Kinnie, 2002; see Holtgrewe *et al.*, 2002). To quote from Bolton and Houlihan's interviewee, Anna, again (2007, p.253):

> If I feel that I've got to get so many [targets] in an hour, I've got to rush the quantity through well – then the customer starts to annoy me . . . It's not a nice feeling, and it's something that makes you not like yourself in a way.

This tension between quality and quantity is experienced in many service work settings. Research into health care show both spaces and tensions in the experience of this work. Spaces are there and can be used for autonomy, humanity and meaning:

> I just love the contact with the patient. I love the chance to be involved in their lives.
> (Nurse in Wicks, 1998, p.85)

> A couple of years ago there was one lady in particular who was a . . . stroke patient and when she finally walked out the door I knew it was through us busting our guts and her really trying and that was one of the happiest days of my life.
> (Nurse in Wicks, 1998, p.84)

But tension is experienced between quality and quantity, with the quantity targets strongly emphasized:

> The most frustrating thing for me is the time thing. The tension between the time allocated for duties and the time to offer comfort in doing those duties.
> I feel myself constantly torn between those two and compromising, staying for five minutes and perhaps racing through the observations and not asking the next lady how she is.
> (Nurses in Wicks, 1998, pp.112–14)

### Service Work Organization as Customer-Oriented Bureaucracy

If there is considerable evidence that the lived experience of many service workers is a contradictory one, involving tensions and spaces in which the customer is both friend and enemy, then what is needed is a theoretical lens which allows us to capture these systematic contradictions. The simple argument, put forward by some critical authors, that service work is *dominated* by McDonaldization (Ritzer, 2006), or by the systematic application of Taylorism (see Taylor and Bain, 1999), is not a lens that allows us to grasp these contradictions. Taylor and Bain's metaphor of the call center as "an assembly line in the head" (1999), whilst startling and elegant, denies us the conceptual space to see the pleasures and spaces of call center work noted above, and to see these existing simultaneously with the pains and the tensions.

The idea of seeing service work organization as a *customer-oriented bureaucracy*, is one that allows us to understand and conceptualize the contradictory lived experiences of service workers. The contradictory experiences of service workers are informed by dual, and potentially contradictory, logics underpinning how service work is organized and managed. On the one hand, service firms compete on the basis of price and efficiency of service delivery. This means that there are systematic and strong rationalizing pressures acting on service organizations. In order to compete, they are obliged to rationalize their work structures to lower costs and maximize efficiency. Thus, there is an important logic pushing service firms towards *bureaucracy – a term used here in the Weberian tradition of describing a purely rational, efficiency-focused organization.* On the other hand, service firms compete on the basis of service quality, such that firms can no longer compete *simply* by treating a customer as an object to be pushed along an assembly-line. Consider Du Puy's description of a customer journey in a pure bureaucracy:

> The customer . . . has to follow a complex process of rules and procedures, running from one place to the next, all because the system was not designed for the customer's convenience, but for the bureaucrats who have certain tasks to do . . . The key symbolic word in the Kafkaesque world of bureaucracies might well be "file": "I have your file" . . . "Your file is incomplete"; "Your file was not sent over to me" and so on.
>
> (1999, p.56)

Competition forces firms away from treating customers this way, such that firms increasingly compete by offering service quality (Parasuraman *et al.* 1992), or by being *customer-oriented*. There is a considerable literature in marketing on the logic of customer-orientation, but the essential element of customer-orientation involves orientation to the non-rational aspects of customers, towards customers' sense of emotions, individuality and power. Applying sociological imagination, it can be seen that the key aspect offered within the service delivery is an *enchanting myth of sovereignty* (see Korczynski and Ott, 2004). The service is organized such that customers can feel a sense of sovereignty in two ways – a sense of relational superiority over the server, and a sense of being in charge. Consider the simple scenario of you entering a restaurant, and a waiter saying to you: "Would you like to follow me to a table that is free, Sir/Madam?" The address of "Sir/Madam" positions you, the customer, as a relational superior, and the form of words, "would you like to, . . ." positions you, the customer, as in charge, as not being dictated to, not being treated as a "file" nor as a nut on an assembly line.

Service work organization, therefore, is structured by the dual and potentially contradictory logics of bureaucratization and customer-orientation. On each dimension of work organization, service management is forced to try to organize work to accommodate to both logics. Table 5.1 puts forward a summary of the "customer-oriented bureaucracy" along key dimensions of work organization. The concept and the table leave open the question of how management may seek to resolve the tensions arising from the dual logics at play in the organization of front line service work. The discussion of each dimension in turn below, however, indicates some ways in which management has approached these dilemmas in practice in a range of service settings.

The concept of the customer-oriented bureaucracy can be seen, in part, as an extension of Weberian thinking.[2] Weber, writing in the early twentieth century, argued that bureaucracies, formally rational organizations centered on creating internal efficiency, would come to dominate social life. Formal rationality is a term Weber used to describe the emphasis on creating an efficient means of doing something. In his theory of bureaucracy, he argued that this emphasis on formal rationality would make the organization one focused on creating internal efficiencies, and would tend to make the organization one in which there is a marginalization of consideration of the substantive outcomes of the organization. In short, an overwhelming focus on means leads to a neglect of the ends of an organization's actions. In a bureaucracy, rules that are seen as promoting efficiency, or as

**Table 5.1** Mapping the customer-oriented bureaucracy against key dimensions of work organization

| Dimension of work Organization | Customer-oriented bureaucracy Dual focus on | |
|---|---|---|
| | Customer-orientation Logic | Bureaucratic logic |
| Dominant organizing principles | Orientation to formally irrational aspect of customers | Rationalization |
| Labor process | Qualitative focus | Quantitative focus |
| Basis of division of labor | Customer relationship | Efficient task completion |
| Basis of authority | Customer-related norms | Rational-legal rules |
| Means/ends status and emotions | Focus on customers as ends of actions | Focus on efficient means |
| Key management role | Creating and maintaining fragile social order that allows creation of profit | |

formally rational, come to be seen as right and legitimate. These "rational-legal rules" come to be seen as the key basis of authority, in fact. Weber presented an essentially pessimistic vision of modern societies dominated by bureaucratic organizations which could give us efficiency but which would create soul-less, disenchanted, iron cages for us to inhabit. Updating Weber's visions, I argue that, particularly in service settings, there is not just the bureaucratic logic at play, but also the customer-oriented logic at play. The nature of market competition has led to service firms to compete not only on the basis of low costs and efficiencies but also by offering to treat the customer as more than a file – by offering to re-enchant the customer through the delivery of pleasurable service quality. The discussion below along each important dimension of work organization examines the simultaneous playing out of these two logics.

*Dominant Organizing Principles*

The ideal-type of the customer-oriented bureaucracy contains within it the dual logics of rationalization, and orientation to the formally irrational aspects of customers. Work is organized to be competitively efficient, to appeal to the utilitarian sense of the customer. In addition, work is organized to enchant the sensibility of the customer, particularly through the enchanting myth of customer sovereignty. The concept points to an essential tension at the heart of contemporary service work. On the one hand, rationalization implies routinization. On the other, orientation to formally irrational customers means embracing and coping with unpredictability and variability. Management's ability to routinize the behavior of customers is systematically limited because of the need to perpetuate the myth of customer sovereignty. Management can organize matters to guide and teach customers, but the need to perpetuate the myth of sovereignty means that the control management has over customers in front line interactions is incomplete. The myth of sovereignty systematically creates the possibility that the customer will step outside the routines that management attempts to impose upon him or her. For instance, Benson's (1986) excellent account of work within a department store argues convincingly that "managers had little, if any, success . . . in controlling the substance of customer-salesperson interactions; the attempt to maximize and satisfy each customer's needs enduringly resisted routinization" (p. 286). Front line service work, therefore, is organized in order to cope with this systematic potential "variability of the customer input" (Riddle, 1990, p.52).

*Labor Process*

The model of the customer-oriented bureaucracy highlights that management demands that service workers have both a qualitative and a quantitative focus in the work that they do. They must maintain the enchanting myth of customer sovereignty but they must do this efficiently and as quickly as possible. There is now a voluminous literature on call center work which highlights the dual demands of quantity and quality made upon call center workers (see Deery and Kinnie 2002, for an overview). Not only are call center workers expected to deal with a high number of customer calls per day (resulting in many cases in call length targets), but they are also expected to deliver a high degree of service quality to these customers (often measured by supervisors listening in on calls and assessing the calls against service quality criteria). As Holtgrewe and Kerst (2002, p.141) argue,

> call centers do not follow an unambiguously (neo-)Taylorist logic of rationalization. As boundary-spanning units of organizations call centers are caught in a dilemma between efficiency and quality – at least if they follow the high road of quality-oriented service organization. They are the object of rationalization and outsourcing strategies while promising customer orientation to their environment. In call centers this organizational dilemma is translated into dilemmatic demands on work behavior, requiring employees to move competently through the dilemma.

As noted earlier, this tension within the labor process, within the key demands of the work undertaken, is a key underpinning for the contradictions within the lived experience of service work that has been noted in so much research. There are tensions to be experienced when these dual pressures clash against each other, when a worker wants to give quality, but is forced to forego this in search of quantity. But there are also potentially spaces in that workers are able to call on management rhetoric of customer-orientation in justifying a prioritizing of quality aims, for instance.

*Basis of Division of Labor*

A key aspect of a bureaucracy is its complex division of labor based on the aim of maximizing the efficiency of task completion. Adam Smith's description of the minute division of tasks and jobs in a pin factory is perhaps the most famous example of this basis of division of labor in practice. Within the customer-oriented bureaucracy, however, the division of labor is also structured around the need to cater to the formally irrational nature of the customer. Specifically, in front line work, the enchanting myth of customer sovereignty must be maintained. The enchanting myth of sovereignty is unlikely to be achieved if the customer is passed around the organization on an (opaque) assembly-line journey. The enchanting myth of sovereignty is more likely to be achieved if the maintenance of customer relationship is a guiding principle for the division of labor.

Gutek (1995) summarizes the encounter/relationship difference, pointing out that in encounters each service interaction is complete in itself, and front line workers are, in the eyes of both the customers and the workers, interchangeable. Relationships, by contrast, happen in the context of an ongoing series of transactions in which a particular front line worker and particular customer become known to each other and expect continued interaction in the future. Gutek's concept of a "pseudo-relationship" also captures a way in which management may typically attempt to create a fragile social order out of the potentially contradictory approaches to the division of labor. As also described by Winslow and Bramer (1994), management are able to use expert systems to allow front line workers to instantly call-up a range and depth of information on customers to allow them to "make encounters feel more personal," and to allow a "simulation" of a relationship. Indeed, in front line work, Business Process Reengineering (BPR) can be seen as exactly suited to creation of pseudo-relationships. As described by Hammer and Champy (1995), BPR tends to involve the creation of one block of front line workers in an organization – so as to prevent the bureaucratic shunting of customers and their files around the organization – supported by expert systems that can rationalize jobs, and store a range of customer information to better allow the front line worker to simulate a relationship with the customer. While pseudo-relationships may create a form of social order between the two logics this is likely to be a fragile one. The line between a simulation of a relationship and an encounter may be a thin one, easily crossed over in service interactions.

*Basis of Authority*

For Weber (1968), in a bureaucracy the basis of authority is rational-legal authority – the idea that power, as formalized in rules and procedures, is legitimized because those rules are seen as encapsulating formal rationality. In the customer-oriented bureaucracy, authority also derives from the customer. Power can become legitimate if it is seen as acting for the customer. The dual bases of authority underlie the perception of "two bosses" found in many service settings. Mars *et al.* (1979) note that in the hotel and catering industry the role of the customer means that, "the effect is that instead of working for one boss the employee is working for two" (p. 84), and that the role of the customer in tipping "both expresses and supports a split in managerial authority" (p. 85). Shamir (1980, p.748) similarly refers to the "two bosses dilemma" faced by front line workers.

Total Quality Management is an approach by management (often, but not exclusively in front line settings) to draw these two, potentially contradictory, bases of authority symbiotically together. As Legge (1995, p.219) notes, at the heart of TQM is a managerial prioritization of quality in which quality is defined, at least rhetorically, as "conformance to the requirements of the *customer*" (emphasis added). What is important about TQM is that it connects with the rise of the customer as a figure of authority at a societal level (Abercrombie, 1991; Gabriel and Lang, 2006). In Weberian terms, the genius of TQM's appropriation of the customer for legitimating power within organizations appears to be that it potentially unites both substantive (or value) rationality and formal rationality. TQM contains within it both substantive rationality, in terms of acting in the interests of the customer, a key authority figure of society, and formal rationality, in terms of "hard" rational techniques to achieve efficiency within production. Its attraction to management is that it seeks to make symbiotic the relationship between these two forms of rationality. In this way, TQM appears to create a hermetically sealed space of legitimizing discourses. BPR, has similar goals. For instance, Hammer and Champy (1995, p.74) argue that BPR requires that "employees deeply believe that they work for their customers, not their bosses." Implicitly, they suggest that employees will go along with the reengineering changes in the organization, many centrally based on the application of principles of formal rationality, because they will see them as working for the customer.

The great sleight of hand in these sophisticated attempts to create a fragile social order out of the dual logics is that the "customer" whom management is holding up as the figure of authority is defined in such a way as to prioritize his/her formally rational nature. TQM rests upon an image of a customer whose behavior and attitudes can be measured, predicted and managed. TQM and BPR rest uneasily with the customer as having the value rationality and unpredictability of a human.

*Means/end Status and Emotions*

An important attribute of the organization informed by the bureaucratic logic is the prioritization of the means of action over the ends of the action (Bauman, 1989). For the front line workforce, this attribute means that there is marginalization of affect to be displayed to the ends of action, and the prioritization of a logic of impersonality in job behavior (Prottas, 1979). The concept of the customer-oriented bureaucracy highlights that the tendency to prioritize the ends of action exists alongside the bureaucratic prioritization of the means of action. The formally rational part of the customer may be satisfied by the emphasis on efficient means and the consequent impersonal interactions with front line staff, but this is not the case for the formally irrational part of the customer, particularly in relation to the enchanting myth of sovereignty. To cope with this aspect of the customer, the organization must also prioritize the ends of actions and consequently its front line workforce are expected to act with emotion, particularly empathy, towards the customer.

In the service management literature, the dual emphasis on means and ends of actions in contemporary service organizations is manifest through the reframing of the continued bureaucratic emphasis on measurement. According to this literature the "metrics" to be used in managing the organization should no longer be "internal" ones related to efficient means, but must be customer-based ones (Heskett *et al.*, 1997; Schneider and Bowen, 1995). The ends of the action enter as organizational priority through the emphasis on the measurement of the customer's perception and behavior. For the front line workforce, the bureaucratic code of impersonality is replaced by the requirement to deliver rationalized emotional labor. Martin *et al.* (1998) and Putnam and Mumby (1993) highlight the rationalized nature of emotional labor in many contemporary service settings by contrasting it with the qualities of the expression of emotions in "feminist" non-rationalized organizations. Management does not just require positive emotions expressed to the customers; but also needs these emotions delivered efficiently. In Hochschild's (1983) study the management need for rationalized emotional labor comes through most clearly in her discussion of the emotions required of flight attendants during the competition-inspired "speed-up" of the 1970s and 1980s. She writes (p.126) that, "before the speed-up, most workers sustained the cheerful good will that food service requires. They did so for the most part proudly." It is only after the speed-up, "when asked to make personal human cost at an inhuman speed," that the tensions of emotional labor become significant.

In many contemporary customer service organizations the contradictions of asking for an efficient display of emotions are implicitly acknowledged by management. Management increasingly seek to maintain the fragile social order through such approaches as creating "downtime" for staff away from customers, developing calming strategies and promoting "cognitive restructuring" among staff (Mann, 1999). An important approach to the creation of downtime in some settings is the creation of "off-stage" areas. As Fineman and Sturdy (2001) note,

> Rest rooms, galleys, corridors and other "off-stage" areas provide an opportunity for employees to drop their corporate mask, free from the scrutiny of supervisors and customers. "Undesirable" emotions, such as fear, anger, hurt and frustration can be vented or expressed. In such settings the otherwise consented-to social order can be attacked, deprecated, or ridiculed in the presence of a "willing" audience of colleagues.

The wider organizational social order may thus be maintained by creating a delimited forum for its breakdown. In these spaces, often implicitly ceded by management, workers frequently form deep bonds of social support among their peers – relationships which have been labeled *communities of coping* (Korczynski, 2003). Although, front line service work appears often to have a highly individualized labor process, with one worker dealing with one customer, the tendency for communities of coping to develop shows that there is an important collective element to the rationalized emotional labor demanded of contemporary service workers. Such communities of coping have been explicitly identified in a range of service settings – hospitals (Lewis, 2005), call centers (Frenkel *et al.*, 1999, Simms, 2005), pubs (Seymour and Sandiford, 2005) unemployment benefit centers (Bishop *et al.*, 2005), retails work and casinos (Simms, 2005).

*Key Management Role*

The presence of the logics of rationalization and orientation towards the formally irrational aspects of the customer means that management is placed in the structural position of attempting to keep tensions latent to facilitate the creation of profit through the orderly functioning of the organization. The customer-oriented bureaucracy suggests that a key management role becomes the establishment of a surface calm above the dual logics of the organization. Any such order created should be seen as fragile in the sense that it does not do away with the essential tension underlying the organization. Contradictions and tensions are there ready to surface at any time. Wicks' (1998, p.132) study of heath care work captures this point well:

> It is in work environments, such the hospital ward that supposedly functional work arrangement can be seen to be conflictual at their very core. In such an environment deeply felt latent and over tensions are unavoidable.

Equally unavoidable is that management will attempt to fashion a situation in which tensions are more often latent than overt.

Shamir's (1978) study of hotels suggests that management may address the dual logics at play by creating a dualistic organizational structure, parts of which are tightly bureaucratic, and parts of which are oriented to cope with the unmanageable and idiosyncratic aspects of customers. This approach, however, may not eliminate tension, but merely alter the place and manner of its manifestation. Typically tension may become manifest in the *lateral* conflict between parts of the organization that are structured by the different logics. In hospitality, the deep personal antagonisms that can arise between front line staff and those in the back-of-house (Whyte, 1948; Wood, 1992) stem from this managerial attempt to create a social order out of the dual logics at play.

In attempting to fashion a fragile social order, to keep tensions latent, a key management tool is also likely to be rhetoric and symbolism. As such it is little surprise to witness the increasing management use in service settings of a win:win:win human resource management rhetoric for customers, workers, and management. This can create a form of discourse in which tensions seem to be redefined away. For instance, the tensions of maintaining a dual focus can be made less visible by redefining the issue as one of "balance" (Heskett *et al.*, 1997). Another way in which HRM can assist in promoting dual-focused behavior is through its use of rhetoric. Indeed, a number of commentators suggest that HRM's importance lies in its rhetorical and symbolic roles (Legge, 1995). The point made is that the power of HRM lies not so much in its substantive content, in terms of, for instance, actual training and hiring practices, but rather in the language and symbols it uses and the effect that these have on the workforce. If management devises mission statements which stress commitment to the workforce, to their development, training and career, and if management continually reinforces this through forums such as team meetings and performance appraisals, then this may have an effect on engendering a level of workforce commitment regardless, to a degree, of whether this rhetoric is actually matched by concrete practices. A key rhetorical aspect of HRM is the creation of a language which suggests shared interests between management and workforce. Thus training is discussed in terms of the mutual benefits that it brings to the organization and to the individual worker. The language of teamwork is stressed since this suggests working together towards a shared goal. In the context of front line work, management can also present customer-orientation as a shared value. Skillfully management may be able to use language to delegitmize a sphere of separate workforce interests by so emphasizing the confluence of worker and customer interests that the former become subsumed into the latter.

## The Customer-Oriented Bureaucracy as an Analytical Tool: Uses and Limitations

The key use of the model of service work organization that is the customer-oriented bureaucracy is as a heuristic device that allows us to understand the deep-seated contradictions that exist in the experience of service workers across many types of service work. It is put forward in the sociological tradition of ideal-types – theoretical constructs that do not necessarily exist anywhere in the pure form in real life. In this section, I want first to stress the role of ideal-types in sociological analysis and then to highlight some necessary limitations in the *sole* use of this ideal-type in the analysis of service work.

The concept of the customer-oriented bureaucracy is put forward, in the tradition of Weber, as an ideal type, a logically derived model to illuminate analysis. Let me consider, then, the main charge against the use of ideal types. Clegg (1989, pp.197–8) makes the case against the use of ideal types, arguing that:

> Organizations should not be conceptualized as the phenomenal expression of some inner principle such as economic exploitation or rationality . . . [but are] locales in which negotiation, contestation and struggle between organizationally divided and linked agencies is a routine occurrence.

Clegg's dichotomy here is a false one. Organizations can both be informed and structured by dominant logics and be locales for negotiation, contestation, and struggle. The concept of the customer-oriented bureaucracy argues that customer service organizations are structured by the dual logics of rationalization and orientation to the formally irrational aspect of customers. How these structuring logics are played out in practice is not seen as pre-determined. The model suggests that structurally, a key management role is to attempt to fashion a fragile social order out of the dual logics, but the model does not presume to outline how, or if, such a social order is established in practice. Rather the model suggests the fragility of any social order created. Also, the discussion has implicitly portrayed the service organization as an arena for negotiation, contestation, struggle (and potentially meaning and pleasure [Benner and Wrubel, 1989]).

Ideal types can aid analysis as long as they are not seen as suggesting that exactly the same dynamics are played out in exactly the same way in organizations. An ideal type is a heuristic device, a way in to examine organizations. As Eliaeson(2000) states:

> "ideal types are deliberately accentuated. Ideal types . . . are an aid to the interpreter and should help the interpreter to depict reality, without reflecting reality directly. The representation of reality given by the ideal-type is disproportionate and serves to make central features of reality more visible and intelligible". (p.250)

Ideal types are thus located at a high level of abstraction. The customer-oriented bureaucracy ideal type is no exception to this. When analysis descends in levels of abstraction towards the more concrete, then problems necessarily arise in the *sole* use of ideal types for analysis. Again, the customer-oriented bureaucracy ideal type is no exception. Further to this, it is useful to highlight such problems when the level of analysis descends to the level of different political economies of nation-states. Regarding the former, Taylor and Bain have argued cogently for the need for the analysis of call center work, and by extension all service work, to be located "within the wider political economy" (2005, p.264). Their implicit argument is that the nature of service work organization may vary in important ways according to the different political economy of nation-states. For instance, service work organization in a short-term neo-liberal economy such as the USA is likely to differ from that in longer-term, socially embedded economies such as Sweden. For the analyst who concentrates on this level of analysis, the concept of the customer-oriented bureaucracy can appear of little use. The concept, on its own, presents a uniform ideal type, and thus could be seen as obscuring differences in service work organization across different political economic regimes. The appropriate reply to this point is that the customer-oriented bureaucracy ideal type *on its own* is indeed of little use at this level of abstraction. Used as a heuristic device in *conjunction with* political economic theory, however, it can aid analysis. The aid to analysis can be framed thus: customer-oriented bureaucracy theory posits the overall dual logics of rationalization and customer-orientation, and articulates how for dimensions of work organization management are faced with the task of trying to fashion a social order. For analysis at the level of political economy, informed by customer-oriented bureaucracy theory, the question is how the different political economic regimes affect the way in which managements in different countries try to fashion a social order. For instance, on the dimension of flexibility, short-termism is likely to pressure more managers to address the need for both (bureaucratic) stability and (customer-oriented) flexibility through labor stretching (Korczynski, 2002, p.74), while being located in long-termist socially embedded economies creates pressures for management to find joint stability and flexibility through training.[3] It should be further noted that just as the concept of the customer-oriented bureaucracy can be used as an analytical tool in conjunction with political economic analysis, so it can be used in conjunction with a focus on gender. Kerfoot and Korczynski (2005) argue that the model helps us understand how gender may be structured within the logics of customer-orientation and rationalization, and may be played out within these structures by the key actors, the workers and the customers. An adequate understanding of other key aspects of service work, therefore, can be found by supplementing the lens of the customer-oriented bureaucracy with other forms of sociological analysis, such as feminist analysis and political economic analysis.

## Notes

1 The focus of this chapter is upon workers who deal with service-recipients as a key part of their job. These are often referred to as front line workers. Here this will be simplified to service workers.

2 For a full statement on the intellectual provenance of this concept as resting in a critical economic sociology, see Korczynski (2007).

3 A similar point about customer-oriented bureaucracy theory and levels of

analysis can be made of analysis which focuses on particular service occupations, such as call center workers, or retail workers, for instance. The point is that customer-oriented bureaucracy theory should be used in conjunction with an understanding of the specifics of such occupations (for an example of this approach, see Chapter 5 in Korczynski, 2002).

# References

Abercrombie, N. (1991) "The privilege of the producer," in R. Keat and N. Abercrombie (eds.), *Enterprise Culture*, London: Routledge, 17–42.

Bauman, Z. (1989) *Modernity and the Holocaust*, Cambridge: Polity.

Benner, P. and Wrubel, J. (1989) *The Primacy of Caring*, Melno Park, CA: Addison-Wesley.

Benson, S. (1986) *Counter Cultures*, Chicago: University of Illinois Press.

Bishop, V., Korczynski, M. and Cohen, L. (2005) "Invisibility of violence: Constructing violence out of the job centre workplace in the UK," *Work, Employment and Society*, 19, 3, 583–602.

Bolton, S.C. and Houlihan, M. (2005) "The (mis) representation of customer service," *Work, Employment and Society*, 19, 4, 685–703.

Bolton, S. and Houlihan, M. (2007) "Risky business: Rethinking the human in interactive service work," in S. Bolton and M. Houlihan (eds.), *Searching for the Human in Human Resource Management*, Basingstoke: Palgrave Macmillan, 245–62.

Clegg, S. (1989) *Frameworks of Power*, London: Sage.

Deery, S. and Kinnie, N. (2002) "Call centers and beyond: a thematic evaluation" *Human Resource Management Journal*, 12, 4, 3–13.

DuPuy, F. (1999) *The Customer's Victory*, Basingstoke: Macmillan.

Eaton, S. (1996) "The customer is always interesting," in C. Macdonald and C. Sirianni (eds.), *Working in the Service Society*, Philadelphia: Temple University Press, 291–332.

Eliaeson, S. (2000) "Max Weber's methodology: An ideal type," *Journal of the History of the Behavioral Sciences*, 36, 241–63.

Fineman, S. and Sturdy, A. (2001) "Struggles for the control of affect," in A. Sturdy, I. Grugulis and H. Willmott (eds.), *Consuming Services*, Basingstoke: Macmillan, 135–56.

Frenkel, S., Korczynski, M., Shire, K., and Tam, M. (1999) *On the Front Line*, Ithaca, NY: ILR/Cornell University Press.

Gabriel, Y. and Lang, T. (2006) *The Unmanageable Consumer*, London: Sage.

Gutek, B. (1995) *The Dynamics of Service*, San Francisco: Jossey-Bass.

Hammer, M. and Champy, J. (1995) *Reengineering the Corporation*, London: Nicholas Brealey.

Heskett, J., Sasser, W. and Schlesinger, L. (1997) *The Service Profit Chain*, New York: The Free Press.

Hochschild, A. (1983) *The Managed Heart*, Berkeley, CA: University of California Press.

Hodson, R. and Sullivan, T. (1997) *The Social Organization of Work*, Washington, DC: Wadsworth.

Holtgrewe, U. and Kerst, C. (2002) "Between customer orientation and organizational efficiency – boundary management in call centers," *Soziale Welt-Zeitschrift für Socialwiseensdschaftliche Forschung und Praxis*, 53, 2, 141–58.

Holtgrewe, U., Shire, K. and Kerst, C. (ed.) (2002) *Re-Organising Service Work*, Aldershot: Ashgate.

Kerfoot, D. and Korczynski, M. (2005) "Gender and service work: new directions for the study of front-line service work," *Gender, Work and Organization*, 12, 5, 387–99.

Korczynski, M. (2002) *Human Resource Management in Service Work*, Basingstoke: Palgrave Macmillan.

Korczynski, M. (2003) "Communities of coping: collective emotional labor in service work," *Organization*, 10, 1, 55–79.

Korczynski, M. (2007) "Service work, social theory and collectivism," *Work, Employment and Society*, 21, 3, 577–88.

Korczynski, M. and Ott, U. (2004) "When production and consumption meet," *Journal of Management Studies*, 41 4, 575–99.

Korczynski, M. and Bishop, V. (2008) "The job centre: abuse, violence and fear on the front line," in S. Fineman (ed.), *Emotions in Organizations: Critical Voices*, Oxford: Blackwell, 74–87.

Legge, K. (1995) *Human Resource Management*, Basingstoke: Macmillan.

Leidner, R. (1993) *Fast Food, Fast Talk*, Berkeley, CA: University of California Press.

Lewis, P. (2005) "Suppression or expression: an exploration of emotion management in a special care baby unit," *Work, Employment and Society*, 19, 3, 565–81.

Lopez, S. (2006) "Emotional labor and organized emotional care," *Work and Occupations*, 33, 2, 133–60.

Mann, S. (1999) *Hiding What We Feel, Faking What We Don't*, Boston: Element.

Mars, G., Bryant, D. and Mitchell, P. (1979) *Manpower Problems in the Hotel and Catering Industry*, Farnborough: Gower.

Martin, J., Knopoff, K. and Beckman, C. (1998) "An alternative to bureaucratic impersonality and emotional labor: bounded emotionality at the Body Shop," *Administrative Science Quarterly*, 43, 2, 429–69.

O'Donohue, S. and Turley, D. (2006) "Compassion at the counter: service providers and bereaved consumers," *Human Relations*, 59, 10, 1429–48.

Parasuraman, A., Berry, L. and Zeithaml, V. (1991) "Understanding customer expectations of service," *Sloan Management Review*, 32, 3, 39–48.

Prottas, J.M. (1979) *People-Processing*, Lexington, MA: Lexington Books.

Putnam, L. and Mumby, D. (1993) "Organizations, emotion and the myth of rationality," in S. Fineman (ed.), *Emotion in Organizations*, London: Sage, 36–57.

Riddle, D. (1990) "Key strategic decisions for service firms," in D. Bowan, R. Chase, T. Cummings (ed.), *Service Management Effectiveness*, San Francisco: Jossey-Bass, 47–58.

Ritzer, G. (2006) *The McDonaldization of Society*, Thousand Oaks, CA: Pine Forge Press.

Schneider, B. and Bowen, D. (1995) *Winning the Service Game*, Boston: Harvard Business School Press.

Seymour, D. and Sandiford, P. (2005) "Learning emotion rules in service organizations: socialization and training in the UK public-house sector," *Work, Employment and Society*, 19, 3, 547–64.

Shamir, B. (1978) "Between bureaucracy and hospitality – some organizational characteristics of hotels," *Journal of Management Studies*, 15, 3, 285–307.

Shamir, B. (1980) "Between service and servility: role conflict in subordinate service roles," *Human Relations*, 33, 10, 138–57.

Simms, M. (2005) "Organising service sector workers," PhD thesis, Cardiff Business School.

Stein, M. (2007) "Toxicity and the unconscious experience of the body at the employee–customer interface," *Organization Studies*, 28, 8, 1223–41.

Taylor, P. and Bain, P. (1999) "An assembly-line in the head: The call center labor process," *Industrial Relations Journal*, 30, 2, 101–17.

Taylor, P. and Bain, P. (2005) " 'India calling to a far away town'," *Work, Employment and Society*, 19, 2, 261–82.

Terkel, S. (1999) *American Dreams: Lost and Found*, Toronto: Hoddon and Stoughton.

Tolich, M. (1993) "Alienating and liberating emotions at work," *Journal of Contemporary Ethnography*, 22, 3, 361–81.

Weatherly, K. and Tanskik, D. (1992) "Tactics used by customer-contact workers," *International Journal of Service Industry Management*, 4, 3, 4–17.

Weber, M. (1921/1968) *Economy and Society*, Totowa, NJ: Bedminster Press.

Whyte, W.F. (1948) *Human Relations in the Restaurant Industry*, New York: McGraw-Hill.

Wicks, D. (1998) *Nurses and Doctors at Work*, Buckingham: Open University Press.

Williams, C. (1987) *Blue, White and Pink Collar Workers in Australia*, Sydney: Allen and Unwin.

Winslow, C.D. and Bramer, W. (1994). *Futurework*, New York, Free Press.

Wood, R. (1992) *Working in Hotels and Catering*, London: Routledge.

# CHAPTER 6

# Labor Process Theory

## *Putting the Materialism Back into the Meaning of Service Work*

CHRIS WARHURST, PAUL THOMPSON

AND DENNIS NICKSON

### Introduction

Service jobs now account for around three-quarters of all jobs in the advanced economies generally. Indeed, if Britain was once a nation of shop-keepers, it is now a nation of shop-workers, with over one in ten of the working population employed in retail (Wilson *et al.*, 2006). Retail is also predicted to have the largest expansion of jobs for the next ten years, further consolidating the dominance of services in Britain. That manufacturing is in decline and displaced by services jobs is not doubted – though caution must be exercised about the "newness" of some of these services (see Warhurst and Thompson, 1998). Retail companies such as Gap and McDonald's are held up as icons of this shift, replacing the big four auto companies as emblematic of economic development and stability (Friedman, 1999). Manufacturing-associated paradigms used to both describe and explain the structure and operation of the capitalist economy have been jettisoned in favor of those associated with services, and a number jostle each other for attention, most obviously "McDonaldization" (Ritzer, 1993) and, more recently, Disneyization (Bryman, 2004).

If the shift to services is not in doubt, what is contested is the meaning of this change and how it is to be interpreted and researched. Because, unlike manufacturing, service work often, but not always, entails interaction with a "third party" – the customer or client – it is often claimed that service work is unique and analysis must be distinct (see for example Korczynski, 2002; Leidner, 2006). Sturdy (2001, p. 5) on the other hand notes that the "distinctions between service and manufacturing labor processes are sometimes overdrawn." However, there is a further and more wide ranging claim, made particularly by post-modernists that the shift to a service economy is associated with a new capitalism in which production itself is said to have been displaced by consumption as the site of meaning and so the focus of analysis. We challenge this position in this chapter through an exposition and interpretation of Labor Process Theory (LPT) and services. What our analysis demonstrates, aside from the continuing utility of LPT as a framework for analysis of services, is that work and employment have not lost their meaning, and that the employment relationship and the labor process remain central to the production and reproduction of capitalism.

The chapter is divided into three main parts. We start with an outline of the post-modern position on services, consumption and the new capitalism We draw into this discussion Ritzer's (2001; 2004, this volume) latest takes on the service economy, which whilst not post-modernist per se offers a sociology of consumption in which production is displaced analytically and work is negated empirically. We demonstrate the weaknesses of these approaches before moving on to outline LPT and affirming the centrality of materialism to its analysis, which, it should be noted, from its origins with Harry Braverman (1974) included services in its account of capitalism. We then illustrate how and why LPT informs key conceptual and empirical developments in the analysis of emotional labor and aesthetic labor in services. We conclude by emphasizing the continuing relevance of LPT for current and future analysis of services.

## Services, Consumption and the Eclipse of the Employment Relationship

We would argue that there is a difference between services being the dominant feature of a capitalist economy and claims that a service economy marks a qualitative break in the system of production. Such thinking has a long history in post-war social science. In the immediate post-war period a "logic of industrialism" (Kerr et al., 1963) was posited with which common organizational and technological imperatives requiring more and better educated labor was displacing capitalism. This argument could only exert influence as long as industrialism itself was seen to be the characteristic form of modernity. That assumption was largely abandoned as increasing numbers of social theorists embraced some variant of theories of post-industrial society. Though it took various forms, a personal service (Halmos, 1970) or service class society (Dahrendorf, 1959) was pushed to the fore in such arguments. By the 1970s, social science became enveloped in debate about the "post-industrial" social division of labor and the class consciousness and cohesiveness of these service workers; more particularly whether or not, as educated labor, these workers comprised a new middle class usurping or supporting capitalism (see Darr and Warhurst, 2008).

Within these debates emphasis was sometimes placed on the individualized nature of service work, its scope for the exercise of personal discretion and interaction with other employees rather than machines. However, the concern continued to be class rather than work. True, stylized contrast was made between manufacturing and service work. Bell (1973) for example argued that the "game against fabricated nature" had been usurped by the "game between persons." In this respect, post-industrial theorists such as Bell tended to emphasize the shift to highly skilled and specialized professionals but only brief indication is made of their work – that these workers "handle people" and are involved in "some phase of research and development" or "teaching" (p.230). In this respect, Kumar (1978, p.206) notes an, "apparently inescapable tendency on the part of writers on the service economy to take as the general pattern of work the conditions in the most attractive and prestigious parts of the service sector."

Elsewhere, we have criticized this tendency to either simply ignore work in favor of occupational label-gazing (Darr and Warhurst, 2008) or focus on the "better" service jobs and overlook the working reality of the more prevalent routine service jobs (Thompson et al., 2001). Occupational and skill trends indicate a polarization of jobs as an hour glass economy emerges with expanded management, professional and associate professional labor at the top and expanded caring, cleaning, waiting and selling jobs at the bottom. Within this polarization, Frenkel (2005, pp.357 and 369) states that most service work is "located at the lower range of the skills, creativity and knowledge continuum [and is] indecent in the sense that it is often poorly rewarded and provides little intrinsic satisfaction." This is a point with which even Reich (1993) and Florida (2002), surprisingly, agree if readers care to continue beyond the headlines of "symbolic analysts" in *The Work of Nations* and the "creative class" in Florida's *The Rise of the Creative Class*. In both cases, a larger number of "personalized service workers" (Reich) or "decreatified," "menial" workers (Florida) involving cooking, cleaning, clerical and caring work are recognized to exist and be required to support the privileged, headline occupations.

For Lash and Urry (1994), this shift to the creating and trading of non-material products with services has a more profound implication: a "weightless economy" now exists. The products of this economy are of two types; first, "post-industrial goods" such as software programs with a cognitive content based on knowledge and information and, second, "post-modern goods" such as film and music with an aesthetic or symbolic content based on signs and symbols. Both claims suggest an increased importance being attached to consumption and the inconvenient truths about the extent of job shifts within production are an irrelevance. Instead, the focus on services leads not just to the marginalization of production but to the eclipse of the employment relationship in all forms of work, for the hallmark of a service economy is consumption.

The term "consumer society" has been around since the 1950s but, in its Fordist context, primarily referred to the virtuous circle of mass production and mass consumption. Now, according to post-modernists, the meaning and identities that individuals once derived from production have been displaced by meaning and identity derived from consumption: we are no longer what we make but what we buy. Of course consumption matters, particularly "competitive consumption" that exacerbates existing social inequalities and gives rise to spiraling personal debt amongst those who can least bear it (Schor, 2000). However it is a huge leap from acknowledging the importance of consumption within capitalism to suggest that consumption heralds a new form of capitalism. Nevertheless, such claims are made as part of post-modernist claims of consumption-driven, status-centered societies (see for example Pakulski and Waters, 1996; Bauman, 1998). In making a critique of this perspective, two qualifications need to be made at this point. First, LPT has nothing to say about consumption and consumers per se. Its core concepts have been developed to analyze work and employment relations. Second, it does not seek to dismiss or downgrade analyses of consumption, and recognizes the full circuit of capital (see Kelly, 1985). What LPT does seek to do is refute the argument that (the rise of) consumption is at the expense of production of goods and services, and instead seeks to develop frameworks that can explain the interface between workers and customers in the provision of services. This distinction is important. In an influential contribution Bauman (1998) argues that late modern or post-modern society is characterized as a "society of consumers" (p.2). In this passage from a producer to a consumer society, the most profound change is the way in which "people are groomed and trained to meet the demands of their social identities" (p.24). In Bauman's world, with the death of the work ethic, work is decentered, and meaning, cast as "identity," is no longer derived from production. Instead, Bauman believes "the aesthetic of consumption" and what is "currently available in the shops" (p.29) now provides individuals with their identity. As Frank (2002) wryly notes, in this approach, consumption is cast as democracy, market populism as human liberation; and both offered as the triumph of the popular will. We all now have the power, and are either driving or subverting the corporates, defining our own meaning through consumption.

Returning to inconvenient truths, Bauman's decentering of work has been challenged by Bradley *et al.* (2000) who, by contrast, suggest that a "cult of work" exists in long working hours,[1] the permeation of work into home life and the multiple jobs held by some workers (see also Warhurst *et al.*, 2008). Bauman's claim to the end of job stability also falls at the first hurdle of evidence (see for example Auer and Cazes [2003] for data on the stability, not decline, of job tenure). In addition the immaterial argument is often over-stated and the material in services under-appreciated. Whilst it is true that much service provision centers on self-service, the most obvious example being supermarkets, and that other services require sales to be made by workers and so might involve the "enchantment of customers" suggested by Korczynski (2005), the provision of service requires a range of other tasks additional to actual selling and much of these other tasks involve engagement with material commodities. Many workers in interactive services make beds, stack shelves and flip burgers – all of which involve tangibles being bought by consumers. Pettinger (2006, p.48) also points out that shops are the end point of a long chain of tasks involving material objects, from design with computers to garment manufacturing machines in factories to haulage trucks that delivery the clothes to the shop for sale. "All of this work is fundamental to economic exchange," Pettinger asserts, "as it creates products as objects of consumption and precedes both self-service work done by consumers and customer service provided to consumers by workers" (p.60). Claims of intangibility in services therefore provide inadequate understanding of the nature, not just of work, but also of industry.

It is easy to rail against the excesses of post-modernism. A more fruitful engagement is with Ritzer's (2001) work on the sociology of consumption, given the prominence of his Weberian analysis of rationalized service work (Ritzer, 1993). Ritzer's earlier work has considerable overlaps with LPT and he continues to make explicit parallels between the control and exploitation of workers and consumers. However he now proclaims a kind of paradigm break: "In twentieth-century capitalism, the focus shifted increasingly from production to consumption, resulting in a parallel shift from control and exploitation of workers to that of consumers" (2001, pp.111–12). This new focus too requires a shift of analytical focus from the means of production to the means of consumption. The latter consist of those things – notably shopping malls, superstores, home shopping television, theme parks and cruise ships – that supply goods and services for exploitable hyper-consumption.

Though borrowing from Weber and Marx for some of this terminology, Ritzer is attracted by the post-modern emphasis on consumption as spectacle (as in "cathedrals of consumption") and work in services as simulation and performance. With reference to the latter, he gives the usual examples of people dressing up as Mickey Mouse and the like, extending the illustration to the claim that "most of the people we encounter in the new means of consumption are simulations, even if they are not wearing costumes . . . [and] are all playing well defined roles" (2001, p.137).[2] This is a theme that has also been taken up by Bryman (2004; this volume) with Disneyization. This is "the process by which the principles of the Disney theme parks are coming to dominate more and more sectors of American society as well as the rest of the world," creating "the highly sought after template for the service sector" (pp.1 and 12). Again its focus is primarily consumption and, in "a post-Fordist world," the creation of "spectacular" shopping and leisure experiences for consumers (pp.5 and 76). No substantive evidence is offered of this "spectacularization," only marketing and marketing executive hype. Nevertheless, elsewhere Bryman does provide evidence, drawing heavily on the empirical research of writers closely associated with LPT, to make his points about the strictures of these Disneyized jobs (for example citing Bain and Taylor, 2000; Callaghan and Thompson, 2002; Warhurst and Thompson, 1998). As a consequence there is no evidence that performative labor is as spectacularly transformed as the places in which it takes place, and Bryman, thankfully, is less seduced by the claims of "fun factory" jobs. Rather than being spectacular, performative labor is standardized and no less tightly controlled by management than any burger flipper in McDonald's. Performative laborers' feelings and bodies are "formally prescribed" to elicit appropriate behavior, attitudes and appearance and "inculcate the demeanor that Walt wanted to engender" (pp. 109 and 110).

Such careful qualification is not present in Ritzer's recent trajectory, claiming to have identified another "general historical trend" in which the loss of meaning in work now reaches its apotheosis (see Ritzer, 2004). This trend is towards "nothing" by which he means, applying the concept to work, it is "devoid of distinctive substantive content" (p. 32). Thus as those employees of Disney World step into their costumes they now become "a high degree of nothingness" (p. 37). The same is true for fast-food, call center and retail workers; he claims; they are "non-persons" employed to perform "non-services." Despite the rhetorical claim of being "relatively content-less" (p.6), given his previous analysis of fast food jobs it would be amnesic of Ritzer to claim that such work is not physically and psychologically demanding. Instead Ritzer argues that because of the high degree of job content predetermination by employers, the individual human element is "squeezed out" leaving only automatons, whose actions and interactions with customers are "controlled and decided in advance by the corporation" (p. 37).

Both positions – that work is "nothing," or at least nothing more than simulation and performance – are typical of the Ritzerian methodology of excessive generalization from a minority trend. Most of the people with whom we have service interactions are either doing routine things (selling us a product such as a newspaper) or are experts (selling us a specialized service such as legal advice). And the "total control thesis" has already been countered, noting that claims of the death of worker resistance for example, whether individualized or collectivized, are greatly exaggerated (Ackroyd and Thompson 1999; see also Taylor and Bain, 2003, for call centers and Paules, 1991, for restaurant workers). Indeed, there is plenty of evidence that Disney workers also resist or reshape their employer's demands – for example being more or less helpful and courteous to customers than is required, so "disabling" any required simulation or performance – unless of course workers stealing, taking drugs and having sex dressed as Minnie and Mickey Mouse is all part of the script (Project on Disney, 1995; Van Maanen, 1991). Employers may seek to predefine such jobs, but they cannot be made "inhuman" in the sense of completely stripping out worker discretion and achieving total conformity, as Ritzer claims. For employees, the Project on Disney (1995, p.127) claims, "The stricter the rule the greater the challenge in breaking them."

For Ritzer, the focus on simulation derives from an attempt to foreground those acts of consumption most compatible with the overall paradigm break thesis. This pattern continues as Ritzer moves to analysis of new sites of immaterial consumption. E-tail and the e-net provide dematerialized consumption sites, where "the electronic impulses emanating from a cybermall are a far cry from the bricks and mortar of a shopping mall or a superstore" (2001, p.146). This move is bad for the consumer who cannot tell where the transaction has taken place but is good for the capitalist who no longer has to contend with the indeterminacy of labor: "no matter how scripted, the human employee can never be as controlled as the completely automated process in cyberspace" (p.150).

This impossibility of human control may be true, but e-tail is not a simple tale of de-materialization. In a capitalist economy, materiality is based on the commodification process and should not be confused with the physical (as in "bricks and mortar"). As Ritzer (2001) admits, many of the biggest firms in the electronic marketplace (Amazon for example) have conventional work settings with an invisible army of employees in warehouses and offices carrying out routine work in conventional employment relationships. Whilst download music sites are a better fit for the chosen narrative of change, Ritzer's emphasis invokes another set of unrepresentative examples that discount or marginalize the employment relationship. Towards the end of the book, he quotes a consultant addressing advertisers who boasts about how consumers can be persuaded to pay $37 for a $3 item. Whilst the mysteries of merchandising and marketing may account for this deception, sociologists of work should surely focus on revealing what goes on in production and employment relations to enable such transactions to take place. In casting consumption as revolution and shifting the gaze away from production, residual structural antagonisms are overlooked, making post-modernists kindred spirits with free market eulogists and, ultimately, conservative in their thinking (Frank, 2002). This perceptual deficit is the gap that LPT continues to fill in its research programs and to which we now turn.

## A Material(ist) World: Labor Process Theory and Service Work

The labor process is sometimes loosely termed "work organization" but was defined by Marx (1946 [1887]) as consisting of three elements; the act of working, a predefined product being worked upon (a good or service) and the instruments, usually some form of technology, through which working creates the product. These products have a "use value" but within capitalism, as commodities, also attain an "exchange value" on the market. LPT proceeds from a series of claims concerning the central features of the labor process under capitalism. These claims comprise what has been described as a core theory. Space prevents a full description here (though see Thompson and Smith, 2001; Thompson and Newsome, 2004), but it is worth emphasizing the centrality given to the nature of labor as a commodity. That commodity is unique in that it is indeterminate – labor power is a potential for work that has to be converted into profitable labor. LPT therefore prioritizes the capital-labor relationship as a focus for analysis of work and employment relations; sees the transformation of the labor process and labor power as central to capital accumulation; argues that there is a control imperative arising from the need to reduce indeterminacy; and that such dynamics and potentially divergent interests generate the conditions for resistance, compliance, and consent. None of these tendencies tell us anything about the specific forms of control, conflict or skill utilization operative in a particular workplace, sector or time period. Although Braverman (1974) stated that deskilling through Taylorism was the form of control, the subsequent second wave of analysis, principally A. Friedman (1977), Burawoy (1979), Edwards (1979) and Littler (1982), demonstrated that other forms exist, though for the same purpose. These forms can only be identified and explained by linking the core theory to concrete analyses of work and employment relations in the context of particular conditions and categories of capitalist political economy.

As we have shown, there has been a continual tendency to present service work as somehow involving a break with one or more of the features of the capitalist labor process. Yet, for LPT in principle, these features apply equally to manufacturing or services, though they may be manifested in different ways. For example, the presence of the consumer does not obviate the requirement for control of the employee but may influence the concrete practices through which control is affected. LPT is a dynamic body of work that cannot be reduced to Braverman or any specific contingent claims. We will demonstrate that LPT not only can incorporate analysis of service work into its research programs, but has already done so.

Whilst much research has continued to focus on developments in manufacturing, services too have been a feature of labor process analysis from Braverman onwards. Kitay (1995) points out that ideas from labor process have become mainstreamed in much Anglo-Saxon academia and suggests that "it is hard to imagine non-managerial research in the broad areas of work and employment which is not influenced by labor process insights." Leidner (2006), for example, has recently acknowledged the influence of LPT on her earlier research, principally that focused on fast work and insurance workers (Leidner, 1993) and further echoes, particularly that of Friedman, resonate in Frenkel's (2005) recent review of interactive service work and his positing of empowerment or rationalization as managerial strategies.

In this respect it is important to note that Braverman's starting point in 1974 was also the "heralded 'service economy'," though he questioned the optimistic thesis that it was supposed to "free workers from the tyranny of industry" (p.373). In a chapter on services, he makes a familiar case that if we look beneath the hype about educated labor within service occupations; we find the reality of routine clerical and sales workers. Moreover he argued that service jobs could be Taylorized, noting that the majority of what are now called the "3Cs" jobs of cleaning, caretaking and caring were being standardized, reutilized, rationalized and subject to the same processes of organization and control as factory labor. "The capitalist," Braverman argued, does not care "whether he [sic] hires workers to produce automobiles, wash them, repair them, repaint them, fill them with gasoline and oil, rent them by the day, drive them for hire, park them, or convert them into scrap metal" (p.364); what is important is not whether goods or services are produced, only that this labor is made profitable. As a corrective, his conceptual point is well made. However Braverman was also trapped within traditional, over-generalized class categories. Determined to counterpoise proletarianization to professionalization, he enrolled service workers in "the giant mass of workers who are relatively homogeneous" (p.359). From this viewpoint, low pay and limited skill is the characteristic feature for all but elite groups such as police and firefighters. Worse, rationalization, new technologies and standardization are leading to mechanized self-service[3] and disappearing crafts for chefs and others: "So far as retail trade is concerned . . . a revolution is now being prepared which will make of retail workers, by and large, something closer to factory operatives than anyone had ever imagined possible" (p.371).

Whilst Braverman failed to offer any credible empirical analysis of the distinctive operation of service labor, particularly where it has an interactive character, his broader theoretical argument does make useful distinctions. Braverman explains the growth of services in the conventional Marxist way – by referring to the penetration of the commodity form into areas that were once dominated by our own labor or that of servants. When making this case, he incorporates the consumer as a distinctive facet, without producing the fallacious argument that "intangibility" marks the essential characteristic of a service. He rightly observes that many factory workers do not directly manufacture an object with their own hands but may design or move it about. Similarly the labor of chambermaids produces a tangible and vendible commodity and the labor process is organized in a similar manner to manufacturing – indeed, there may be little difference to the work of cleaners in a factory: "When ... chambermaids in hotels ... make beds they do an assembly operation which is not different from many factory assembly operations – a fact recognized by management when it conducts time and motion studies of both on the same principles" (p.361). Certainly the continued imposition of standard operating procedures for hotel room cleaning would suggest that Braverman's observation still has analytical purchase (see Dutton et al., 2008).

Irrespective of any similarities, Braverman regards the conceptual mistake as trying to classify labor by its determinate form. Instead, what matters is "its social form, its capacity to produce, as wage labor, a profit for the capitalist" (p.362).

Commodification thus creates one form of tangibility. However, whilst Braverman was correct to observe that the capitalist is indifferent to the particular form of labor, the consumer is not and this other interaction may make a difference to the way profits can be made – as the groundbreaking research of Fuller and Smith (1991) highlights with an additional form of managerial control of employees enabled by customers in interactive services. Even this recognition, however, does not lead to a categorical difference between manufacturing and services. There are two principal ways in which the capitalist seeks to ensure a profit from (interactive) service labor. First, this is undertaken by seeking to remove as much of the indeterminacy as possible. As this labor is simultaneously produced and consumed, the most likely means is to impose standardized scripts and verbal or aesthetic recipes. Second, management is compelled to seek a more intensive utilization of labor power. For example, it not only seeks to appropriate and transmute workers' knowledge, as Braverman highlighted, but also workers' feelings and bodies. LPT has long accepted that required new conceptualizations. Warhurst and Thompson (1998: 10) argued that there are two important innovations – emotional labor and the extension of normative controls.

In some areas, notably though not exclusively in the service sector, capital has also sought to mobilize the emotional labor and "extra-functional" skills of employees. By moving away from a predominantly technical and task-based definition of skills in favor of a broader range of social competencies, employers aim to stretch and broaden performance criteria (Thompson 2003, pp.362–3). Such arguments and other features of contemporary labor process research are best examined within the context of particular case examples.

## Suits You Sir! Applying Labor Process Theory to Contemporary Interactive Services

If in the early stages of the services dominated economy, employers simply bought personality on the labor market (Mills, 1956), employers have since sought to intervene in the labor process to affect the employee attitudes and appearance that comprise this personality (Hochschild, 1983; Nickson et al., 2001; cf. Mills, 1956). Recent research of interactive services, particularly call center, retail and hospitality work, whilst analyzed through the paradigms of emotional labor and, more recently, aesthetic labor, draw extensively on LPT to explain how and why such work is organized and controlled.

### Case Study 1: Call Centers and Emotional Labor

Frenkel et al.'s (1998, 1999) influential work on front-line service workers criticized labor process approaches for neglecting such workers and the growth of knowledge work, arguing that the need to meet diverse customer requirements places constraints on the extent to which work can be reutilized. Though partly bureaucratized, call centers include elements associated with professional or knowledge-intensive settings. Whilst the accusation of neglect of customer-facing service work may have some degree of truth, it is inaccurate with respect to call centers. A decade after the emergence of a significant literature on call centers, Ellis and Taylor (2006, p.107) could confidently assert, "We now know a great deal about work organization, surveillance, managerial control strategies and other central concerns of labor process analysis." In one sense this claim is not surprising as LPT-influenced researchers, notably Bain and Taylor (2000), were at the forefront of this field of enquiry.

A simplistic reading of this analysis would see LPT proclaiming the rise of industrialized, mass services and high tech office factories as confirmation of the tight control and deskilling theses (wrongly) associated with the perspective. Such arguments do exist – but not from LPT. For example, Poynter (2000, p.151) resuscitates the proletarianization thesis once popular in Marxist treatments of office work. Mental labor has become variously Taylorized, de-professionalized, reutilized and manual, "sharing many of the characteristics of the assembly line," he claims.

By contrast, labor process research has tried to chart a path that recognizes elements of continuity and change. Although there are examples of knowledge-intensive operations, the vast majority of call centers operate at the mass, standardized transaction end. This positioning is primarily due to the underlying economic drive to gain economies of scale in restructured, rationalized and de-regulated markets in the finance and related sectors. It also reflects the opportunities available to management to fashion a socio-technical system that combines capacity to handle high call volumes and high surveillance of performance.

However, skills and control show distinctive patterns that are different from classic Taylorist, factory-like organization. Potential customer service representatives typically lack job-specific qualifications but are not unskilled. Call centers, like many other services, put considerable emphasis into identifying potential employees who are predisposed to become effective customer service representatives. The perceived centrality of social skills and competencies leads management to use rigorous selection and training procedures more usually associated with high discretion jobs. To use terms such as deskilling not only under-estimates the importance of those qualities, which companies do seek to identify and develop, it is also based on a false comparison with traditional white-collar occupations such as those in banking. Interactive service work is distinct from rather than a debased version of such work. One key difference is the centrality of emotional labor, which clearly does not fit neatly into the classic manual/mental divide.

Researchers utilizing LPT have consistently drawn on and extended concepts of emotional labor as a key explanatory tool (Taylor and Bain, 1999; Taylor, 1998; Callaghan and Thompson, 2002). Stephen Taylor's (1998) account of telesales employees at "Flightpath" was one of the earliest applications of emotional labor to interactive service work and he is careful to link Hochschild's work on emotional labor to core LPT, including the indeterminacy of labor – in this case the tendency of enhanced emotional demands to provoke strong resistance from employees. Consistent with the labor process perspective on workers as active agents and Bolton's (2005) new typology of emotion work, such studies have demonstrated that far from being passive providers of management requirements, employees can be active and skilled emotion managers in their own right. There is, therefore, an emotional effort bargain that constitutes a hidden and contested dimension of the call center labor process. As Hochschild

(1983, p.89) notes, "Emotional labor is . . . about how to feel and how to express feelings . . . set by management, . . . when deep and surface acting are forms of labor to be sold."

As for control, and replaying wider debates, labor process researchers spent some time refuting the early Foucauldian "total control" line, and illustrating the capacity for formal and informal resistance by call center workers (Bain and Taylor, 2000; Taylor and Bain, 2003). Whilst acknowledging the significance of surveillance, studies have drawn on the one of the greatest strengths of LPT – its ability to identify a variety of modes on control – to identify the distinctive features of new systems in call centers. Callaghan and Thompson's (2001) article has been the most explicit attempt to locate new developments within the corpus of material on control. They use their Telebank case study to develop a view that call centers operate through integrated systems of technical, bureaucratic and normative controls. The practical process of integrating bureaucratic and technical control systems emerges from the supposedly "objective" statistical information, which is combined with bureaucratic standards concerning values and behavior.

One of the key points of emphasis in such studies is the significance of normative controls. Though intensive technical and bureaucratic controls are available, they are insufficient to handle the complexities of the process (Deery and Kinnie, 2002). As Taylor and Bain's (1999) classic paper memorably put it, this time the assembly line is also in the heads of employees. Employers recruit attitude, then seek to shape and specify appropriate social competencies (Callaghan and Thompson, 2001). Aside from selection and training process, normative controls are most obvious in the attention paid to social and recreational events inside and outside work designed to ameliorate the intense nature of call center working and persuade employees to identify with the company and its brand (Baldry *et al.*, 2007), as well as in the widespread use of teams. There is little or no teamwork in call centers but teams provide a further normative control opportunity for management (Thompson *et al.*, 2004).

Overall, the call center labor process is based on a distinctive hybrid that Houlihan (2002) labels a high commitment, low discretion model. In her four case studies, a variety of human resource practices and normative control measures were used to generate commitment and mediate the tensions arising from the organization and control of the labor process. Ultimately the latter outweighed the former: "The common theme to these cases was low discretion, reutilized customer service" (p.82). The central role assigned to human resource management by a number of key commentators to cope with the tensions between serving customers and managing employees (Korczynski, 2002) has not come to pass. It could be argued that off-shoring strategies offer the advantages of the existing high commitment, low discretion model by transferring operations to countries such as India, which can supply high quality but much cheaper employees (Taylor and Bain, 2005). These authors also note however the limitations of this off-shoring as the supply of appropriate labor shrinks, impacting negatively on the quality of the employee-customer interaction.

The hybrid labor process has similarities with the customer-oriented bureaucracy conceptualization. However, the latter (Korczynski, 2002; also this volume) is underpinned by the idea of a "dual logic" of efficiency and bureaucratic standardization versus customer-oriented service quality. Whereas it is relatively straightforward to identify an "efficiency" logic that flows through economies of scale, standardization and surveillance of employees, a customer equivalent appears to lack a mechanism other than a vague inference of a desire for quality and diversity. Whilst the (indirect) presence of the customer does impact on the work, what is notable is that customers are managed through the same technology and management system as employees. For example, software streaming technologies allow the identification of customers with a specific profile or who fit high value criteria, who can then be cross-sold other products or diverted to more specialist staff.

*Case Study 2: Retail, Hospitality and Aesthetic Labor*

If, over recent years, emotions have been discovered to be here, there and everywhere in the workplace (Bolton, 2000), the same might now be said for aesthetics (see Felstead *et al.* 2005, pp.78–96). With many front-line service workers now expected to embody the company image or required service, it is the commodification of workers' corporeality, not just their feelings that is becoming the analytical focus.

Indeed, although less eloquent (or verbally convoluted) than Bauman but probably selling more copies as a *New York Times* bestseller, Postrel (2003) claims a "major ideological shift" as we reach the "tipping point" into an aesthetic economy, heralding the age of look and feel. Now, form usurps function and sensory perception is the new organizing principle. This aesthetic economy is allegedly driven by consumers' alleged demand for beauty and pleasure and a belief that aesthetics and design, not price and performance, create product differentiation in highly competitive markets.

Labor is part of this shift. Referring to Warhurst and Nickson (2001), Postrel states; "When style is strategy . . . how employees look can be as much a part of the atmosphere [of companies] as the grain of the furniture or the beat of the background music" (p.127). The employment relationship is regarded as unproblematic and uncontested. Employers choose stylish and handsome employees because of those employees fit with the organizational aesthetic; stylish and handsome employees choose to work for an organization because it fits their aesthetic identity. Where aesthetic dissonance occurs, employers should be free to sack employees; employees can vote with their feet and choose another employer.

However, long before claims of an aesthetic economy, the importance of employee appearance at work was recognized. In McKinlay's analysis of the hiring of the "model" bank clerk in the nineteenth century, management appraisal entries refer repeatedly to potential employees' looks. In one, the ideal senior banker is described as being "handsome" with "hazel eyes, aquiline nose, iron-gray hair, firm moustache, oval chin [and] cheeks slightly tinged with red" (2002, p.607). C. Wright Mills' 1950s classic account of white-collar workers notes a female department store worker who "focuses the customer less upon her stock of goods than upon herself . . . attract[ing] the customer with modulated voice, artful attire and stance" (1951, p.175). What is clear from such research is that despite employers appreciating the importance of employee appearance for obtaining and doing jobs, managerial intervention to shape this appearance was absent. Appearance was bought as is, and was devoid of organizational intervention.

It is assumed in some accounts that this "hands off" approach still exists. For example, Tyler and her colleagues, whilst making a useful contribution to analyze the gendering of bodies in the recruitment, training and management of female flight attendants still conceptualize the required "body work" as "invisible," with the demand to be aesthetically pleasing to customers argued to be "beyond contract" (Tyler and Taylor, 1998, p.165). Instead, the deployment of personal aesthetics by female flight attendants is deemed to occur "by virtue of being women" (Tyler and Abbott, 1998, p.440); the presenting and performance of the body by these female flight attendants as a "gift" to men. It is an "aesthetic exchange" that takes place "outside of formal, contractual relations" (Tyler and Taylor 1998, p.166).[4] Hancock and Tyler (2000a, p.97) claim too that, whilst it is "central to the maintenance of working bodies," body work "is carried out outside of the formal domain of wage labor." Hancock and Tyler suggest that there is "no actual training or instruction" in this aesthetic labor, as it is now termed, and is "neither remunerated nor particularly acknowledged by management, clients or even the flight attendants themselves" (2000b, pp.119–120). In sum, this body work or aesthetic labor is "unworked" (Hancock and Tyler, 2000b, p.119) and so unrecognized, untrained and unrewarded by management.

Materialist accounts, however, recognize that what is happening now, as services dominate the advanced economies, is that organizational intervention in workers' corporeality is occurring. As Wolkowitz (2006, p.96) notes, "In customer services . . . there seems to be a new, or at least more explicit, emphasis on bodily discipline and appearance." What Postrell and Tyler and her colleagues fail to recognize is how the workers are now being controlled by management in an attempt to ensure aesthetic labor.

As first conceived by Warhurst *et al.* (2000), aesthetic labor refers to employees' bodies being organizationally produced or "made up" to embody the desired aesthetic of the organization and intended to provide for organizational benefit. This aesthetic labor rests on embodied "dispositions" (Bourdieu, 1984). Such dispositions, in the form of embodied capacities and attributes are, to some extent, possessed by workers at the point of entry into employment. However, crucially, employers then mobilize, develop, and commodify these embodied dispositions through processes of recruitment, selection, training and management, transforming them into "skills" which are geared towards producing a "style" of service encounter that appeals to the senses of the customer. In other words, aesthetic labor is a key feature of such employees' wage-effort bargain.

In a survey of UK retail and hospitality employers reported in Nickson *et al.* (2005), 90 per cent rated employee appearance as critical or important in recruitment and selection. Significantly, 61 percent thereafter offered training in dress sense and style, 56 percent provided other appearance training including employee body language and 34 percent provide training in personal grooming. It is clear therefore that employers are concerned now with not only recruiting appearance, but they also intervene to ensure that appearance is mobilized as part of the service encounter. As with emotional labor (see Hochschild, 1983), different "looks" can be required of employees through their aesthetic laboring by different organizations targeting different market segments (see for example Pettinger, 2004; Warhurst and Nickson, 2007). As such, these organizations are attempting to convert that potential into actual, desired labor, prescribing, most obviously, the sight and sound of their employees in exchange for wages. Employees, for example, are hired because of the way they look and talk; once employed, staff are instructed how to stand whilst working, what to wear and how to wear it and even what to say and how to say it to customers.

This emphasis on employees having the right appearance does not shunt but complement the demand for employees having the right attitudes. Other UK surveys as well as those from the US and Australia reveal that retail and hospitality employers want customer-facing employees with the right attitude and good appearance, both of which employers perceive of as skills to be employed and then deployed at work (HtF, 2000; Martin and Grove, 2002; Jackson and Briggs, 2003). What aesthetic labor highlights is that in interacting with customers, many employees not only have to be skilled emotion managers but also manage their appearance in order to "make the body more visible in customer service" (Wolkowitz, 2006: 86). Employees are required to be "the animate component of . . . the corporate landscape" according to Witz *et al.* (2003, p.44) and, in this process of becoming "human hardware," their corporality is appropriated and transmuted by the organization. Moreover, as with emotional labor, aesthetic labor has a clear purpose – corporate commercial gain (Nickson *et al.*, 2001). What Taylorism sought to do with employee knowledge and emotional labor with employee feelings, aesthetic labor does with employee corporeality. Thus with aesthetic labor, employee heads, hearts and now bodies feature in the wage-effort bargain, and are appropriated and transmuted within the employment relationship of interactive services in a attempt to overcome the indeterminacy of labor and secure market competitiveness for some employers.

## Concluding Remarks: The Continued Relevance of Labor Process Theory

We have argued two fundamental points in this chapter. First, that qualitative breaks associated with service work, or particular aspects of it, are over-stated and that LPT has operated as a vital source of critique of such claims. Although services jobs now dominate the advanced economies, these services do not herald a new capitalism centered on the consumption of intangibles. Given its core theory, LPT is inherently skeptical of any attempt to assert the existence of a distinctive service economy outside the dynamics of capitalist political economy, whether in post-industrial or post-modern forms. With this in mind, much service is still focused on the provision and preparation for sale to customers of materiality – beds, burgers and handbags for example. Likewise, production is not irrelevant and meaning has not been stripped out of work. Ritzer's claim that work is now "nothing" or nothing but a simulation or performance, confuses the topical (Disney) with the typical and is evidence-lite in asserting that workers have become no more than marionettes controlled by management. Spectacle makes money, or at least organizations believe that it will but to generate and secure that profit, employers must ensure that employees convert their potential labor into actual labor – hence the provision by management of scripts and role descriptors that prescribe the performance or simulation. But even when dressed as Mickey Mouse workers are real people who may be willing or unwilling to provide the labor required: hence both management's need to control and workers' capacity to resist. Understanding these processes has been the strength of LPT. Far from being decentered, the organization and control of the labor process of services remain central to employers' generation of profit, and reveal why workers' feelings and bodies are being commodified and therefore why the employment relationship matters. As such, LPT helps bend back the stick from consumption to production, from analysis that over-sells the role of the customer or unquestionably accepts the hype of marketing executives to one that foregrounds the demands of management and the experiences of workers.

Second, LPT has always provided a focus on services. Its associated research has been innovative, whilst emphasizing the continuity of concepts centered on issues such as the transformation of labor power, control and resistance. For example, emotional labor has been the dominant research paradigm of interactive services research for the past decade or so and aesthetic labor is emerging as a key, new concept being applied in this research. Whilst both are cited as "the primary forms" (p.127) of the "performative labor" in the latest "ization" claimed for the service economy – Bryman's (2004) Disneyization – as we have shown, they have been used and developed in a materialist manner by labor process researchers. We would argue that whilst the theoretical influences are diverse, the focus on labor power and its commodification has provided a key resource for the development of both concepts. At the same time, the characteristics of labor power, as understood by LPT, provides a corrective to claims that capital can engineer the transmutation of feelings in a relatively unproblematic way. As Bolton (2005, p.63) notes, "Hochschild fails to recognize is that the indeterminacy of labor is further exacerbated within the contested terrain of the emotional labor process." This contestation is not simply a matter of the persistence of resistance but, as Bolton has demonstrated in her work, that employees can be active emotion managers within the varied constraints of capitalist and non-capitalist employment relations. In this sense, contrary to Hochschild, workers need not be conceptualized as necessarily being alienated or estranged from their own feelings given that they own the means of this particular production.

Whilst LPT has sought to incorporate new developments in services and society more generally into its body of concepts, those who search for something new to say about labor often over-interpret empirical trends. For example, even the "new" forms of labor control cited by Bryman (2004) as featuring in Disneyized jobs are largely familiar: direct by managers, indirect through mystery shoppers and real customers and remote via technology, usually CCTV. In addition, aside from being a natty nomenclature, "performative labor" adds little conceptual understanding of contemporary interactive service jobs beyond that already provided by LPT.

In sum, LPT has long folded services into its analysis of workplace developments. Indeed, the expansion of services, the growth of educated labor and assumptions of better technical-scientific jobs were the stimulus in Braverman coming to write *Labor and Monopoly Capital* and also his point of departure from those, optimistic writers such as Daniel Bell. Research informed by LPT has been at the forefront of recent path-breaking developments in analyses of services and has helped put back the meaning in the interactive service *work*.

## Notes

1  Though we would qualify this judgment by reference to household and female working hours rather than aggregate hours (see Roberts 2007).
2  Our emphasis added.
3  Pre-dating Ritzer by twenty years, Braverman referred to the "displacement of labor" occurring in automated service functions that also incorporate the labor of customers.
4  Authors' emphasis.

## References

Ackroyd, S. and Thompson, P. (1999) *Organization Misbehaviour*, London: Sage.
Auer, P. and Cazes, S. (eds.) (2003) *Employment Stability in an Age of Flexibility*, Geneva: ILO.
Bain, P. and Taylor, P. (2000) "Entrapped by the 'electronic panopticon'? Worker resistance in the call center," *New Technology, Work and Employment*, 15,1, 2–18.
Baldry, C., Bain, P., Taylor, P., Hyman, J., Scholarios, D., Marks, A., Watson, A., Gilbert, K., Gall, G. and Bunzel, D. (2007) *The Meaning of Work in the New Economy*, London: Palgrave.
Bauman, Z. (1998) *Work, Consumerism and the New Poor*, Cambridge: Polity.
Bell, D. (1973) *The Coming of Post-Industrial Society*, New York: Basic Books.
Bolton, S. (2000) "Emotions here, emotions there, emotional organizations everywhere," *Critical Perspectives on Accounting*, 11, 2, 115–71.
Bolton, S. (2005) *Emotion Management*, London: Palgrave.
Bourdieu, P. (1984) *Distinction*, London: Routledge & Kegan Paul.
Bradley, H., Erickson, M., Stephenson, C. and Williams, S. (2000) *Myths at Work*, Cambridge: Polity Press.
Braverman, H. (1974) *Labor and Monopoly Capital*, New York: Monthly Review Press.
Bryman, A. (2004) *The Disneyization of Society*, London: Sage.
Burawoy, M. (1979) *Manufacturing Consent*, Chicago: Chicago University Press.
Callaghan, G. and Thompson, P. (2001) "Edwards revisited: Technical control in call centers," *Economic and Industrial Democracy*, 22, 1, 13–37.
Callaghan, G. and Thompson, P. (2002) " 'We recruit attitude': The selection and shaping of call center labor," *Journal of Management Studies*, 39, 2, 233–54.
Dahrendorf, R. (1959) *Class and Class Conflict in an Industrial Society*, New York: Stanford University Press.
Darr, A. and Warhurst, C. (2008) "Assumptions, assertions and the need for evidence: Debugging debates about knowledge workers," *Current Sociology*, 56, 1, 25–45.
Deery, S. and Kinnie, N. (2002) "Call centers and beyond: a thematic evaluation," *Human Resource Management Journal*, 12, 4, 3–13.
Dutton, E., Warhurst, C., Lloyd, C., James, S., Commander, J. and Nickson, D. (2008) "Just like the elves in Harry Potter: Room attendants in UK hotels," in C. Lloyd, G. Mason, and K. Mayhew (eds.), *Low Wage Work in the UK*, New York: Russell Sage Foundation.
Edwards, R. (1979) *Contest Terrain*, London: Heinemann.
Ellis, V. and Taylor, P. (2006) "You don't know what you've got till it's gone: Re-contextualising the origins, development and impact of the call center," *New Technology, Work and Employment*, 21, 2, 107–22.
Felstead, A., Jewson, N. and Walters, S. (2005) *Changing Places of Work*, London: Palgrave.
Florida, R. (2002) *The Rise of the Creative Class*, New York: Basic Books.
Frank, T. (2002) *New Consensus for Old*, Chicago: Prickly Paradigm Press.

Frenkel, S. (2005) "Service workers in search of decent work," in S. Ackroyd, R. Batt, P. Thompson, and P.S. Tolbert (eds.), *Oxford Handbook of Work and Organization*, Oxford: Oxford University Press.

Frenkel, S., Korczynski, M., Shire, K. and Tam, M. (1998) "Beyond bureaucracy? Work organization in call centers," *International Journal of Human Resource Management*, 9, 6, 957–79.

Frenkel, S., Korczynski, M., Shire, K. and Tam, M. (1999) *On the Front Line*, Ithaca, NY: Cornell University Press.

Friedman, A. (1977) *Industry and Labor*, London: Macmillan.

Friedman, T. (1999) *The Lexus and the Olive Tree*, London: HarperCollins.

Fuller, L. and Smith, V. (1991) "Customers' reports: Management by customers in a changing economy," *Work, Employment and Society*, 5, 1, 1–16.

Halmos, P. (1970) *The Personal Service Society*, London: Constable.

Hancock, P. and Tyler, M. (2000a) "Working bodies," in P. Hancock, B. Hughes, E. Jagger, K. Patterson, R. Russell, E. Tulle-Winton and M. Tyler (eds.), *The Body, Culture and Society*, Buckingham: Open University Press.

Hancock, P. and Tyler, M. (2000b) "The look of love: Gender and the organization of aesthetics," in J. Hassard, R. Holliday, and H. Willmott (eds.), *Body and Organization*, London: Sage.

Hochschild, A.R. (1983) *The Managed Heart*, Berkeley, CA: University of California Press.

Hospitality Training Foundation (HtF) (2000) *Skills and Employment Forecasts 2000 for the Hospitality Industry*. London: HtF.

Houlihan, M. (2002). "Tensions and variations in call center management strategies," *Human Resource Management Journal*, 12, 4, 67–85.

Jackson, S. and Briggs, C. (2003) "Tourism and hospitality," in *Beyond VET: The Changing Skill Needs of the Victorian Services Industries. Vol.2*, ACIRRT, University of Sydney.

Kelly, J. (1985) "Management's redesign of work: labor process, labor markets and product markets," in D. Knights, H. Willmott, and D. Collinson (eds.), *Job Redesign*, Aldershot: Gower.

Kerr, C., Dunlop, J.T., Harbison, F.H. and Mayers, C.A. (1963) *Industrialism and Industrial Man*, Harmondsworth: Pelican.

Kitay, J. (1995) "The labor process: Still stuck? Still a perspective? Still useful?," *Electronic Journal of Radical Organization Theory*, 3, 1, available at http://www.mngt.waikato.ac.nz/ejrot/vol3_1/kitay.asp

Korczynski, M. (2002) *Human Resource Management and Service Work*, London: Palgrave.

Korczynski, M. (2005) "The point of selling: capitalism, consumption and contradictions," *Organization*, 12, 1, 69–88.

Kumar, K. (1978) *Prophecy and Progress: The Sociology of Industrial and Post-Industrial Society*, Harmondsworth: Penguin Books.

Lash, S. and Urry, J. (1994) *Economies of Signs and Space*, London: Sage.

Leidner, R. (1993) *Fast Food, Fast Talk*, Berkeley, CA: University of California Press.

Leidner, R. (2006) "Identity and work," in M. Korczynski, R. Hodson, and P. Edwards (eds.), *Social Theory at Work*, Oxford: Oxford University Press.

Littler, C. (1982) *The Development of the Labor Process in Capitalist Societies*, London: Heinemann.

McKinlay, A. (2002) "Dead selves: the birth of the modern career," *Organization*, 9, 4, 595–614.

Martin, L. and Grove, J. (2002) "Interview as a selection tool for entry-level hospitality employees," *Journal of Human Resources in Hospitality and Tourism*, 1, 1, 41–7.

Marx, K. (1946[1887]) *Capital vol.1*, London: Allen and Unwin.

Mills, C.W. (1956) *White Collar*, New York: Oxford University Press.

Nickson, D., Warhurst, C. and Dutton, E. (2005) "The importance of attitude and appearance in the service encounter in retail and hospitality," *Managing Service Quality*, 15, 2, 195–208.

Nickson, D., Warhurst, C., Witz, A. and Cullen, A.M. (2001) "The importance of being aesthetic: work, employment and service organization," in A. Sturdy, I. Grugulis, and H. Wilmott (eds.), *Customer Service*, Basingstoke: Palgrave.

Pakulski, J. and Waters, M. (1996) *The Death of Class*, London: Sage.

Paules, G. (1991) *Dishing it Out – Power and Resistance among Waitresses in a New Jersey Restaurant*, Philadelphia: Temple University Press.

Pettinger, L. (2004) "Brand culture and branded workers: service work and aesthetic labor in fashion retail," *Consumption, Markets and Culture*, 7, 2, 165–84.

Pettinger, L. (2006) "On the materiality of service work," *The Sociological Review*, 54, 1, 48–65.

Postrel, V. (2003) *The Substance of Style*, New York: HarperCollins.

Poynter, G. (2000) "Thank you for calling: The ideology of work in the service economy," *Soundings*, 14, Spring, 151–60.

Project on Disney (1995) *Inside The Mouse: Work and Play at Disney World*, London: Rivers Oram Press.

Reich, R. (1993) *The Work of Nations*, London: Simon & Schuster.

Ritzer, G. (1993) *The McDonaldization of Society*, London: Sage.

Ritzer, G. (2001) *Explorations in the Sociology of Consumption*, London: Sage.

Ritzer, G. (2004) *The Globalization of Nothing*, London: Pine Forge Press.

Roberts, K. (2007) "Work-life balance – the sources of the contemporary problem and the probable outcomes: a review and interpretation of the evidence," *Employee Relations*, 29, 4, 334–51.

Schor, J. (2000) *Do Americans Shop Too Much?*, Boston: Beacon Press.

Sturdy, A. (2001) "Servicing societies: colonisation, control, contradiction and contestation," in A. Sturdy, I. Grugulis, and H. Willmott (eds.), *Customer Service*, London: Palgrave.

Taylor, P. and Bain, P. (1999) " 'An assembly-line in the head': work and employee relations in the call center," *Industrial Relations Journal*, 30, 2, 101–17.

Taylor, P. and Bain, P. (2003) "Subterranean worksick blues: humour as subversion in two call centers," *Organization Studies*, 24, 9, 1487–509.

Taylor, P. and Bain, P. (2005) "Call center off-shoring to India: the revenge of history?" *Labor and Industry*, 14, 3, 15–38.

Taylor, S. (1998) "Emotional labor and the new workplace," in P. Thompson and C. Warhurst (eds.), *Workplaces of the Future*, London: Macmillan.

Thompson, P. (2003) "Disconnected capitalism: or why employers can't keep their side of the bargain," *Work, Employment and Society*, 17, 2, 359–78.

Thompson, P. and Smith, C. (2001) "Follow the redbrick road: reflections on the pathways in and out of the labor process debate," *International Studies of Management and Organization*, 30, 4, 40–67.

Thompson, P. and Newsome, K. (2004) "LPT, work and the employment relation," in B.E. Kaufman (ed.), *Theoretical Perspectives on Work and the Employment Relationship*, Ithaca, NY: Cornell University Press.

Thompson, P., Warhurst, C. and Callaghan, G. (2001) "Ignorant theory and knowledgeable workers: interrogating the connections between knowledge, skills and services," *Journal of Management Studies*, 38, 7, 923–42.

Thompson, P., van den Broek, D. and Callaghan, G. (2004) "Keeping up appearances: recruitment, skills and normative controls in call centers," in S. Deery and N. Kinne (eds.), *Human Resource Management in Call Centers*, London: Palgrave.

Tyler, M. and Abbott, P. (1998) "Chocs away: Weight watching in the contemporary airline industry," *Sociology*, 32, 3, 433–50.

Tyler, M. and Taylor, S. (1998) "The exchange of aesthetics: women's work and 'The gift' ", *Gender, Work and Organization*, 5:3, 165–71.

Van Maanen, J. (1991) "The smile factory: work at Disneyland," in P. Frost, L. Moore, M. Louis, C. Lundberg and J. Martin (eds.), *Reframing Organizational Culture*, New Park, CA: Sage Publications.

Warhurst, C. and Nickson, D. (2001) *Looking Good and Sounding Right: Style Counselling and the Aesthetics of the New Economy*, London: The Industrial Society.

Warhurst, C. and Nickson, D. (2007) "Employee experience of aesthetic labor in retail and hospitality," *Work, Employment and Society*, 21, 1, 103–20.

Warhurst, C. and Thompson, P. (1998) "Hands, hearts and minds: changing work and workers at the end of the century," in P. Thompson and C. Warhurst (eds.), *Workplaces of the Future*, London: Macmillan.

Warhurst, C., Nickson, D., Witz, A. and Cullen, A. (2000) "Aesthetic labor in interactive service work: some case study evidence from the 'New' Glasgow," *Service Industries Journal*, 20, 3, 1–18.

Warhurst, C., Eikhof, D.R. and Haunschild, A. (2008) "Out of balance or just out of bounds? Analysing the relationship between work and life," in C. Warhurst, D.R. Eikhof, and A. Haunschild (eds.), *Work Less, Live More?*, London: Palgrave.

Wilson, R., Homenidou, K. and Dickerson, A. (2006) *Working Futures 2004–2014: National Report*, Wath on Dearne: Sector Skills Development Agency.

Witz, A., Warhurst, C. and Nickson, D. (2003) "The labor of aesthetics and the aesthetics of organization," *Organization*, 10, 1, 33–54.

Wolkowitz, C. (2006) *Bodies at Work*, London: Sage.

# CHAPTER 7

# Intersectionality in the Emotional Proletariat

## A New Lens on Employment Discrimination in Service Work

CAMERON LYNNE MACDONALD AND DAVID MERRILL

## Introduction

Feminist theorists were among the first to speak to the significance of the rise of the service sector. It is well established that the vast majority of service sector jobs are held by women, and most of these can be said to be "typed" female. In fact, the growth in services in industrialized nations coincides nicely with the rise in female labor force participation, creating a cycle in which women left home to enter predominantly female jobs (teaching, nursing, social work, etc.), leaving behind a gap in reproductive labor (cleaning, cooking, childcare) that was in turn filled by other women entering these occupations. However, this work was not only gendered, but raced. In her now-famous essay, Evelyn Nakano Glenn (1996) demonstrated that in the U.S, as African American women moved out of domestic work into the lower tiers of the formal service sector, immigrant workers moved in to take their places, working in the homes of middle and upper-middle class White women, who had moved into managerial and professional service work.

We also know that a large proportion of jobs in the service sector require what Hochschild (1983) has termed "emotional labor" and that emotional labor is also sex-typed. In *the Managed Heart*, she studied the emotional labor and feeling rules associated with two gendered occupations, female flight attendants and male bill collectors (Hochschild, 1983). Her findings have been reproduced in numerous studies of interactive service work: women are expected to be "nicer than natural" while men are more likely to be in positions where they are expected to be "nastier than natural," emphasizing stereotypically feminine and masculine characteristics (Forseth, 2005, p.444). Our understanding of the gendered nature of occupations has come a long way since Hochschild's path breaking work, and feminist theorists now seek to understand not just how jobs are gendered, but how gendered jobs intersect with other ascribed characteristics like ethnicity, class, sexuality, and age. In their essay on intersectionality in the labor market, Browne and Misra point out that, "it is precisely in the sorting of individuals into jobs that gender and race appear to intersect in important ways."

When we think of job discrimination, several models come to mind. Social capital theories of discrimination focused on the resources available to individuals that qualify them for various jobs (Becker, 1957). Institutional theories explore the ways in which work organizations and bureaucracies are gendered in ways that reproduce masculine bias in employment (Acker, 1990). Reskin and Roos (1990) expanded queuing theory to argue that employers and employees respectively rank order preferred workers and preferred jobs and these queues generate the labor market segmentation we observe. These queues are constructed based on a variety of factors, including labor supply, race and sex composition of the job, skills required, and other employment opportunities available to a given group of workers.

Occupations can shift in their ethnic and gender compositions as women begin to move into sex-atypical jobs. Once this process begins and the occupations begin to be coded as "women's work," men will place these jobs lower in their queues and attempt to move out of the jobs in favor of work that is not feminized. Further, Christine Williams (1993) and Jennifer Pierce (1995) have studied men in "female" professions, and have argued that not only are jobs sex-typed but that when the job-holder's gender does not fit that of the position, they are treated differently by their colleagues and superiors. This argument becomes even more salient when we explore stereotyping in interactive services, given that employers take customer preferences into account when hiring.[1]

Stereotyping theories fall into two basic categories. In the first, dominant groups control access to employment and provide access to coveted jobs based on membership in "ingroups" and "outgroups," while simultaneously making those inequalities appear "natural" (Sidanius and Pratto, 2001). On the other hand, the cognitive turn in social psychology has shifted our understanding of stereotyping from a practice based on motives, (i.e. excluding out-group members due to hostility or a need to dominate) to a natural human tendency to order a complex world through the use of categories.[2] Individuals use stereotypes as an unconscious "cognitive shortcut" to sort through the barrage of information encountered on a regular basis, and that stereotyping occurs regardless of whether or not the person applying the stereotype carries animosity towards a given group (Ridgeway, 2000).

While human capital theories, theories of gendered institutions, queuing theories, and theories about stereotyping account for some of the gender and ethnic discrimination present in service sector work, it cannot, we argue, account for all of it, especially in what Macdonald and Sirianni (1996) have termed the "emotional proletariat": service workers who perform face-to-face or voice-to-voice service work, but who have no control over the "feeling rules" that guide their emotional labor, and who are in a subservient position vis-à-vis the customer.

In this chapter, we analyze the hiring practices specific to the emotional proletariat, and argue that a full understanding of these practices depends on using intersectionality as an epistemological frame. Labor market segmentation and gender and ethnic "niches" within interactive services are hardly accidental – ethnicity and gender shape hiring decisions because they shape service interactions.

The study of how intersectionality shapes hiring in the emotional proletariat offers a perfect case for applying feminist theories of what Collins (1991) has termed "the matrix of domination" to discrimination in hiring. First, in the front of the house (face-to-face service interactions), the "service triangle" (Leidner, 1993) of management, customer and server is particularly salient in hiring decisions. Managers attempt to match the "type" of service provider with their assumptions concerning the customer's expectations of the nature and meaning of the service. Macdonald calls this process of hiring according to assumed customer preferences in terms of gender and ethnicity and other status markers, ethnic and gender "logics" (Macdonald forthcoming). These logics vary from service to service and from region to region, and therefore do not follow an additive model in which some groups are de facto preferred over others. Rather, they are specific to the meanings inherent in particular services and cultural assumptions about who can best provide them, making ethnic and gender job-typing in the emotional proletariat virtually inevitable.

Second, interactive service work requires that the worker engage in "deep" or "surface" acting (Hochschild, 1983), thus bringing crucial aspects of the self to their work. In our discussion below, we will argue that not only do customer preferences create a segmented labor market in interactive service work, but that the gender and ethnic identities of the workers themselves play a critical role in creating occupational segregation in the service sector. Interactive service workers must "perform" according to certain customer and management expectations, and the service performance may be more or less aligned with the gender and ethnic identity of the worker.

As Hochschild (1983) points out, the manufacturing worker uses his arms in the service of the capitalist, thus alienating his physical labor in creating surplus value. The service worker, however, alienates crucial aspects of her personality, her sexuality, her friendliness, her deference, in the production of profit. In some cases, the service role and the gender and ethnic identity may cohere such that the worker perceives service provision as simply an extension of her "natural" self. In other cases, the service performance may be so incongruent with the gender and ethnic identity of the worker that she may be perceived as unsuitable for the work or that she may choose unemployment over personal debasement.

In the discussion that follows, we will demonstrate how the feminist approach to intersectionality offers insights into both discrimination in hiring and the experience of working in interactive services that would not be evident without this epistemological frame. We select the emotional proletariat as our case study because it represents, in many ways, the "ideal typical" form of service work, and thus reveals the interactions of ethnicity, gender and class in service work in ways that do not operate similarly in other sectors of the labor market.

## Intersectionality

"Intersectionality Theory" (first coined by Kimberly Crenshaw in 1989) has developed into a prominent mode of feminist analysis. While early second-wave feminist theorists attempted to theorize from a univocal "woman's" position, it quickly became clear that not only were the lived experiences of women of color different from the white women's perspective that dominated second-wave feminist theorizing, but that the "higher status and living standards of white women have depended on the subordination and lower living standards of women of color" (Glenn, 1999). Feminist theorizing from the standpoint of women of color is aimed primarily at redressing the injustices associated with treating women as a monolithic category and treating White women as the universal female.

Early attempts at combining race and class with gender analyses resulted in cumbersome and inaccurate additive models. For example, Ransford's "multiple jeopardy-multiple advantage hypothesis suggests that the groups experiencing the most disadvantages in terms of race/gender/class, would cumulatively be the most disadvantaged group" (Ransford, 1980). Applied to the labor market, this hypothesis would suggest, for example, that those on the lower rungs of more than one ethnic/gender/sexuality category would necessarily also occupy the lowest rung of any given labor market.

Feminist theorizing in the 1990s corrected these somewhat simplistic models starting from a relational perspective that viewed various ascribed characteristics as "simultaneous and linked" and by asserting that "race is gendered and gender is racialized, so that race and gender fuse to create unique experiences and opportunities for all groups – not just women of color". However, as Baca Zinn and Thornton Dill (1996, p. 329) have argued, "Race class, gender, and sexuality are not reducible to individual attributes to be measured and assessed for their separate contributions in explaining given social outcomes." For example, Collins developed the concept of the "matrix of domination" based on "interlocking systems of oppression" (Collins, 1991). Within this matrix, an individual may be advantaged or disadvantaged by a combination of markers, including gender, ethnicity, social class, age, sexuality, and disability. Further, these characteristics may intersect to create advantages for an individual in one context while disadvantaging them in another.

These relative advantages and disadvantages are historically and contextually defined. For example, McCall has shown that in numerous economic contexts, White women earn more than Black and Latino men – thus demonstrating that simplistic models of hierarchal domination fail in the face of the complexities of social reality (McCall, 2001). As we will show below, women of color are frequently employed at higher rates than their male counterparts in entry-level service sector jobs. Thus the relevance of certain social markers to an institutional context such as a job market must be studied through an intersectional lens.

In her essay on approaches to the study of intersectionality, McCall demonstrates that intersectionality is not only a theory but an epistemology (McCall, 2005). The majority of feminist theorizing on intersectionality falls into one of two categories. Some argue that social life is too complex to be reduced to the categories of race, gender, and class, and that to treat these categories as extant *in the world* is in itself a reification. McCall terms these approaches, "anticategorical" – that is, rejecting the inherent relevance or tangible reality of categories such as race or gender, as in most postmodern and post-structural approaches.[3] Others argue that while it may be important to recognize the "stable and durable relationships that social categories represent at any given point in time," they also argue in favor of a generally "critical stance towards categories" (McCall 2005, p. 1746). McCall calls this an "intracategorical" approach. In this approach, the experience of a marginalized group is the point of departure, while simultaneously the contingent nature of that marginality is also maintained – as in standpoint theory. In the "intracategorical" approach to the study of intersectionality, "the point is not to deny the importance – both material and discursive – of categories but to focus on the process by which they are produced, experienced, and resisted in everyday life" (McCall 2005, p. 1783).[4]

In her own research, McCall (2001) uses a third approach she calls "intercategorical," using the tools of quantitative social science research to explore inequality among "already constituted social groups, as imperfect and ever changing as they are, and tak[ing] those relationships as the center of analysis" (McCall, 2005, p. 1785). In the discussion that follows, we adopt each of these approaches to show how different intersectional "lenses" reveal aspects of inequality in interactive service work that would not be revealed otherwise. In the next section, we take McCall's "intercategorical" approach, using categories as constituted in the U.S. Current Population Survey to demonstrate the "matrix of domination" at work in various subgroups of service workers.

After that, we discuss how employers' constructs of customer impressions shape hiring in the emotional proletariat. This is an example of an "anticategorcial" approach to intersectionality. Clearly the categories in question exist only in the minds of employers as they try to predict customer's unstated preferences: these hiring decisions are thus based on the thinnest fragment of a chimera. Yet these impressionistic images are real in their consequences for workers. Finally, we take an "intracategorical" approach in exploring the standpoints of workers from various marginalized groups and how these shape their perceptions of "fit" with a given type of service work, and further, how they affect how workers conceptualize possibilities of resistance and collective mobilization.

### Intersectionality and Discrimination in the Emotional Proletariat: Intercategorical Intersectionality – Labor Market Statistics in Action

The emotional proletariat comprises[5] a substantial portion of the labor market: approximately 29 percent of workers in the United States are employed in the emotional proletariat.[6] And this proportion will only continue to increase – employment in the U.S. service sector is projected to increase by 17 percent over the next 10 years (Dohm and Shniper, 2007, p. 91). Of service sector jobs, many of the fastest growing individual occupations are jobs that fall into the emotional proletariat. The two fastest growing occupations, personal and home care aides and home health aides, are expected to grow by 50 percent each (Dohm and Shniper, 2007, p. 94).

However, not every worker has an equal chance of finding work in the emotional proletariat – the intersections of ethnicity, class, and gender sort workers into different niches within this part of the service sector. Table 7.1 shows the percentage of the workers in each ethnic/sex category that work

**Table 7.1** Percentage of total workers by sex and ethnicity that work in the emotional proletariat in the United States

|          | Men   | Women |
|----------|-------|-------|
| White    | 15.9% | 41.8% |
| Black    | 21.0% | 48.1% |
| Hispanic | 18.8% | 49.1% |
| Other    | 18.5% | 39.4% |

in the emotional proletariat in the United States. Even though only 29 percent of the total workforce is employed in the emotional proletariat, there are vast discrepancies among groups. Overall, women are employed in the emotional proletariat at almost twice the rate of men. In addition, substantial differences exist among ethnic groups, with more Black and Latina women employed in the emotional proletariat than White and Asian women.

In addition, the rates of participation in the emotional proletariat are not stable over the life course. Figure 7.1 shows the number of women in

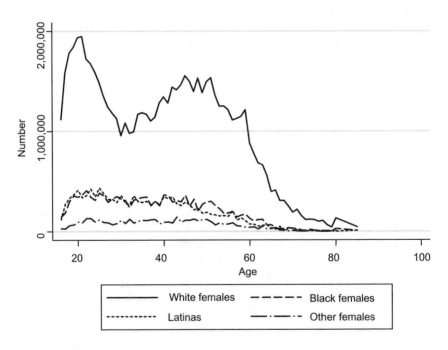

Authors' original analysis of 2006 CPS data

**Figure 7.1** Number of women in emotional proletariat by race and age

the emotional proletariat as a function of age. The most noticeable aspect of this graph is the bimodal distribution of White women. This graph makes clear that there are two different types of White women employed in the emotional proletariat – young women that are most likely working part-time during school and before marriage and childbearing, and older women who entered this sector after raising children. By contrast, Black and Latina women tend to enter the emotional proletariat and remain there.

This pattern shows that some white women have advantages of education, class, and ethnicity that result in remaining in the emotional proletariat as a temporary job prior to moving into another sector of the workforce or into life as a housewife. However, this is not true of all White women and this underscores the necessity of having white women perform some of the work that customers expect to see. The continued employment of white women in the emotional proletariat cannot simply be understood as a "choice" they make. In fact, there are some jobs that would be very difficult to get because they don't meet the "ethnic logics" associated with that job.

There are notable exceptions to the ability of groups to "cross" into jobs that customers do not associate with their ethnicity. For example, there may be very strong feelings on the part of parents about who is suitable to take care of their children. As Macdonald (Macdonald forthcoming) has shown, racial/ethnic groups are preferred by parents based on their presumed qualities that are rooted in their ethnicity. In this situation, it may be difficult for other women to move into these jobs even if they are capable and willing to perform the work. These effects of intersectionality at work are largely missed by conventional theories of labor market segmentation. This is not simply an example of employer discrimination nor is it exclusively an issue of workers' self-selection. Instead, the patterns of distribution within this sector are complicated and structured by multiple forces.

To illustrate the complexity of the patterns of employment within the emotional proletariat, it is worth considering how ethnicity and sex intersect to result in very specific types of distributions within a single setting. Many women work in the dental field, but they are not evenly distributed around the office. In the U.S., 90 percent of the dental hygienists are white women and this is the occupation in which the most over-representation of White women occurs. With very few exceptions, when a customer goes to get her teeth cleaned, it will be done by a White woman. However, the receptionist that schedules appointments and answers the phone is likely to be a woman of color. In fact, Black women are employed as operators at a rate that is three times that of their labor force participation. The same is true of the women dealing with the medical records. The expectations customers have about their face-to-face interactions play a very important role in shaping the decisions employers make and the patterns of employment they encounter. Differences in education alone cannot account for the ethnic differences in employment. Dental hygienists and licensed practical nurses require about the same amount of education. However, 90 percent of the dental hygienists are White compared to only 65 percent of the LPNs that are White. So, for the same educational investment, we find that one occupation has a heavy over-concentration of White women, while the other finds a relative overconcentration of women of color.

Similarly, employers of childcare workers have very specific, but regionally variable ideas about the "type" of person who should care for their children. Macdonald's study of nannies and their employers in one major U.S. urban area showed that employers in one community preferred to hire Irish immigrant nannies and advertised only in newspapers that would target this group. Ten miles away, employers told her that they never sought Irish nannies because "they can't drive, because they're too poor, and they all smoke" (Macdonald forthcoming). In that community, the preferred nanny was a Swedish au pair, referred to as the "European version of the All-American girl." In London, by contrast, employers seek Filipina childcare workers. According to a placement agency owner, "people think that Filipinas are from a different planet where everybody cares about children" (Lister *et al.*, 2007). While in Madrid, "Anti-Muslim sentiment meant that Moroccans were bottom of the hierarchy ... South Americans were thought of as warm-hearted but slow; Eastern Europeans were considered to be hard-working, and as Europeans, more like Spanish people" (Williams and Gavanas, 2008).

Exploring the regional variation among employer preferences reveals how arbitrary these ethnic typifications can be. For a final example, Parreñas (2000) finds that because of variations in international labor queues, Filipina migrant workers find work as domestics in Rome, but work as nurses in Los Angeles. Her findings may speak to the operation of labor shortages in each country, but is as likely to speak to cultural preferences for a given type of worker in a given type of job. While a Filipina nurse may be perfectly acceptable, and even preferable, to patients and hospital administrators in the U.S., in Rome she would be unthinkable. On the one hand, it is clear that the mix of employees reflects the mix of the pool of available workers. On the other hand, how they are ranked and sorted by employers reflects regionally specific cultural logics that can only be revealed through an intersectional lens. Our point is that global labor queues are not shaped only by economic supply and demand, but also by cultural supply and demand.

## Anticategorical Intersectionality: Customer Preferences and the Service Triangle

In studying employer hiring preferences, we see a cognitive approach to stereotyping taken to an extreme, both in that employers calculate customer preferences and hire based on these rather fuzzy assumptions, and in that they manipulate assumed stereotypes to create a product. Employers take customers' stereotypes into account and then hire a person who will fit these stereotypes or fulfill their corporate "brand." This approach to hiring based on intersectional characteristics is particularly evident in what Warhust, Witz, and Nickson have variously termed "aesthetic labour." Defined as "the mobilization, development and commodification of embodied 'dispositions'" (Witz, 2003), aesthetic labor speaks to the importance in face-to-face service interactions of "packaging the service provider" (Solomon, 1985, quoted in Warhust and Nickson, 2007, p. 112). Like emotional labor and "soft skills," aesthetic labor is shaped by intersectionality. As Witz points out, "the kinds of embodied dispositions that acquire an exchange value are not equally distributed socially, but fractured by class, gender, age and racialized positions or locations" (Witz, 2003, p. 41). Scholars of aesthetic labor have pointed out that by emphasizing the "feeling work" of emotional labor and the "attitudes" inherent in employers' views of soft skills, scholars have missed the salience of the embodied nature of service work.

We concur, but also suggest, that previous applications of the concept of aesthetic labor have not gone far enough in conceptualizing how race, class, gender and age serve as signifiers in the service encounter. Like the concept of "Soft Skills" or employers' search for employees who display the "right attitudes" (Moss and Tilly, 2001; Warhust et al., 2000), research on aesthetic labor employs an implicit assumption that appearance, demeanor, and attitude fall along a continuum from worse to better, and that this continuum applies similarly regardless of the service provided. An intersectional lens, however, reveals that like the regional variations in employer preferences described above, employers seek gender, ethnic and class "markers" in employees that will signify to the service recipient the nature of the service they are about to consume.

Demand for these aesthetic skills and competencies are becoming more prevalent because of their perceived commercial utility. For example "the employer may know there is no real difference in competence between an attractive an unattractive employee, but there *may* be a difference in how they are perceived by the public or the client that could mean a difference in profit" (Warhust et al., 2000, p. 5), quoting Hatfield and Sprecher). As a case in point, Hooters "unashamedly uses nubile young waitresses dressed in skimpy tops to attract customers – seeking the 'Florida beach girl look' "

(Golding, p. 7 quoted in Warhust *et al.*, 2000, p. 5). In fact, Hooters recently sued a competitor, claiming infringement on what it considered its trademark rights to its uniforms. In his ruling, the superior court judge argued that the uniforms did not qualify for trademark protection since the Hooters' trademark is not the white tank tops and orange short shorts, but the type of person who will adequately fill them.[7] Just as the Hooters' "girl" symbolizes the Hooters' experience, other service interactions are signified by the type of person who performs them. Instead, the judge pointed out,

> The overwhelmingly predominant feature of Hooters' trade dress is the Hooters Girl. As the Plaintiffs themselves have said, "the Hooters Girls *are* Hooters. They are not simply a marketing tool; they are the essence of the business" whose "predominant function is to provide vicarious sexual recreation, to titillate, entice, and arouse male customers" fantasies.
>
> (*Hooters, Inc v. Winghouse*, 347 F. Supp. 2d 1256)

The specific nature of service work and the particulars of different service occupations shape employers' visions of the "type" of worker who will ideally fit particular service needs. In the UK, such labor market discrimination is legitimized by companies having the right to determine appearance if a business case for the appearance is made (Hays and Middlemiss, 2003, quoted in Warhust and Nickson, 2007). Numerous studies and court cases demonstrate how attractive young women are given preferential treatment in hiring in certain types of face-to-face service work (Entwhistle and Wissinger, 2006; Warhust and Nickson, 2007).

Yet how is aesthetic labor raced, classed and gendered? Unfortunately, most extant studies on aesthetic labor emphasize businesses such as high-end retail, expensive hotels, and couture fashion, creating perhaps a mistaken notion that aesthetic labor occurs only at the high end of retail services or that it exists along a continuum. Aesthetic labor is presented as hierarchical – assuming that young, white, middle-class, attractive workers are hired for better-paying, better status jobs.

We argue instead that aesthetic labor exists in all customer service jobs, and that rather than existing along a continuum from least valued to most valued, race, gender class and age coalesce in different job settings to create a norm of the worker who will "look the part" given a particular service. For example, although Warhust and Nickson (2007), Entwhistle and Wissinger (2006), and Witz (2003) have found a preference for young women presenting a middle-class "doxa" in high-end clothing sales, we also find evidence of preferences for older men in other sectors.[8] For example, Foster's study of customer preferences in a prominent "Do-it-yourself" (DIY) store chain, indicates that customers preferred older, working-class men as service providers because they appeared to have "been in that trade all of his life, instead of someone younger who's done botched up jobs all their life" (Foster 2004). Focus groups on customer perceptions of the ideal DIY man described the ideal sales worker as "a Bob the builder type," "a Texan, a John Wayne, or Clint Eastwood." Similarly, all workers wore orange "workman's aprons," with a nametag suggesting the worker's expertise, if he had one. There were no female experts (Foster, 2004).

Customer preference for male service workers in this environment went so far that a male worker stated, "I used to work on tools. I think it's perceived that males know more about tools than women. There's many a time when I've been on hardware and a female member of staff was stand-ing 200 yards in front of me and the customer would pass her and ask me instead (Foster, 2004)." The layout of the store consciously reflected this gendered division of expertise, with the masculine heavy equipment and contractors' sections at one end, moving to the smaller tools and finally to the more feminine carpets and paint sections. Similarly, customers showed a marked preference for age over youth, regardless of gender. One worker commented, "The assumption is that age means experience and men know and women don't. I can be stood with a young lad and a young female member of the staff and they'll always come to me." Thus, we find that a desirable employee "look" is neither uniformly young, attractive, nor middle-class, but rather serves a signaling function based on the nature of the service provided.

We can find this kind of diversity in customer preferences in studies of tourism as well. (Desmond, 1999; Sherman, 2007; Thompson, 2002; Wells, 2000). For example, In their study of resort workers in Hawaii, Adler and Adler draw on Lieberson's (1980) argument that racial/ethnic groups enter occupational niches because: "they have some cultural characteristic (per-ceived physical, mental, or social ability) that is associated with a given job, or they find a ripe opportunity structure available for this job at the time they enter the employment market" (Adler and Adler, 2004). The authors point out that among other sorting mechanisms, personnel managers fun-nel workers of various races into different parts of the hotel based on what Adler and Adler call "ethnic typicifications."

Although they do not define this term, they do report its effects. The labor force in Hawaiian resorts are ethnically stratified: local and mainland "Haole's" were funneled into key guest contact positions;[9] natives were funneled two ways – into "token positions commodifying Hawaiian cul-ture for the guests" (generally women) and into positions that exploited their physical strength (generally men). Leis and hula lessons were given by locals who "fulfilled the objectified, commercialized notion of Hawaiians as ideal natives" (Adler and Adler 2004, p. 226). Immigrants of color worked in "back of the house" ghettoes in which they had little or no guest contact. Acknowledging the commoditization of culture that formed these job queues, Adler and Adler also argue that these "rationalizations are based . . . on a customer service orientation that sweeps inequality under the rug in the name of pleasing the client." We argue, however, that "customer service orientation is not an obfuscation, but rather a driving force behind the creation of labor market inequalities in the emotional proletariat." In attempting to please the client, employers draw on existing stereotypes, many of which are based on existing power inequalities.

For example, certain workers are virtually excluded from jobs in the emotional proletariat because of how they are perceived. While the shift to a service-based economy has opened up low-skill and low-wage jobs for women of color, men of color, particularly African-American men, have been excluded from entry-level interactive service jobs. Scholars argue that this re-shuffling of labor-market segmentation is, at least in part, the product of a heightened emphasis on "soft skills," or interpersonal abilities. The increase in the number of interactive service jobs has placed customer's racial-ethnic preferences high on the list of employer preferences.

We might ask, however if "soft skills" can be measured as human capital the way that the ability to read, write, or use a calculator are, since these skills exist as much in the eyes of the consumer/employer as in the capacities of the employee. "Skills" like the ability to appear deferent, nurturing, or sexy, are not so much abilities that prospective workers can invest in as they are attributes cued by physical appearance. One can accentuate them, but they are as much in the eye of the beholder as in the incumbent. Racial/ethnic identity or gender identity can in fact trump those skills. For example, according to Tilly and Moss, African American men rarely get the chance to try to perform "soft skills" because employers simply assume that they cannot. Although interpersonal interactions are managed *jointly* by the customer and provider, employers surveyed "genuinely view interaction and motivation as skills" that inhere in the incumbent alone (Moss and Tilly, 1996, p. 45; Moss and Tilly, 2001).

Viewed through the lens of anticategorical intersectionality, we can see how employers use signifiers, such as race and ethnicity, as well as gender, age, and social class, as proxies for the kinds of emotional labor, cultural and aesthetic displays they believe a worker can successfully perform, as well as what their "type" may signify to customers. Employers and service recipients translate race and ethnic markers into indicators of the nature of the service itself. Can the customer expect kindness, deference, flirtation? The famed "Singapore Girl" of the airlines advertisement speaks to how cultural codes inflect the combination of a particular Asian ethnicity with gender to connote a pleasant (and perhaps sexually charged) flying experience.

Some of these expectations have been shaped by how members of various groups have formed "an immigrant niche" in certain occupations. The Chinese laundry and the Korean or Vietnamese nail salon are examples of how an ethnic group may specialize in certain skills and then engage in what Waldinger (1996; 2003) terms "occupational closure" through ethnic networks. This "niche" may then translate into a self-perpetuating stereotype from the perspective of future employers or consumers who then expect to find a certain "type" of person performing a given service. Here we see the shift from ethnicity and gender as part of a given "group-making" and networking strategy to the reification of a given ethnic/gender category that ultimately becomes an occupational ghetto and a new form of discrimination.

But are ethnic and gender logics simply examples of employers deploying stereotypes? As discussed above, scholars of the "cognitive turn" in stereotyping research argue that stereotypes and other forms of categorization are the raw socio-cultural material from which actors select strategically to make sense of the world. Stereotypes draw heavily on schematic thinking, but not, as has been previously assumed, because groups exist in the world as distinct entities, but because "grouping and group-making" are human activities: "they are not things *in* the world, but perspectives *on* the world – not ontological, but epistemological realities" (Brubaker *et al.*, 2004). In interactive service work, the customer's perception of the worker *is* in many respects the service; therefore this kind of ethnic and gender stereotyping is likely to be particularly resistant to change.

### Intracategorical Intersectionality: Ethnic and Gender Identities

For many workers in the emotional proletariat, their work is not simply a job, but an extension of their identity. Just as customers presume that certain workers are capable of providing the service because of their race and gender, so the employees think that their ability to do the work is rooted in some deeper part of themselves. Being a nurse is not simply an issue of learning how to administer medicine, change dressings, and start an IV. Instead, it is the combination of technical skills and emotional labor that is connected with many nurses' self-identity as a caring and compassionate person who wants to make a positive difference for their patients. The ways that emotional labor, ethnic and gender identities and employment categories intersect have profound implications both for how workers select jobs and for their resistance and mobilization strategies.

For example, although we have pointed out above that employers use customer preferences as a justification for discriminating against inner-city men, arguing that they lack the requisite "soft skills," it may also be the case that working class and poor men find the deference and feigned friendliness inherent in most interactive service jobs incompatible with an already damaged sense of masculinity (Lindsay and McQuaid, 2004; Nixon, forthcoming, 2009). Socially and economically excluded from enacting forms of highly-educated high-earning corporate "hegemonic" masculinity (Connell, 1995), poor and working class men establish a masculine identities based on toughness and an anti-middle class style of embodiment. For example, Lamont's (2000) research shows how working class men enact a particular masculine "doxa" to define and reinforce their own sense of gender and class identity. Similarly, Anderson (1999) shows how "street" men enact a particular African-American male doxa, both to signify belonging and to keep themselves safe in a hostile environment.

We do not suggest a "blame the victim" approach to ethnic and gender identity in service work. On the contrary, as discussed above, urban males face employment discrimination before they walk in the door. However, it is clear that certain masculinities are internally incompatible with jobs in the emotional proletariat. For example, Leidner found that male workers at McDonald's preferred the hot and dirty work of the grill to the subservient role of order-taker and cashier. Male workers explained the aversion to working the register or the window because "that job required swallowing one's pride and accepting abuse calmly." As one noted, "women are afraid of getting burned (on the grill), and men are afraid of getting aggravated and going over the counter and smacking someone" (Leidner, 1991, p. 163). Those male workers who did work the window reframed the work as masculine by assuming the "cool pose . . . enacting and imperviousness to hurt" (Leidner 1991, p. 164). Although male workers at McDonald's could re-frame Black masculinity to include interactive service work, this took more re-framing of identity than it did for women. As Leidner points out,

> The job requirements of smiling and otherwise demonstrating deference are not in keeping with the cool pose. Those committed to that stance might well find such behavior demeaning, especially in interactions with White customers or those of higher status.
>
> (Leidner, 1991)

Thus gender and ethnic identity become salient not in *whether* the worker can produce the expected emotional display, but in *how much* emotional labor this requires, and in how congruent or incongruent this display is with their sense of identity and dignity.

We can see the relevance of intersectionality also in worker's explanations of why they choose to remain in a certain line of work. Childcare is among the most poorly paid and least respected jobs in the United States. However, workers bring particular gendered and ethnic "vocabularies of motive" to their internal and external accounts of their choice to remain in this line of work. Since virtually all childcare workers are female, gender identity is particularly salient to accounts of the meaning of working in childcare.

The nannies Macdonald studied adhered to a strong belief in "intensive mothering," (Hays, 1996) explaining that they chose nanny work over working in a day care center because they could provide the children in their care with the "kind of mothering the children deserve," and which their employers did not. At the same time, they created their own class-inflected version of "intensive mothering," disdaining the plethora of enrichment activities that their employers insisted on for their children. Instead of the middle-class version of childrearing as "concerted cultivation," they created a work ethic and a sense of dignity in their work by combining ideologies of "intensive mothering" with working-class beliefs in the "accomplishment of natural growth" (Lareau, 2003).

These workers deployed the language of motherhood and of a class-based view of childrearing to criticize their employers and thus valorize their own work. As a White, working-class nanny explained, "I just think they need to have a little more time with their kids – QUALITY time. Not time running them around to their activities. . . ." We gotta go to baseball. We gotta go to hockey. We gotta go here and there." Like most of the nannies Macdonald interviewed, this nanny enacted a resistance strategy based on "outmothering the mother" and being more nurturing than their employers towards their employers' children. If her work was devalued because of social class and its association with "natural" femininity, then she would emphasize those class and gendered aspects of the work in her efforts to dignify it.

On the other hand, we can see how race informs the motivations of childcare workers in the African-American childcare workers Tuominen studied. They drew on an ethnically specific vocabulary to valorize their often underpaid and underappreciated work. They explained that they were motivated by both their identities as African American women and as Christian women to care for the children in their communities.

As one caregiver explained, "my meaning is that I'm putting back into my community. Just being an asset to my community" (Tuominen, 2003, p. 168). In their view, they played an important role as "community other mothers," that justified the sacrifices they made, while simultaneously arguing that this role was important enough to warrant fair pay (Collins, 1991; Tuominen, 2003). As Tuominen points out, "Other mothering encompasses community activism to address the needs of the children and the community" (Tuominen, 2003, p.168). Thus the intersection of race and gender provides a specific meaning and set of motivations for one set of childcare workers that is specific to their social location.

The ways in which self-identity is intertwined with their job make mobilization for change particularly difficult. In England et al.'s (2002) work, the wages of caregivers, she shows that people that work in caring professions (including high status jobs such as doctors, university professors, and therapists) suffer a "care penalty." Workers experience this penalty even when controlling for education, experience, and several occupation and industry characteristics. For many of these workers, they are willing to accept this wage penalty because they feel that the rewards of their work extend beyond wages and benefits. Instead, being a good caregiver is central to their own sense of self.

Cobble and Merrill's chapter in this book highlights some of the difficulties in trying to mobilize this segment of the labor force in light of the fact that both their institutional locations and refusal to adopt a directly confrontational approach render conventional unionization efforts ineffective. We have also touched on this conflict in our discussion of the need for workers to obtain both higher wages and intersubjective recognition. We argue that many caregivers suffer a double penalty both in terms of the wage penalty identified by England *et al* . . . as well as a failure on the part of their employers (and some times the recipient of their care) to grant recognition to the work that is rooted in their self-conception. Many of the soft skills performed by caregivers are simply assumed to be a natural part of their ethnic heritage or the fact that they are a woman. In our research on mobilization among care workers, we found that caregivers faced internal conflicts between their view of themselves as "worthy workers" and as "altruistic careers." The intersection of gender and other characteristics often made their service to the community more important to them than their rights as workers. Successful campaigns were those that involved demonstrating that their needs for fair treatment as workers coincided with their clients' needs for quality care (Macdonald and Merrill, 2002).

## Conclusion

Both of us have "served time" in the emotional proletariat. Macdonald worked variously as a waitress, a hotel desk clerk, an exercise instructor, and as a nanny. In writing this chapter, she was reminded of an odd interaction: the manager of the hotel that employed her on the night shift of the front desk was walking across the spacious lobby one evening, glanced at the seven or eight workers on duty, paused, smiled, and said, "Ahhh, the Hyatt look in action." The workers gave one another bemused looks. What did he mean? The workers were White women, two Ethiopian women, a Filipina, and two demonstrably gay men – one White and one Black. What did we have in common besides our polyester pseudo-tuxedos?

The question of what comprises the "Hyatt look in action" remains a mystery. However, applying the feminist intersectional lens, we can see that this collection of workers was sorted into this relatively high-paying, unionized job according to characteristics that went far beyond our education (none of us had more than a little college), training (minimal, at best), or even our "soft skills" (pretty darned good): something about the way that ethnicity, social class, gender and sexuality appealed to management. On the surface, at least, individually and collectively, we fit an image that Hyatt management believed their customers wanted to see when they checked into the hotel. Aspects of our gender and ethnic identities also made the job acceptable to us. We generally didn't mind calling the guest "sir" or "ma'am," wearing a straight face when we assigned a room to an inebriated guest with his third prostitute of the night, or accommodating the poor business traveler who had been bumped from his flight, forced to pay for a higher-priced rental car than he had reserved, only to arrive at our desk to find that there was no room left at the inn.

In the preceding analysis we have made a case for the particular salience of intersectional analyses in understanding how discrimination operates in interactive service work. The "personal qualities" of the worker – both as constructed by management and the customer and perceived internally by the incumbent – are inextricably interwoven with the nature of the service provided. Therefore, jobs in the emotional proletariat are segmented by gender, race, and other status markers in sometimes irrational ways. Further, the sorting of workers into these jobs may be more intractable than other forms of discrimination in employment precisely *because* of the interconnected nature of server and service. As more and more jobs are created within the emotional proletariat, the social cost of these subtle forms of discrimination will increase. It is the authors' hope that increased awareness of these issues will create a dialog in which we can critically address these problems.

## Notes

1  In the discussion that follows, we do not discount the power of labor queues and aspects of human capital such as education in shaping labor markets. However, we do suggest that these theories cannot fully explain the ethnic and gender stratification we observe in the emotional proletariat.
2  See e.g. Fiske (1998) for a useful overview of the Social Psychology literature.
3  For example, Fausto-Sterling (2000), Fuss (1989) and Butler (2004).
4  For examples, see Glenn (1999), Hondagneu-Sotelo (2001) and Crenshaw (1989).
5  For the empirical analysis of the Current Population Survey, we operationalize the concept of the emotional proletariat by examining the 2000 Census occupation codes. Based on the occupations and descriptions of the individual occupations, we selected those occupations that met the following criteria: (1) involved face-to-face or voice-to-voice interaction with customers where the employee is required to engage in emotional labor, where (2) the employee

has little or no autonomy in setting the "feeling rules" in the job description and where (3) the employee is in a subordinate position vis-à-vis the customer and is not able to control the conditions under which the interaction occurs. Based on these criteria, we selected 73 occupations that made up the emotional proletariat.

6　All of the statistical analyses in this chapter are original analyses of the 2006 outgoing rotation groups of the United States Current Population Survey (Current population survey merged outgoing rotation groups [MORG] annual files: 1979–2006 extracts. [machine-readable data file] / U.S. Department of Commerce. Bureau of the Census [principal investigator(s)] / Cambridge, Massachusetts: National Bureau of Economic Research [distributor]). The outgoing rotation group is a common subset of the yearly CPS data that is used to conduct statistical analyses. For more information on the usage of the CPS outgoing rotation group, see Appendix B in Mishel *et al.* (2007).

7　Ironically, because Hooters' girls and their uniforms "serve a function", the Eleventh Circuit Court of Appeals held that they could not legally "protect something that serves a legal purpose" (Porter 2006). For more on US Antidiscrimination law and appearance, see Post (2000).

8　For a definition of Doxa, see Bourdieu (1990).

9　White, non-natives.

# References

Acker, J. (1990) "Hierarchies, jobs, bodies: A theory of gendered organizations," *Gender and Society*, 4, 139–58.

Adler, P and Adler, P. (2004) *Paradise Laborers: Hotel Work in the Global Economy*, Ithaca, NY: ILR Press.

Anderson, E. (1999) *Code of the Street: Decency, Violence, and the Moral Life of the Inner City*, New York: W. W. Norton & Company.

Baca Zinn, M. and Thornton Dill, B. (1996) "Theorizing difference from multicultural feminism," *Feminist Studies*, 22, 321–31.

Becker, G. (1957) *The Economics of Discrimination*, Chicago: University of Chicago Press.

Bourdieu, P. (1990) *The Logic of Practice*, Translated by R. Nice, Cambridge: Polity Press.

Browne, I. and Misra, J. (2003) "The intersection of gender and race in the labor market," *Annual Review of Sociology*, 29, 487–513.

Brubaker, R., Loveman, M. and Stamatov, P. (2004) "Ethnicity as cognition," *Theory and Society*, 33, 31–64.

Butler, J. (2004) *Undoing Gender*, New York: Routledge.

Collins, P.H. (1991) *Black Feminist Thought: Knowledge, Consciousness, and the Politics of Empowerment*, New York: Routledge.

Connell, R.W. (1995) *Masculinities*, Berkeley, CA: University of California Press.

Crenshaw, K. (1989) "Demarginalizing the intersection of race and sex: A black feminist critique of antidiscrimination doctrine, feminist theory, and antiracist politics," *University of Chicago Legal Forum*, 139–67.

Desmond, J.C. (1999) *Staging Tourism: Bodies on Display from Waikiki to Sea World*, Chicago: University of Chicago Press.

Dohm, A. and Shniper, L. (2007) "Occupational Employment Projections to 2016," *Monthly Labor Review*, 130, 86–125.

England, P., Budig, M. and Folbre, N. (2002) "Wages of virtue: The relative pay of care work," *Social Problems*, 49, 455–73.

Entwistle, J. and Wissinger, E. (2006) "Keeping up appearances: Aesthetic labour in the fashion modelling industries of London and New York," *The Sociological Review*, 54, 774–94.

Fausto-Sterling, A. (2000) *Sexing the Body: Gender Politics and the Construction of Sexuality*, New York: Basic Books.

Fiske, S. (1998) "Stereotyping, prejudice, and discrimination," in S.T.F.D.T. Gilbert and G. Lindzey (eds.), *The Handbook of Social Psychology*, Boston, MA: McGraw-Hill, 357–411.

Forseth, U. (2005) "Gender matters? Exploring how gender is negotiated in service encounters," *Gender, Work and Organization*, 12, 441–59.

Foster, C. (2004) "Gendered retailing: A study of customer perceptions of front-line staff in the DIY sector," *International Journal of Retail and Distribution Management*, 32, 442–7.

Fuss, D. (1989) *Essentially Speaking: Feminism, Nature and Difference*, New York: Routledge.

Glenn, E.N. (1996) "From servitude to service work: Historical continuities in the racial division of paid reproductive labor," in C.L. Macdonald and C. Sirianni (eds.), *Working in the Service Society*, Philadelphia: Temple University Press, 115–56.

Glenn, E.N. (1999) "The social construction and institutionalization of gender and race," in M.M. Ferree, J. Lorber, and B.B. Hess (eds.), *Revisioning Gender*, Thousands Oaks, CA: Sage Publications, 3–43.

Golding, C. (1998) "Britain gets first look at Hooters," *Caterer and Hotelkeeper 30 April*, 7.

Hay, O. and Middlemiss, S. (2003) "Fashion victims, dress to conform to the norm or else? Comparative analysis of legal protection against employers" appearance codes in the United Kingdom and United States," *International Journal of Discrimination and Law*, 6(3), 69–102.

Hays, S. (1996) *The Cultural Contradictions of Motherhood*, New Haven, CT: Yale University Press.

Hochschild, A. (1983) *The Managed Heart: Commercialization of Human Feeling*, Berkeley, CA: University of California Press.

Hondagneu-Sotelo, P. (2001) *Domestica: Immigrant Workers Cleaning and Caring in the Shadows of Affluence*, Berkeley, CA: University of California Press.

*Hooters Inc v. Winghouse*, 347 F Supp. 2d, 1256.

Lamont, M. (2000) "Meaning making in cultural sociology: Broadening our agenda," *Contemporary Sociology*, 29, 602–7.

Lareau, A. (2003) *Unequal Childhoods: Class, Race, and Family Life*, Berkeley, CA: University of California Press.

Leidner, R. (1991) "Serving hamburgers and selling insurance: Gender, work, and identity in interactive service jobs," *Gender and Society*, 5, 154–77.

Leidner, R. (1993) *Fast Food, Fast Talk: Service Work and the Routinization of Everyday Life*, Berkeley, CA: University of California Press.

Lieberson, S. (1980) *A Piece of the Pie: Blacks and While Immigrants since 1880*, Berkeley, CA: University of California Press.

Lindsay, C. and McQuaid, R. (2004) "Avoiding the Mcjobs: Unemployed jobseekers and attitudes to service work," *Work, Employment and Society*, 18, 297–319.

Lister, R., Williams, F., Anttonen, A., and Bussmaker, J. (2007) *Gendering Citizenship in Western Europe*, Bristol, UK: Polity Press.

Macdonald, C.L. (Forthcoming) *Shadow Mothers: Nannies, Au Pairs, and the Micropolitics of Motherhood*, Berkeley, CA: University of California Press.

Macdonald, C.L. and Merrill, D.A. (2002) "It shouldn't have to be a trade: Recognition and redistribution in care work advocacy," *Hypatia: A Journal of Feminist Philosophy*, 17, 67–83.

Macdonald, C.L. and Sirianni, C. (1996) "The service society and the changing nature of work," in C.L. Macdonald and C. Sirianni (eds.), *Working in the Service Society*, Philadelphia: Temple University Press, 1–26.

McCall, L. (2001) *Complex Inequalities: Gender, Class, and Race in the New Economy*, New York: Routledge.

McCall, L. (2005) "The complexity of intersectionality," *Signs: Journal of Women, Culture and Society*, 30, 1271–800.

Mishel, L., Bernstein, J.and Allegretto, S. (2007) *The State of Working America 2006/2007*, Ithaca, NY: ILR Press.

Moss, P.and Tilly, C. (1996) " 'Soft' skills and race: An investigation of black men's employment problems," *Work and Occupations*, 23, 252–76.

Moss, P. and Tilly, C. (2001) *Stories Employers Tell*, New York: Russell Sage Foundation.

Nixon, D. (Forthcoming 2009) "I Can't Put a Smiley Face On: Working-class masculinity, emotional labor and service work in the 'New Economy'," *Gender, Work and Organization*.

Parreñas, R.S. (2000) "Migrant Filipina domestic workers and the international division of reproductive labor," *Gender and Society*, 14, 560–80.

Pierce, J.L. (1995) *Gender Trials: Emotional Lives in Contemporary Law Firms*, Berkeley, CA: University of California Press.

Porter, J. (2006) "Hooters girls are 'Functional'," *The Writ*, November 1, 2006, pp. 1–4.

Post, R. (2000) "Prejudicial appearances: The logic of American antidiscrimination law," *Working Papers*, Institute of Governmental Studies.

Ransford, E. (1980) "The prediction of social behavior and attitudes: The correlates tradition" in V. Jeffries and H.E. Ransford (eds.), *Social Stratification: A Multiple Hierarchy Approach*, Boston: Allyn & Bacon, 265–303.

Reskin, B.F. and Roos, P.A. (1990) *Job Queues, Gender Queues: Explaining Women's Inroads into Male Occupations*, Philadelphia: Temple University Press.

Ridgeway, C. and Correll, S.J. (2000) "Limiting inequality through interaction: The end(s) of gender," *Contemporary Sociology*, 29, 110–20.

Sherman, R. (2007) *Class Acts: Service and Inequality in Luxury Hotels*, Berkeley, CA: University of California Press.

Sidanius, J. and Pratto, F. (2001) *Social Dominance: An Intergroup Theory of Social Hierarchy and Oppression*, Cambridge: Cambridge University Press.

Solomon, M. (1985) "Packaging the service provider," *Service Industries Journal*, 5(1), 65–72.

Thompson, E. (2002) "Engineered corporate culture on a cruise ship," *Sociological Focus*, 35, 331–44.

Tuominen, M.C. (2003) *We Are Not Babysitters: Family Child Care Providers Redefine Work and Care*, New Brunswick: Rutgers University Press.

Waldinger, R. (1996) *Still the Promised City: African-Americans and New Immigrants in Postindustrial New York*, Cambridge, MA: Harvard University Press.

Waldringer, R. (2003) "Networks and niches: The continuing significance of ethnic connections," in G. Loury, T. Modood and S. Teles (eds.), *Race, Ethnicity and Social Mobility in the US and UK*, New York: Cambridge University Press.

Warhust, C. and Nickson, D. (2007) "Employee experience of aesthetic labour in retail and hospitality," *Work, Employment and Society*, 21, 103–19.

Warhust, C., Nickson, D., Witz, A. and Cullen, A.M. (2000) "Aesthetic labour in interactive service work: Some case study evidence from the 'New' Glasgow," *The Service Industries Journal*, 20, 1–18.

Wells, M.J. (2000) "Unionization and immigrant incorporation in San Francisco hotels," *Social Problems*, 47, 241–65.

Williams, C.L. (1993) *Doing "Women's Work": Men in Nontraditional Occupations*, Newbury Park, CA: Sage Publications.

Williams, F. and Gavanas, A. (2008) "The intersection of childcare regimes and migration regimes: At three-country study" in H. Lutz (ed.), *Migration and Domestic Work: A European Perspective on a Global Theme*, Aldershot, UK: Ashgate.

Witz, A., Warhurst, C. and Nickson, D. (2003) "The labour of aesthetics and the aesthetics of organization," *Organization*, 10, 33–54.

# CHAPTER 8

# The Globalization of Care Work

RHACEL SALAZAR PARREÑAS

"Migration has a woman's face," announces a recent educational poster released by the United Nations. The poster declares that close to 70 percent of Filipino and Indonesian emigrants are women, while half of labor migrants around the globe are women. In 2002, approximately 175 million people – 2.3 percent of the world's population – lived outside their country of birth (United Nations Population Division, 2002). Women have historically migrated as wives and dependents of men (Donato, 1992; Hondagneu-Sotelo, 1994). Today, marriage still motivates the migration of women. Contemporary marriage migrants include but are not limited to "pen pal" brides that relocate West from Asian and Eastern Europe, military brides, as well as co-ethnic brides who subsequently follow male migrants abroad (Constable, 2003; Thai, 2003; Yuh, 2002). Yet, more than brides, women now migrate mostly as independent labor migrants. The majority of them are provisional migrants with temporary working visas that allow them to do the care work necessary to maintain the population of richer nations of Asia, the Americas and Europe (Anderson, 2000; Parreñas, 2001). From their performance of elderly care, housecleaning and childcare, migrant care workers arguably meet all of the dependency needs of many industrialized nations.

Because of the dependence of industrialized nations on the care work of migrant women, no longer do men who seek low-wage jobs in construction or heavy manufacturing solely lead the flow of workers from poorer to richer nations in the new global economy. Men still seek labor migration. For instance, they respond to the demand for agricultural workers in richer countries in the North and West. For example, in Spain, 99 percent of Algerian men, 83 percent of Moroccan men, and 86 percent of Senegalese men are in the agricultural sector (Ribas-Mateos, 2000: 176–7). Yet, with or without them, women are relocating across nation-states and entering the global labor market independently. Migrant women do not just respond to the demand for care work but also for low-wage manufacturing work, for instance as garment workers and factory assembly line workers in richer nations the world over (Chang, 2000; Parreñas, 2001: Gamburd, 2000; Hondagneu-Sotelo, 2001). Migration occurs mostly from South to South (Oishi, 2005) but also takes place from South to North and from East to West. As such, a global flow of domestic workers and care workers has emerged with women from Mexico and Central America relocating to clean the households of working families, take care of the children and elderly, in the United States (Hondagneu-Sotelo, 2001); Indonesian women to richer nations in Asia and the Middle East (Silvey, 2004); Sri Lankan women to Greece and the Middle East (Gamburd, 2000); Polish and Ukranian women to Germany and other nations of Western Europe (Misra et al., 2004); and Caribbean women to the United States and Canada (Bakan and Stasiulis, 1997).

In a much wider and greater scale, women from the Philippines have also responded to the demand for migrant care workers. Providing their services in more than 160 countries, Filipino women are the domestic workers par excellence of globalization (Parreñas, 2001). In Europe alone, a fairly large number of them work in the private households of middle to upper-income families in Great Britain, France, the Netherlands, Spain, Greece, and Italy. While in Asia, they toil in private households in Taiwan, Singapore, and Hong Kong (Lan, 2006; Constable, 1997). The flow of migrant domestic workers from poor to rich nations speaks of what Pierrette Hondagneu-Sotelo (2001) calls a "new world domestic order," meaning an unequal division of care labor between the global south and global north. This flow of labor raises our attention to new forms of inequalities between women; particularly care labor inequalities that result in the "international division of reproductive labor"[1] or "global care chains" of women purchasing the care of their children from women with lesser resources in the global economy (Parreñas, 2000; Hochschild, 2000). Freed by migrant workers of their care responsibilities in the family, employing women in turn can avoid the penalty of the "mommy tax" or more generally the "caregiver tax" that stalls the advancement of women in the labor market (Crittenden, 2001). As such, migrant care workers enable them to pursue careers without penalty.

The rise in the labor migration of domestic workers speaks of the globalization of care work or what we could more specifically refer to as the global flow of care workers. This flow speaks of a different aspect of the globalization of service work than the outsourcing of service jobs, such as of call-center operators, addressed by George Ritzer in this volume. In this chapter, I do not address the movement of jobs but of workers. As Ritzer (this volume) acknowledges, certain service jobs cannot be off-shored as they depend on face-to-face interaction. Certainly the care of children and elderly are examples of such work.

In this chapter, I address what the global flow of domestic workers tells us about the status of women in the family as well as relations between women in globalization. As I establish, the globalization of service work generates unequal relationships between women across nation-states. This is because to unleash the burden of housework, women, as Evelyn Nakano Glenn (1992) points out, rely on the commodification of this work and purchase the low-wage services of poorer women. This bears significant consequences for relations between women. The advancement of one group of women is at the cost of another group of women. At the same time, as I wish to show in this chapter, the globalization of service work, i.e. the demand for migrant domestic workers, also speaks of women's oppressions in neoliberal states and the failure of states to meet the needs of women who choose to enter the labor force. Across nations, caring for the family remains a private and not a public responsibility, but more precisely a private responsibility designated to women (Conroy, 2000). Despite the increase in their labor market participation in both developing and advanced capitalist countries, women still remain primarily responsible for housework (Hochschild and Machung, 1989; Rai, 2002). Men have not taken up their share of housework, and likewise, states with neoliberal regimes have failed to respond to the welfare needs of the rising number of women in the labor force. Consequently, the gendered burden of housework plagues the possible advancements of women in the labor market and places them at a disadvantage vis-à-vis men.

In this chapter, I explain the social implications of the globalization of service work by first explaining the relations of inequality it engenders with a discussion of the international division of reproductive labor and the exportation of care. Then, I explain how neoliberal regimes contribute to the globalization of service work, and continue with an explanation of how the exclusion of foreign domestic workers locks the inequality of the international division of reproductive labor. I end by analyzing the implications of the inequalities engendered by the globalization of service work to transnational feminist relations between women.

## The International Division of Care Work

The flow of migrant domestic workers from poor to rich nations generates troubling care inequities that speak of race and class hierarchies between women and nations. First, it gives rise to the inequality of the international division of reproductive labor, a three-tier transfer of care among women in sending and receiving countries of migration (Parreñas, 2001). Second, it leads to the exportation of care and the consequent unequal distribution of care resources in the global economy.

In the international division of reproductive labor, women with privilege in rich countries pass down the care of their families to migrant domestic workers as migrant domestic workers simultaneously pass down the care of their own families – most of whom are left behind in the country of origin – to their relatives or sometimes even poorer women who they hire as their own domestic workers. The case of Carmen Ronquillo, a domestic worker in Rome, provides us with a good illustration of the international division of carework. Carmen is simultaneously a domestic worker for a professional woman in Rome and an employer of a domestic worker in the Philippines. Carmen describes her relationship to each one of these women:

> When coming here, I mentally surrendered myself and forced my pride away from me to prepare myself. But I lost a lot of weight. I was not used to the work. You see, I had maids in the Philippines. I have a maid in the Philippines that has worked for me since my daughter was born twenty-four years ago. She is still with me. I paid her three hundred pesos before, and now I pay her 1000 pesos. I am a little bit luckier than others because I run the entire household. My employer is a divorced woman who is an architect. She does not have time to run her household so I do all the shopping. I am the one budgeting. I am the one cooking. [Laughs.] And I am the one cleaning too. She has a twenty four and twenty six year old. The older one graduated already and is an electrical engineer. The other one is taking up philosophy. They still live with her ... She has been my only employer. I stayed with her because I feel at home with her.
>
> (Parreñas, 2001: 74–5)

It is quite striking to observe the formation of parallel relationships of loyalty between Carmen (the employer) and her domestic in the Philippines and Carmen (the domestic) and her employer in Italy. Also striking is the fact that Carmen's domestic worker does exactly the same work that Carmen does for her own employer. Yet, more striking is the wide discrepancy in wages between Carmen and her own domestic worker.

Their wage differences illuminate the economic disparity among nations in transnational capitalism. A domestic worker in Italy such as Carmen could receive U.S.$1,000 a month for her labor. As Carmen describes,

> I earn 1,500,000 (U.S.$1000) and she pays for my benefits. On Sundays, I have a part-time. I clean her office in the morning and she

pays me 300,000 lira (U.S.$200). I am very fortunate because she always gives me my holiday pay in August and my thirteenth month pay in December. Plus, she gives me my liquidation pay at the end of the year.

(Parreñas, 2001: 75)

Carmen's wages easily enable her to hire a domestic worker in the Philippines, who on average only earns what is the equivalent of $40 during the time of my interviews. Moreover, the domestic worker in the Philippines, in exchange for her labor, does not receive the additional work benefits that Carmen receives for the same labor.[2]

Under the international division of care work, there is a gradational decline in the worth of care. As sociologist Barbara Rothman poignantly describes, "When performed by mothers, we call this mothering . . .; when performed by hired hands, we call it unskilled" (Rothman, 1989: 43). Commodified care work is not only low-paid work but declines in market value as it gets passed down the hierarchical chain. As care is made into a commodity, women with greater resources in the global economy can afford the best-quality care for their families. Conversely, the care given to those with fewer resources is usually worth less.

Consequently, the quality of family life progressively declines as care is passed down the international division of care work. Freed of household constraints, those on top can earn more and consequently afford better-quality care than the domestic workers whom they hire. With their wages relatively low, these domestic workers cannot afford to provide the same kind of care for their family. They in turn leave them behind in the Philippines to be cared for by even lesser paid domestic workers. Relegated to the bottom of the three-tier hierarchy of care work, domestic workers left in the Third World have far fewer material resources to ensure the quality care of their own family.

Another inequality that emerges in the globalization of care work is the exportation of care from the sending countries of migrant domestic workers. For example, in the Philippines, care work is now the largest export and source of foreign currency for the country. In fact, the migrant flow of domestic workers indicates a contemporary colonial trade relationship with the global south, sending neither raw materials nor manufactured goods but rather a (female) labor supply of care workers to the global north. Remittances – mostly from migrant care workers – to the Philippines totaled almost $7 billion in 1999 and generated more foreign currency than manufactured exports including garments and electronics (Bureau of Employment and Labor Statistics, 1999). Most migrant workers from the Philippines, more than half of them, are women and the labor that they provide to the citizenry of other nations is mostly care work.

As a result of the systematic extraction of care from the Philippines, a great number of children are growing up without the physical presence of their (migrant) parents. Assuming that women with children can provide better quality care than other women, employers often prefer their migrant nannies to be mothers themselves. What this means is that migrant mothers who work as nannies often face the painful prospect of caring for other people's children while being unable to tend to their own. Rosemarie Samaniego, a transnational mother working in Rome, describes this predicament.

> When the girl that I take care of calls her mother "Mama," my heart jumps all the time because my children also call me "Mama." I feel the gap caused by our physical separation especially in the morning, when I pack (her) lunch, because that's what I used to do for my children . . . I used to do that very same thing for them. I begin thinking that at this hour I should be taking care of my very own children and not someone else's, someone who is not related to me in any way, shape, or form . . . The work that I do here is done for my family, but the problem is they are not close to me but are far away in the Philippines. Sometimes, you feel the separation and you start to cry. Some days, I just start crying while I am sweeping the floor because I am thinking about my children in the Philippines. Sometimes, when I receive a letter from my children telling me that they are sick, I look up out the window and ask the Lord to look after them and make sure they get better even without me around to care after them. [Starts crying.] If I had wings, I would fly home to my children. Just for a moment, to see my children and take care of their needs, help them, then fly back over here to continue my work.
>
> (Parreñas, 2001: 119)

For a large number of women, the experience of migration involves the pain of family separation. This emotional burden is one that directly results from the exportation of care and its consequent effect of transnational motherhood. In pointing out the pain of transnational mothering, I do not intend to naturalize mothering. Instead, I point to the fact that transnational mothering is not a preferred choice for many low wage migrant workers, but a result of the structural inequalities that limit the labor market choices of women from poor countries such as the Philippines to foreign domestic work. Because foreign domestic work is often not a preferred choice in the global labor market, distance mothering engenders feelings of pain and loss for many of those who pursue this type of work.

It is not just mothers but also children who lose out from this separation. Between 2000 and 2002, I spent 18 non-continuous months in the Philippines where I conducted 69 in depth interviews with children of migrant workers. Among these children, I found a great number have come to expect a lesser amount of care from their migrant mothers. This includes Ellen Seneriches,[3] a 21-year-old medical student in the Philippines and daughter of a domestic worker in New York. She states,

> There are times when you want to talk to her, but she is not there. That is really hard, very difficult ... There are times when I want to call her, speak to her, cry to her, and I cannot. It is difficult. The only thing that I can do is write to her. And I cannot cry through the e-mails and sometimes I just want to cry on her shoulders.

Children such as Ellen, only 10 years old when her mother left for New York, often repress their longing to reunite with their mothers. Understanding the limited financial options available to families in the Philippines, they sacrifice by putting their emotional needs aside. This is often done with the knowledge that their mother diverts her care to other children in the global economy of care work. As Ellen describes,

> Very jealous. I am very, very jealous. There was even a time when she told the children who she was caring for that they are very lucky that she was taking care of them, while her children back in the Philippines don't even have a mom to take care of them. It's pathetic, but it's true. We were left alone by ourselves and we had to be responsible at a very young age without a mother. Can you imagine?

While their mothers give their care and attention to other children, children such as Ellen receive a lesser amount of care from their mothers, a sacrifice made more painful by their jealousy over these other children.

As shown by the story of Ellen, geographical distance in transnational family life engenders emotional strife among children. By asserting this claim, I do not mean to imply that migrant mothers do not attempt to ease the difficulties of children. Yet, despite these efforts of migrant mothers, children in transnational families still do suffer as they lose out in family intimacy. They can only wait for the opportunity to spend quality time with migrant parents. Yet, waiting tends to be a painful process. As Theresa Bascara, an 18 year old college student whose mother has worked in Hong Kong since 1984, describes:

> When my mother is home, I just sit next to her. I stare at her face, to see the changes in her face, to see how she aged during the years that she was away from us. But when she is about to go back to Hong Kong, it's like my heart is going to burst. I would just cry and cry. I

really can't explain the feeling. Sometimes, when my mother is home, preparing to leave for Hong Kong, I would just start crying, because I already start missing her. I ask myself, how many more years will it be until we see each other again?

In general, children in transnational families do lose out. They are denied the intimacy of the daily routine of family life. Theresa continues,

Telephone calls. That's not enough. You can't hug her, kiss her, feel her, everything. You can't feel her presence. It's just words that you have. What I want is to have my mother close to me, to see her grow older, and when she is sick, you are the one taking care of her and when you are sick, she is the one taking care of you.

Sacrificing the routine pleasures of receiving and giving emotional care is what a great number of children in the Philippines are doing to help keep their families intact. This sacrifice works to the benefit of those at the receiving end of the global transfer of care work – the employer, their family, and the local economies that utilize the freed employer's labor.

## Regressive State Welfare Regimes

In various industrialized countries around the world, the number of gainfully employed women has climbed dramatically in the last 40 years. For instance, in France, an additional 2 million women entered the labor force between 1979 and 1993, a 21 percent increase in the number of employed women (Conroy, 2000). Mothers are also more likely to work. For instance, in the United States, three out of four mothers with school-age children are in the paid labor force, the majority working fulltime (Coltrane and Galt, 2000). This is also the case in Italy, where an increasing number of married women are in the labor force (Goddard, 1996). In Italy and Spain, women tend to keep their full-time jobs even when they have young children at home (Conroy, 2000).

For the most part, men have not responded to women's income contributions to the household with a marked increase in housework. This is the case in countries such as the United States (Hochschild and Machung, 1989) as well as in countries known to have gender egalitarian welfare policies such as those in Nordic countries (Orloff, 2006). For instance, women more so than men are likely to take advantage of parental leave options in countries such as Sweden. A multi-country study of the division of labor in European families shows that women still do the majority of parental childcare. In Denmark, Belgium, and Spain, for instance, women bear the responsibility for 65 to 87 percent of care work (Ghysels, 2004: 248). As such, they are more likely to hold part-time jobs than men, or less likely to seek high ranking positions than men. This is for instance the case in Nordic countries, which are considered to provide women with more progressive support to balance work and family responsibilities than countries with neoliberal welfare regimes (Orloff, 2006).

Socialist welfare regimes differ from most other countries as they, unlike countries with neoliberal regimes, provide extensive access to publicly supported care. Support begins with highly subsidized parental leave periods in the first three years of a child's life and continues with the provision of centralized care services in centers or through supervised family child-minders. Moreover, children have the option of spending all or part of the day in preschool programs (Gornick and Meyers, 2003). Universal entitlement for care is provided in Finland and Denmark. In Sweden, children have access to publicly subsidized or public care until the age of 12.

Yet, state welfare support for the family in most other countries does not reflect the generous childcare provisions in Nordic countries. For the most part, the state has not adequately responded to the changes brought by the entrance of women, particularly mothers, to the labor force. Instead, in various countries in Europe, Asia, and the Americas, the state has imposed neoliberal policies in response to women's labor market participation. Welfare support in many countries does not provide the new familial needs of single-parents as well as dual-earning or dual-career couples (Heymann, 2000).[4] Examples of such support would include long postpartum family leaves, after-school programs and extended school days for children in the year (Conroy, 2000; Heymann, 2000; Tronto, 2002). Without a "public family welfare system," government assistance keeps childcare a private and not public responsibility (Conroy, 2000). For instance, in the United States, government assistance for the childcare needs of dual income households remain restricted to an income tax credit. Notably, the private sector usually does not pick up the slack of the welfare system. In the United States, employers often penalize members of working families instead of providing working families with the flexibility to handle their caring needs. For instance, non-managerial employees often do not have the flexibility to take a sick relative to the doctor or to meet their child's teacher during work hours (Heymann, 2000).

In countries such as the United States, the inadequacy of state welfare support is one of the greatest burdens of women in the labor force. Moreover, it instigates care inequalities between women and nations. Privatization engenders the commodification of care and the search for affordable care workers. Many of these care workers are from poorer countries in the global south. This is the case in the United States, which notably has the least welfare provisions among rich nations in the global economy as families are without access to universal health care, paid maternity and parental leave, government-provided childcare, or family care giving allowances (Cancian and Oliker, 2000: 116). Although generally boasting a more social democratic welfare regime than that in the United States, European nations are not immune to the growing trend of privatization. Domestic workers are present in European countries such as: the United Kingdom, where markets have assumed a greater role in welfare regimes; the Netherlands, where single mothers are forced to seek paid employment and are without choice but to remunerate lower paid workers for the care of their children; the Mediterranean region, e.g. Greece, Italy, and Spain, where dual wage earning families do not have market options for care; and France, where the universal care for children by the state is not mirrored in elderly care provisions (Daly and Lewis, 2000: 292). Generally, domestic workers can be found in regions where care is kept a private family matter, which includes most developed nations in the world today.

Countries with high welfare provisions are not exempt from this group, as we more and more see them implement a less universal, more privatized form of welfare with the reduction in publicly controlled care services for families and the increase in the use of cash subsidies as well as paid care leave for mothers (Morgan and Zippel, 2003). Addressing how the state assists time pressed dual earner couples in their efforts to negotiate child care, Rianne Mahon (2002) notes that state welfare assistance largely maintains the privatization of care and fails to secure a gender egalitarian system for employed women. For instance, the new familialism approach found in nations such as France features a decrease in publicly funded collective child care provisions and an increase in cash benefits. A system that truly secures public responsibility for care, one that provides generous parental leaves and universal non-parental childcare services, is adopted in very few countries (e.g. Denmark).

In addition to the absence of public accountability for care, gender inequities in the family also fuel the need for domestic workers. As I noted earlier, the division of labor in most families still does not mirror the increase in women's labor market participation. For instance, a recent survey of dual wage earning families with children in Canada found that women were still responsible for all of the daily housework in 52 percent of households (Rai, 2002: 101). The increase in women's labor market participation usually translates to the dwindling supply of family care providers (Hochschild and Machung, 1989) and consequently goes hand in hand with the commodification of care work. We see this in France, where the comprehensive publicly funded preschool system stabilizes the family life of dual wage earning couples, but still where women suffer from the burden of daily housework as well as elderly care falling mainly on their shoulders, as the latter responsibility is not supported with residential care provisions (Koffman et al., 2000: 143). This burden has created an economic niche for privately hired care workers (Mozere, 2003). In contrast, socially democratic Scandinavian nations depend less on domestic workers as they provide the most gender sensitive public benefits for families including gender-neutral parental leave and universal entitlements in the form of allowances, subsidies, and direct services for the elderly and single parent households (Cancian and Oliker, 2000: 18).

Ruth Milkman and her colleagues note that economic inequities direct the flow of domestic workers: they found that urban centers with the greatest economic inequities in the United States have a higher rate of domestic service employment (Milkman *et al.*, 1998). I would add to their observation that social patterns of welfare provisions also influence the direction of the migratory flows of foreign domestic workers. Looking at the migration patterns of migrant Filipina domestic workers, the more countries keep the care of the family a private responsibility, the greater the reliance on the low wage work of migrant care workers. This seems to be the case in the Americas and Europe, where the presence of migrant Filipina domestic workers is more strongly felt in countries with the most inadequate welfare provisions. Nations with very low welfare provisions, i.e. nations that keep the care of the family a private responsibility, particularly the United States and southern European nations such as Spain, Greece, and Italy have a greater presence of foreign domestic workers (Koffman *et al.*, 2000). We also see their presence in countries where comprehensive publicly funded welfare programs are threatened by being replaced with the use of cash subsidy benefits such as France (Misra *et al.*, 2004). In contrast, countries with social democratic regimes such as those in Scandinavia, where the benefit system abides by universalism and provides large-scale institutional support for mothers and families, are less likely to rely on foreign domestic workers.

Thus, it seems that the less public accountability there is for the family the greater the need for the labor of foreign domestic workers. This suggests that a movement against neoliberal state regimes would lead to greater recognition of the high worth of care and the lesser burden of the double day on women in the labor force. It would also mean a lesser need to devalue into low-paid labor the caring work required in the family. The implementation of a public family welfare system, as feminist scholars have argued, would not only benefit double burdened women in the labor force and give greater value to the work of privately hired care workers but would translate to the good of society as a whole (Folbre, 2001; Tronto, 2002). As economist Nancy Folbre argues, public responsibility for parental support would optimize the care of children and consequently increase the likelihood of their healthy and productive labor force participation in the future (2001: 111). This translates to the greater ability of children to physically care for us in the future and pay the taxes needed to cover the social security benefits we are working for today (Folbre, 2001: 110). As had been recognized with the implementation of universal public education in the nineteenth century, the optimal care of children translates to the welfare of society as a whole. It cuts to the core of democracy, helping provide equal opportunities for children to succeed so they may contribute the most to the economy.

The inadequacy of welfare support for dual income families goes against the principles of democracy and universal educational opportunities for our children. As Joan Tronto (2002) further argues, individual accountability for children increases competition between mothers and families and concomitantly decreases the ethic of care. Hiring private domestic workers, tutors, and other care workers creates incredible disparities between families. Those with private care workers can ensure that their children are those best equipped and developed to be competitive members of society. In contrast, other children are less likely to succeed as they are left with less guidance and adult supervision. As Tronto states, "individualized accounts of mothering make us inured to the social structures that contribute to the growing gaps among advantaged and less advantaged children" (2002: 48). Thus, the privatization of care reinforces inequalities of race, class, and citizenship among women – employers and employees – as it furthers the disparities in the prospects available to children in industrialized countries.

With the individual responsibility for care imposed upon them, and denied the utmost benefits of a truly democratic regime, women in industrialized countries have come to take advantage of the greater economic resources that they have than women from developing countries: they do this by unloading the care giving responsibilities of their families to these other women. Those who receive less gender-sensitive welfare provisions from the state do so much more than others. And those who are able to negotiate with their male counterparts in the family for a fairer gendered division of labor are equally less likely to do so. Finally, as I show in the next section, those whose governments deny the human rights of migrant workers are also more able to depend on the low wage work of other women.

## The Human Rights of Migrant Domestic Workers

The denial of the human rights of migrant domestic workers eases the process of the care chain. By denying migrants their human rights, states avoid the cost and responsibility for care. States do so by securing a pool of privately hired and affordable care workers for working families, an act which also allows states to avoid the need to expand welfare provisions. Despite their economic contributions, migrant domestic workers suffer from their limited incorporation as partial citizens of various receiving nations (Parreñas, 2001). As I have defined elsewhere, this means they face restrictive measures that stunt their political, civil, and social incorporation into host societies (Parreñas, 2001). From an economic standpoint, this is not surprising. Receiving nations restrict the social incorporation of migrants so as to guarantee their economies a secure source of cheap labor. By containing the costs of reproduction in sending countries, wages of migrant workers can be kept to a minimum. This is because migrants do not have the burden of having to afford the greater costs of reproducing their families in host societies. Moreover, by restricting the incorporation of migrants, receiving nations can secure for their economies a ready supply of low-wage workers who could easily be repatriated whenever the economy is low. For instance, countries often recognize that many immigrants illegally fill the demand for various low wage jobs, but they still do not give work visas for some of these jobs (Misra et al., 2004).

This is the case with care work in France and Germany. In France, the increase in individualized private care among upper middle class families and the reliance on migrant women for such private care is not mirrored in immigration policies. Migrant care workers in France do not qualify for temporary work permits and consequently are subject to the insecurities of the informal economy (Misra et al., 2004). In contrast, Germany grants work permits to domestic workers but only to elderly caregivers and not to housecleaners and childcare workers. This restriction keeps a large number of care workers in Germany ineligible for legal residence status.

Other countries of Europe grant legal residence to domestic workers. However, as migrants, they are usually relegated to the status of guest workers limited to the duration of their labor contracts. Often, they cannot sponsor the migration of their families. This is also the case in Middle Eastern and Asian receiving nations, which are much more stringent than other countries. For example, in Taiwan, state policies deny entry to the spouses and children of the migrant worker (Lan, 2006). Singapore even prohibits the marriage or cohabitation of migrant workers with native citizens (Bakan and Stasiulis, 1997). The restriction of family migration comes in different gradations of exclusion. For instance, with European countries more accommodating of their legal migrants than Asian countries, temporary residents in Italy have been eligible for family reunification since 1990 (Koffman et al., 2000).

However, family reunification remains a challenge for many immigrants in Europe. Despite the more inclusive policies for migrants in Europe than in Asia, many European nation-states still restrict migrants to the status of "guest workers." With heightened anti-immigrant sentiments in European nations such as Italy, the basis of citizenship is unlikely to become more inclusive of ethnically distinct migrant groups. As a result, most migrant

Filipina workers would still prefer that their children do not join them in Europe, i.e. despite the struggles of transnational family life (Parreñas, 2001). Other migration policies further discourage complete family migration. In France, for instance, migrants are put off by the increase in residence requirements to qualify for family reunion as well as the decrease in the age of eligibility for dependants from 21 to 18 years old (Koffman et al., 2000: 68). Moreover, in Germany, children under 16 years old must obtain a visa to visit their legally resident parents. In the United Kingdom, entry conditions for family visits have become stricter with the rising suspicion of the intent of family members to remain indefinitely (Koffman et al., 2000). In the Netherlands, the state sponsored au pair program, which disguises the flow of migrant domestic workers from the global south, restricts the household helper to a temporary duration of stay that does not allow for family migration (Meerman, 2000).

Eligibility for full citizenship is available in a few receiving nations including Spain, Canada, and the United States. In Spain and Canada, migrant Filipinas are eligible for full citizenship after two years of legal settlement. Despite the seemingly more liberal and inclusive policies in these nations, political and social inequalities still stunt the full incorporation of migrant workers (Bakan and Stasiulis, 1997). In Canada, the Live-in Caregivers Program requires an initial two years of live-in service before foreign domestics can become eligible for landed immigrant status. During this time, foreign domestics are prone to abusive working conditions, subject to split-household arrangements, and restricted to temporary status (Bakan and Stasiulis, 1997). Foreign domestic workers in the United States experience a similar vulnerability. In the United States, obtaining a green card through employer sponsorship, according to Shellee Colen, is like a "form of state-sanctioned indenture-like exploitation" because "the worker is obligated to stay in the sponsored position until the green card is granted (usually two or more years)" (Colen, 1995: 78).

Providing care work often requires migrants to leave their children in the Philippines because the structure and standards of employment in this type of labor[5] and the imposition of partial citizenship usually prevent the migration of kin (Parreñas, 2001). This works to the benefit of employers. The partial citizenship of migrant workers guarantees employers an affordable pool of care workers who can give them the best care for their families, since migrant care workers are freed of care responsibilities in their own families. Yet, the experience of partial citizenship for migrant domestic workers points to an injustice in globalization, one that poses a direct challenge to transnational feminist alliances. Migrant domestic workers care for rich families in the global north as they are imposed with social, economic, and legal restrictions that deny them the right to nurture their own families. The elimination of these restrictive measures would at the very least grant foreign domestic workers the basic human right of caring for their own family.

## Conclusion

The global labor migration of domestic workers attests to the globalization of care work. This global flow speaks of a direct relationship of inequality between women, particularly the unequal relationship between migrant domestic workers and their employers. It also speaks to the different positions of women regarding family care work. In both poor and rich nations, class privileged women are increasingly viewing care work as a burden to be passed on to poorer women. Those to whom they pass it on often view care work as a human right denied to them either by restrictive migration policies that prevent the migration of their kin or by heavy work responsibilities that deny them the time and energy to devote to their own families. However, the division of care labor between women does not completely work to the advantage of the employing women. Though freed of the care work for the family, they are still plagued by the structural gender inequities that relieve men and the state of responsibility for care.

The international division of care work arises not just from relations of inequality between women but also from neoliberal state regimes. Migrant Filipina domestic workers rarely enter Nordic countries with socialist welfare regimes but in various degrees of concentration work in countries that keep the care of the family a private and not a public responsibility. Without adequate state welfare provisions, dual wage earning families in countries with neoliberal state regimes turn to foreign domestic workers. This tells us that the failure of the state to adequately meet the care needs of working families partially accounts for the rise in the use of foreign domestic work. Without doubt, some families may prefer to provide private exclusive care for their children and elderly rather than centralized public facilities. Yet, many families turn to the low-wage labor costs provided by foreign domestic workers and not necessarily the skilled work of highly trained care workers such as British nannies and registered nurses. They turn to low-cost foreign domestic work due to their lack of choices for balancing work and family.

Yet, many foreign domestic workers, at least from the Philippines, are skilled care workers. For instance, many Filipina domestic workers, if not college educated, secure government accredited caregiver certificates with six months of training prior to migration. The training of these workers comes at no cost and to the benefit of the destination countries. This training enables destination countries to continue to ignore providing care provisions for working families. Perhaps then countries that depend on foreign domestic workers should acknowledge the contributions of their labor and bear some of the costs of these workers. Doing so would mean that receiving states would make these workers eligible for permanent residence, grant them a minimum wage rate comparable to native workers, and ensure the protection of their labor by allowing them to report labor violations without penalty or the threat of deportation for illegal workers.

It is likely that the international division of care work would not completely disappear with state acknowledgment of the labor contributions of foreign domestic workers. A marked increase in care work by men, which will only mean a reduction in their working hours, and a notable limit to the working hours of women, would lessen the reliance of families in non-commodified care work. Moreover, only the greater valuation of care work would abolish the inequalities that currently define the international division of care work. State acknowledgment of the high value and contributions of foreign domestic workers would likely mean that the labor conditions of domestic workers would improve and domestic workers would have the option of raising their children up close and not from a distance. If this occurs, the international division of care work and the commodification of care would at the very least not signify severe relations of inequalities between domestic workers and the families that employ them.

## Notes

1 By reproductive labor, I refer to the labor needed to sustain the productive labor force. Reproductive labor primarily refers to caring work required to sustain the (able-bodied) population. Such work includes the task of feeding and nurturing.

2 Migrant domestic workers usually belong in a higher-class stratum than do domestics left in the Philippines. Often professionals in the Philippines, they use their resources to afford the option of seeking the higher wages offered in more developed nations.

3 Ellen Seneriches and the names of the other children who I quote in this chapter are all pseudonyms.

4 By welfare support, I refer to the government's accountability for the social and material well-being of their citizenry.

5 Labor conditions in domestic work usually discourage family reunification. This is especially true of live in domestic workers who are isolated in private homes. Moreover, contracts of "guest workers" usually bind them to stay with their sponsoring employer, which leaves them vulnerable to less than par labor standards.

## References

Anderson, B. (2000) *Doing the Dirty Work? The Global Politics of Domestic Labour*, London and New York: Zed Books.
Bakan, A. and Stasiulis, D. (1997) "Introduction," in A. Bakan and D. Stasiulis (eds.), *Not*

*One of the Family: Foreign Domestic Workers in Canada*, Toronto: University of Toronto Press.

Bureau of Employment and Labor Statistics. "Remittances from overseas Filipino workers by country of origin Philippines: 1997–fourth quarter 1999," *Pinoy Migrants, Shared Government Information System for Migration*. Retrieved 4 April 2004, from http://emisd.web.dfa.gov.ph/~pinoymigrants/.

Cancian, F.M. and Oliker, S.J. (2000) *Caring and Gender*, Thousand Oaks, CA: Pine Forge Press.

Chang, G. (2000) *Disposable Domestics*, Boston: South End Press.

Chin, C. (1998) *Of Service and Servitude*, New York: Columbia University Press.

Colen, S. (1995) "Like a mother to them: stratified reproduction and West Indian childcare workers and employers in New York" in F. Ginsburg, and R. Rapp (eds.), *Conceiving the New World Order: The Global Politics of Reproduction*, Berkeley, CA: University of California Press.

Coltrane, S. and Galt, J. (2000) "The history of men's caring," in M. Harrington Meyer (ed.), *Care Work: Gender, Labour and the Welfare State*, New York and London: Routledge.

Conroy, M. (2000). *Sustaining the New Economy: Work, Family, and Community in the Information Age*, New York: Russell Sage Foundation Press and Cambridge, MA: Harvard University Press.

Constable, N. (1997) *Maid to Order in Hong Kong*, Ithaca, NY: Cornell University Press.

Constable, N. (2003) *Romance on a Global State*, Berkeley, CA: University of California Press.

Crittenden, A. (2001) *The Price of Motherhood: Why the Most Important Job in the World is Still the Least Valued*, New York: Metropolitan Books.

Daly, M. and Lewis, J. (2002) "The concept of social care and the analysis of contemporary welfare states," *British Journal of Sociology*, 51, 2, 281–98.

Donato, K. (1992) "Understanding U.S. immigration: why some countries send women and others send men," in D. Gabbacia (ed.), *Seeking Common Ground: Multidisciplinary Studies of Immigrant Women in the United States*, Westport, CT: Greenwood Press, 159–84.

Folbre, N. (2001) *The Invisible Heart: Economics and Family Values*, New York: The New Press.

Gamburd, M. (2000) *The Kitchen Spoon's Handle*, Ithaca, NY: Cornell.

Ghysels, J. (2004) *Work, Family, and Childcare: An Empirical Analysis of European Households*, Cheltenham, UK and Northampton, MA: Edward Elgar.

Glenn, E.N. (1992) "From servitude to service work: historical continuities in the racial division of paid reproductive labor," *Signs: Journal of Women in Culture and Society*, 18, 1, 1–43.

Goddard, V.A. (1996) *Gender, Family and Work in Naples*, Oxford and Washington, DC: Berg.

Gornick, J. and Meyers, M. (2003) *Families That Work: Policies for Reconciling Parenthood and Employment*, New York: Russell Sage Foundation.

Heymann, J. (2000) *The Widening Gap: Why America's Working Families are in Jeopardy – and What Can Be Done About It*, New York: Basic Books.

Hochschild, A. (2000) "The nanny chain," *American Prospect*, 11, 4. Retrieved 4 April 2004, from http://www.prospect.org/print/V11/4/hochschild-a.html.

Hochschild, A.R. and Machung, A. (1989) *The Second Shift*, New York: Avon Books.

Hondagneu-Sotelo, P. (1994) *Gendered Transitions*, Berkeley, CA: University of California Press.

Hondagneu-Sotelo, P. (2001) *Doméstica*, Berkeley: University of California Press.

Koffman, E., Phizacklea, A., Raghuram, P. and Sales, R. (2000) *Gender and International Migration in Europe: Employment, Welfare and Politics*, New York and London: Routledge.

Lan, P. (2006) *Global Cinderellas*, Durham, NC: Duke University Press.

Mahon, R. (2002) "Child care: toward what kind of 'social Europe?' " *Social Politics*, 9, 343–79.

Meerman, M. (2000) *The Chain of Love*, Amsterdam, Netherlands: VPRO-TV (U.S. Distributor: First Icarus Run).

Milkman, R., Reese, E. and Roth, B. (1998) "The macrosociology of paid domestic labor," *Work and Occupations*, 25, 4, 483–507.

Misra, J., Merz, S. and Woodring, J. (2004) "The globalization of carework: Immigration, economic restructuring, and the world-system," American Sociological Association Meeting, American Sociological Association, San Francisco, CA. 17 August.

Morgan, K. and Zippel, K. (2003) "Paid to care: the origins and effects of care leave policies in Western Europe," *Social Politics*, 10, 49–85.

Mozère, L. (2003) "Filipina women as domestic workers in Paris: a national or transnational labour-market?" (unpublished paper), Department of Sociology, University of Metz, France.

Oishi, N. (2005) *Women in Motion*, Stanford, CA: Stanford University Press.

Orloff, A.S. (2006) "Farewell to maternalism? State policies and mothers' employment," WP-05–10, Institute for Policy Research Northwestern University, *Working Paper Series*.

Parreñas, R.S. (2000) "Migrant Filipina domestic workers and the international division of reproductive labor," *Gender and Society*, 14:4 (August), 560–80.

Parreñas, R.S. (2001) *Servants of Globalization: Women, Migration, and Domestic Work*, Stanford, CA: Stanford University Press.

Rai, S.M. (2002) *Gender and the Political Economy of Development*, Cambridge: Polity Press.

Ribas-Mateos, N. (2000) "Female birds of passage: leaving and settling in Spain," in A. Floya and G. Lazaridis (eds.), *Gender and Migration in Southern Europe: Women on the Move*, Oxford and New York: Berg, 173–98.

Rothman, B.K. (1989). *Recreating Motherhood: Ideology and Technology in a Patriarchal Society*, New York and London: W.W. Norton.

Silvey, R. (2004) "Transnational migration and the gender politics of scale: Indonesian domestic workers in Saudi Arabia," *Singapore Tropical Geography*, 25(2), 141–55.

Thai, H. (2003) "Clashing dreams: highly educated overseas brides and low-wage U.S. husbands," in B. Ehrenreich and A. Hochschild (eds.), *Global Woman: Nannies, Maids, and Sex Workers in the New Economy*, New York: Metropolis Books, 230–53.

Tronto, J. (2002) "The 'Nanny' question in feminism," *Hypatia*, 17, 2, 34–51.

United Nations Population Division. (2002) International Migration, *United Nations Publication*, Sales Number E.03.XIII.3. October. http://www.un.org/esa/population/publications/ittmig2002/WEB_migration_wallchart.xls Accessed 6 September 2005.

Yuh, J. (2002) *Beyond the Shadow of Camptown: Korean Military Brides in America*, New York: New York University Press.

# CHAPTER 9

# The Promise of Service Worker Unionism

### DOROTHY SUE COBBLE AND MICHAEL MERRILL

Despite C. Wright Mills' pioneering efforts in *White Collar* (1951) to draw attention to the "giant salesroom" of employee-customer exchange or Daniel Bell's riveting descriptions of "people work" in his 1973 classic *The Coming of Post-Industrial Society,* labor and industrial relations scholars paid little attention to the service economy until recently. Throughout the 1970s and 1980s, they rarely strayed far from the factory floor; and when they did, service workers were more often than not understood through manufacturing metaphors like "sweatshop," "speed-up," "white-collar proletariat," and the "office assembly line." There were exceptions, of course. Flight attendants, department store clerks, waitresses, and fast food workers, for example, were all subjects of revealing studies by the early 1990s (Hochschild, 1983; Benson, 1988; Cobble, 1991a; Leidner, 1993). But the theoretical frameworks governing studies of workers and work processes in the social sciences as a whole continued, for the most part, to be drawn from an imaginary[1] populated by industrial wage-earners (male) and white-collar salaried managers (male). The knowledge and efforts of the predominantly female service workforce remained largely unacknowledged and unexplored.

Now, writing in 2008, "managing service encounters," "empowering front-line service workers," and piercing the mysteries of the Wal-Mart service economy have taken center stage as topics of academic inquiry and business concern. And despite grousing from some labor leaders that "we'll never build a real labor movement with a bunch of nurses," the conventional wisdom in the U.S. labor movement, particularly in the new

Change-To-Win (CTW) federation, formed in July 2005,[2] is not only that service workers are "organizable" – a premise which had long been in doubt – but also that they are the future of trade unionism.

The new thinking among trade unionists should not be surprising since, as this chapter will detail, almost all the recent growth in union membership in the U.S. has been in service occupations and industries. But do these now substantial union victories among service workers herald the beginnings of a new unionism that could transform service work and service economies? Will the growth of service unions in the twenty-first century have the same impact on the wealth and welfare of wage-earners as the rise of large industrial unions had on working-class fortunes a half century ago? Will this new unionism help revalue service work and raise at least some portion of the millions and millions of low-wage service workers into the middle class? After a brief description of the changing demographics of U.S. labor unions and the new organizing occurring among white and blue-collar service workers, the first part of this chapter takes up these questions by analyzing both the new models of service worker unionism that have emerged and the challenges that service workers and their allies must overcome in their attempts to organize.

The examples in this section of the chapter will be drawn primarily from Cobble's long-term research on the unionization of service workers in the U.S., but we see the general arguments as relevant to many "advanced" industrial countries. As Dolvik and Waddington (2005) have noted, more than 70 percent of employment in many OECD countries is now in service industries, and, of equal importance, with the privatization of services, or the rise of "marketized services" (to use their term), a growing share of workers face the more privatized labor market dynamics common to the United States. In addition, our conclusions have been informed by the insights of the many non-U.S. scholars writing on service work and labor movement revitalization (Dolvik and Waddington, 2005; Korczynski, 2002; Tannock, 2001; Simms, et al., 2000; Simms, 2003).

In the second section of this chapter, we examine the rise of a new service worker unionism, arguing that contract unionism by itself is not enough to reverse the fortunes of those in the lowest-paying service occupations, a disproportionate number of whom are women and minorities. The struggle for union recognition and signed contracts with employers is a crucial aspect of raising the status of service workers. But the movement to transform service work will need to be broad-based. It will need to include workers organizing *outside* the traditional trade unions in community, women's and civil rights organizations and their middle-class allies in government, business, and academe. It also will need to embrace the community unions and worker centers emerging among low-income workers as well as the NGOs and the other global institutions which have sprung up everywhere to advance labor and human rights, institute new international labor standards, and regulate corporate conduct. Thus, in the next section of the chapter, we will take a closer look at these efforts and at what they have to teach us about the limits of a reform strategy based solely on contract unionism.

Finally, in the concluding section of the chapter we argue that raising the standards of service workers will require new ways of thinking about labor and labor movements. In the social imaginary we have inherited, "labor" is a process by which "man" (literally) engages and dominates "nature," creating value by wrestling "goods" out of resistant raw materials with skill, will, and tools. In this imagined world, workers organize themselves to fight a "class war" against their employers, sometimes of "position" and sometimes of "maneuver," so that they may have a determining say in the distribution of the things their labor makes and of the income earned by their sale. This older imaginary captured important elements of the lived realities of earlier generations of wage earners in the industrialized areas of the world, and it still does capture essential truths about the lives of many workers today, especially those in newly industrializing countries. But it obscures the circumstances and aspirations of the growing number of service workers in the new economies of the twenty-first century.

To understand these new economies, and the labor movements they are spawning, we need an imaginary that does not privilege the making of things over the provision of services. In such an imaginary, "labor" would be as much about cooperating with and taking care of one another as about knocking nature into useable shapes; and labor movements would be as much about strengthening the bonds that hold us together and increasing the pleasure we take in each other's company as about ensuring an equitable distribution of goods, whether in the household, the firm, or the wider society. The chapter ends, then, with a discussion of how paying closer attention to the specificities of service labor can enrich our social theory, expand our understanding of work and work processes, and help move us toward a world in which all labor receives the recognition and reward it deserves.

## The Rise of Service Worker Unionism

The power of U.S. unions – as measured by membership figures or by political and economic clout – has seemed to most commentators to be in free fall for the last quarter century. In 1979, organized labor still claimed close to a fourth of all workers, some 23 percent; but by the end of the 1980s the figure had dropped to 15 percent. It has been inching downward ever since. In 2005, union density (the percentage of the labor force that is unionized)[3] stood at 12 percent in the U.S., a drop of 21 points since its high water mark of 33 percent in 1953 (USDL, 2006). One has to go back almost a hundred years, to before World War I, to find figures so low. A similar decline occurred in the U.K. and many other Western European countries, with U.K. union membership slipping from a high of 56 percent in 1979 to around 30 percent today (USDL, 2006; Korczynski, 2002, p. 175).

To take just the U.S. case, the story of unrelenting union decline changes rather dramatically if one looks beneath these generic figures to union membership in various sectors of the economy. Many of the industrial unions in mining and mass production have virtually disappeared in the last quarter century, and unionism in construction and among small manufacturers is similarly diminished. Yet unionism among service workers is far from moribund. Indeed, it has been on the rise since the 1960s, fueled first by the emergence of public sector unions in the 1960s and 1970s and more recently by the continuing growth of unionism among low-wage service workers in both the public and private sectors.

Public sector unionism blossomed in the U.S. in the 1960s and 1970s, as one group of workers after another – most of them in service occupations – turned to unionization. By the early 1980s, when public sector unionism peaked, close to two-fifths of U.S. government workers had organized (Cobble, 2005; USDL, 2006). Over the next quarter century, public sector unionism held steady. In 2005, with private sector unionism hovering at 7 percent, public sector density sat at a respectable 37 percent. Unionism in public services enjoyed a similar resurgence in the U.K. and Europe, with average union densities in public service today of 50 percent in the EU countries (Dolvik and Waddington, 2005: 320).

Teachers were among the first and largest occupational group to embrace unionism in the U.S. The National Education Association (NEA), the nation's largest professional employee association with 2.7 million members, turned to collective bargaining in the 1960s, influenced by the example of its rival, the American Federation of Teachers (AFT), which had been pushing for teacher contracts and bargaining rights since the beginning of the twentieth century (Murphy 1990, Table 6).

Other public sector workers turned to unionism as well in this era, enabled by President Kennedy's 1962 Executive Order 10988 and inspired in part by the civil rights and women's movements. The 1968 Memphis sanitation strike – which ended with a settlement in the workers' favor only after the tragic assassination of Martin Luther King, Jr. riveted world attention to the substandard wages and working conditions of the African-American garbage collectors – was part of an upsurge of organizing among minority and blue-collar workers in municipal service jobs that spread public sector unionism throughout the South, boosting the membership of the American Federation of State, County, and Municipal Employees (AFSCME) over the million mark.

The growth of feminism in the 1970s helped spur a parallel wave of unionism among white and pink-collar women, including thousands of government social workers, librarians, clericals, classroom aides and others. Unionization among these same groups increased in the private sector as well in the 1970s (Cobble, 2005). To be sure, the valiant efforts by the Service Employees International Union (SEIU) District 925 and other unions to organize private sector clericals in insurance and banking floundered. But clerical and administrative staff in quasi-public settings such as colleges and universities, in publishing houses, and elsewhere successfully organized, raising overall office-worker unionization to 16 percent by the end of the 1980s (Cobble, 1999).

Of equal importance was the continuing growth of unionism in the 1980s and 1990s among low-wage service workers in both the private and public sector, led largely by the SEIU. Launched in the early 1980s, SEIU's "Justice for Janitors" campaign succeeded in organizing some 200,000 private sector janitorial and maintenance workers in little over a decade. By the end of the 1990s, re-built and expanded janitorial locals existed in most of the major metropolitan centers outside the South (Cobble, 1996; Milkman and Wong, 2001). SEIU also reached out successfully to the home care aides who assist the elderly and disabled in their homes. By 1995, some 45,000 home care workers, predominantly Black and Latina women, had signed up in California alone and flourishing union locals existed in Chicago, New York, and other cities. In 1999, after a twelve-year campaign, an additional 74,000 home care workers in Los Angeles County voted for union representation, making it one of the largest single union victories since the massive organizing campaigns among mass production workers in the 1930s (Delp and Quan, 2002; Boris and Klein, 2007). Since the 1999 L.A. victory, momentum continues to build with current home care membership topping 300,000 (SEIU, 2007b).

Most recently, SEIU launched a national campaign among child care workers. One of their first large-scale breakthroughs occurred in April 2005 when 49,000 Illinois family child care providers voted to unionize and then, shortly thereafter, secured a historic contract which not only helped more families afford child care but also raised pay and guaranteed training and access to health care for the providers. Although some center-based child care workers organized with the United Child Care Union, an AFSCME-affiliated union based in Philadelphia as well as with SEIU, the successes have been overwhelmingly among home-based child care providers, with 90,000 joining SEIU in the last two years (SEIU, 2007a; SEIU, 2007c; Smith, 2004: 426–30).

Lastly, SEIU, like the AFT and other unions, has sought to expand unionism in the health care field, often by affiliating nurses and other health care workers already organized into professional associations. Although the American Nurses Association (ANA) dropped its opposition to bargaining in the late 1940s, few of its affiliated state nurse associations seriously pursued the union route. Yet in the last decade, as the registered nursing shortage reached crisis proportion and the conditions of staff nurses worsened, dissatisfaction within nurse associations over how to represent the divergent interests of staff nurses and nurse managers flared. In 1995, the 60,000-member California Nurses Association left the ANA over the issue. By 2004, they had set up a new independent national union for registered nurses and had a growing membership outside California. Seventeen percent of nurses are now affiliated with one of the many unions vying to represent them, making them among the more organized occupational groups in the U.S. (Gordon, 2005b).

## Expanding Service Worker Unionism

The obstacles to expanding service worker unionism are formidable, particularly in the U.S. private sector, where employers wield enormous power, largely unconstrained by law or political considerations. Despite polls showing that a majority of U.S. workers desire collective representation at work (Freeman, 2007: 83–5), actually winning a union election and securing a contract is far from easy. The National Labor Relations Act (NLRA), the federal law passed in 1935 to foster private sector collective bargaining, currently exempts from protection some one-third of the private sector labor force, including domestic and agricultural workers; professional, managerial, supervisory and "confidential" employees; and the so-called "independent contractors" or "self-employed" (Cobble, 1994; U.S. General Accounting Office, 2002). In addition, many organizing campaigns conducted under NLRA auspices face legal delays and employer opposition that render guarantees of freedom of choice and the right to collective association farcical. The number of workers fired in organizing campaigns continues to rise in the U.S., and because many employers refuse to negotiate first contracts even *after* a majority of workers has voted for union representation only a third of all union victories currently result in a signed contract (Compa, 2003: 32–52; Freeman 2007: 80–2).

Any expansion of private sector service worker unionism in the U.S. will depend in part on the degree to which this hostile legal and social environment can be modified. Indeed, U.S. labor law presents particular obstacles to organizing many service workers (Cobble, 1994; Cobble and Merrill, 1994). U.S. labor law assumes a long-term, continuous relation to a single employer. Bargaining units are worksite based and elections are conducted over a period of months or years. Yet many service workers move from job site to job site, "working the circuit" as it is known among waitresses. The long, drawn-out election procedures typical under the NLRA framework make organizing a mobile workforce difficult, since few stay with one employer long enough to utilize the conventional election procedures and card-signing associated with NLRA-based worksite organizing. The restraints on secondary boycotts, sympathy and secondary strikes, mass picketing, and other kinds of economic action inscribed in U.S. labor law also make it difficult for workers, particularly those in small establishments or in sectors of the economy where sub-contracting is prevalent, to exert much economic pressure on their employers.

In order to organize successfully in today's service sector, U.S. unions must figure out innovative ways of exerting pressure on recalcitrant employers and bypassing an ill-suited and archaic legal framework. And not surprisingly, many of the most successful campaigns to date in the U.S. have relied on such nontraditional organizing strategies as will be detailed later in this chapter. U.S. unions, both in the CTW federation as well as within the AFL-CIO, also are mounting political and public relations campaigns to call attention to the constricted state of worker rights and freedom of association and to push for a major overhaul of labor law.[4]

These ongoing efforts to address the problems of employer hostility and legal constraints on organizing in the U.S. are necessary and commendable. Yet service worker unionism in the U.S. as well as in many other service economies will remain a marginal and minority movement until there are comparable efforts to transform unions themselves. Labor movements as we know them today arose over a half century ago as institutions premised largely on meeting the needs of a mass production factory workforce. The *majority* of workers, however, are now doing different kinds of work, often in quite different kinds of work settings. In part, the ability of organized labor to recognize these discontinuities and remake itself to attract this new workforce will determine whether this new majority opts for paternalistic, individualistic, or collective strategies to improve the terms and conditions of their employment. The re-making of unions will need to be fundamental, involving a transformation of union institutions, cultures, and values. New models of unionism must be invented – models that are more appropriate for a post-industrial service workforce.[5]

Service workers are often found in work settings that differ dramatically from those common to the manufacturing workforce of the recent past.[6] Many tend to be found in smaller establishments (restaurants, retail shops, dental offices) where employee-employer relations may be personal and collaborative rather than adversarial, formalized, and highly bureaucratic. The employment relationship is not the classic one described by Marx, nor is it even the conventional us-versus-them world view that often prevails in large bureaucratically-run enterprises. The line between employee and employer is more indistinct than in the traditional, blue-collar, mass production factory.[7]

In addition, a new third party, the customer, complicates and transforms the old dyad. Many service workers, in fact, perceive this third party as *more* important in determining their wages and working conditions than the employer (Cobble, 1991a: 44–8). This attitude prevails regardless of whether the worker's income is derived wholly from the customer (the professional in private practice or the self-employed home cleaner), only partially so (the waiter, bartender, or cab driver), or not at all (the nurse or teacher).

Lastly, many jobs in the service sector are occupationally rather than worksite- based, and therefore exist more in an external than an internal labor market. In the former, lateral mobility is crucial for improving one's wages and career prospects as well as for escaping bad management or a declining customer base. Furthermore, the education and training required for these occupations is usually external to the employer and less firm-specific. A unionism modeled on the worksite-based unionism dominant among industrial workers, with its emphasis on job security in an individual firm, firm-based rather than portable benefits, and vertical rather than lateral mobility is a poor fit for today's service workforce. In a break from industrial union traditions, many service workers need a unionism that facilitates rather than retards employee "exit," and that continues to represent and advocate for them as they move from job to job. In other words, they need an organization that provides portable benefits, enhances access to life-long learning and training opportunities and increases their employability and so-called "human capital." Cobble (1991a; 1991b) has called this approach "occupational unionism" and has documented its appeal to waitresses and other non-factory workers before the rise of mass production unionism in the 1930s. Aspects of this model would appeal to a significant portion of the service workforce today.

## New Organizing Strategies

Some unions, as we have seen, have risen to the challenge and successfully organized in the service sector. What lessons can be learned from these successful campaigns? Can they be replicated in other settings, among other groups of service workers? Are these victories the advance guard of a more large-scale revitalization of service worker unionism that might rival the industrial upsurge of the 1930s?

The home care organizing drives of the 1990s offer the richest case for analysis. In many ways, home care unionization is the model for how organizing low-wage service workers, particularly those in front-line or interactive service jobs, can occur. The home care campaigns built on the strategies used in organizing janitors in the 1980s, but they also moved beyond them. The strategic key to the janitorial victory, according to Stephen Lerner (1991), director of the Building Service Division of SEIU, was a rejection of the site-by-site NLRA-style organizing typically used by most unions. Rather than organize the individual subcontractors or cleaning vendors who hire and supervise a janitorial workforce scattered across hundreds of cleaning sites in downtown office buildings, SEIU targeted all janitors in a particular region or labor market.[8] They also used civil disobedience, political pressure, community boycotts, and "shaming" publicity, going after the subcontractor's employer – mainly commercial landlords – and their tenants (Howley, 1990). But they cleverly wielded the carrot as well as the stick, proposing in the recent Houston campaign, as in others, that the wage hikes agreed to by unionized employers would not take effect until a majority of employers in the local labor market had agreed to sign. This awareness of the need to lower the union wage penalty on organized employers helped to gain the initial cooperation of employers and positioned the union as an ally of high-road employers in ensuring that the bottom-feeders would not gain an undue share of the market.[9]

Home care organizers adopted many of these same non-traditional approaches. Home care aides, like janitors, are scattered across various worksites; typically, they work alone in individual homes tending to the needs of the elderly and the disabled. Many of the leaders of the home health-care organizations were steeped in the community-based organizing approaches of the National Welfare Rights Organization, the United Farm Workers, and the Association of Community Organizations for Reform Now (ACORN). These community-based strategies blended well with SEIU's desire to move beyond worksite campaigns in their labor organizing. The union orchestrated campaigns that embraced all home care aides within a particular locale and that drew upon local institutions and community leaders for support (Kelleher, 1986, 1994; Walker, 1994; Boris and Klein, 2007). In the case of janitors and home care aides, ethnic and racial bonds as well as occupational ties helped forge and sustain worker solidarity across worksites. In Los Angeles, for example, where the "Justice for Janitors" campaign secured its initial crucial breakthrough, four-fifths of cleaners were Hispanic, with many recent immigrants from Mexico (Pastreich, 1994). Similarly, home care aides, as noted earlier, are primarily African American and Latina women (Kilborn, 1994).

Many home care groups reached out to the clients as well, making the case that raising wages for aides would help clients secure the best aides and maintain uninterrupted quality service. Since social service agencies often pay the wages of home care aides from Medicaid and other public funds (although clients may hire and supervise their aides), clients could support wage increases for their "employees" without having to pay their increases themselves. Clients did express fear, however, that unionization might lessen their control over aides (Walker, 1994).

In California, SEIU was particularly successful in building alliances with home care clients. In the early stages of organizing, SEIU realized that a political campaign would be necessary simply to overcome the legal obstacles. Home care aides were not "employees" under the NLRA definition; neither was there an "employer" with whom the union could bargain. SEIU therefore began to organize the clients as well as the aides. Many of the clients had been active in the disability movement for years and were not only "organizable" but also politically sophisticated. Their support helped convince the state to set up an "employer of record" who could bargain with the union over the wages and working conditions of home care workers. In other regions, SEIU created important alliances with civil rights organizations, churches, and senior groups (Boris and Klein, 2007).

Many of today's successful organizing drives across a wide range of work settings combine grassroots or "bottom-up" pressure with "top-down" pressure on employers (Milkman and Wong, 2001). The janitorial and home care campaigns confirm the importance of adopting this dual strategy. Yet the home care example points to one of the key reasons why unionization has risen among service occupations since the 1960s and why it continues to outpace unionization in other sectors. Like earlier campaigns among teachers, nurses, and other front-line service workers in health care and education, home care workers were conscious of creating a unionism which could help solve the problems of both service producers and service consumers. Not only would the union work to advance the economic status of its members; it would seek to improve the lives of those in the larger community.

The child care campaigns, now modeled in large part on the winning strategies in home care, reflect this same emphasis. SEIU and other unions organizing child care workers are careful to forge alliances with parents and repeatedly stress the ways in which improving caregiver pay and working conditions enhances the quality of care recipients receive (Whitebook, 2002; Smith, 2004). The first union contracts negotiated by family child care providers in the states of Washington, Illinois, and California translated these ideas into reality by expanding state child care subsidies to working families, increasing the number of nutritious meals available to children, and instituting pay raises based in part on meeting higher standards of quality care (SEIU, 2007c; SEIU, 2007d). The July 2007-June 2009 Collective Bargaining Agreement between SEIU Local 925 and the state of Washington, in addition to guaranteeing higher wages, training and benefits to 12,000 family child care providers, pledges increased access to quality child care for every Washington state family and specifies that "the rights of the Consumer (s) to select, change or terminate their child care provider" will be protected (SEIU 2007d).

## New Representational Practices

Finding innovative ways of relating to all three parties of the "service triangle" – employers, workers, and customers – proved key to successful union organizing in service economies. But unions must transform their representational practices as well as their organizing strategies if they are to win the allegiance of the twenty-first-century workforce. In particular, they will need to move beyond a representational model based on the realities of the mass production factory floor and pay greater attention to the lives and concerns of the new "emotional proletariat" (Macdonald, this volume). Wages will remain an issue, of course, as will restraining abusive employers. Nevertheless, service workers want unions that help them affect the rules governing the employee–customer/client/patient relationship and that help them move toward more of a "bread and roses" unionism – a unionism, that is, which not only secures a decent standard of living but also fosters individual growth and more satisfying relationships between workers and between workers and those they serve. In the section that follows, we will discuss the new models of union representation that are emerging among clericals, teachers, and nurses. Then we will assess the degree to which these new representational practices might be appropriate for other service workers, particularly those in more "working-class" service occupations.

The Harvard Union of Clerical and Technical Workers (HUCTW), organized in 1988 after over a decade of struggle, is one of the best examples of a union that is attuned to the particular needs of the workers it represents (Eaton, 1996; Putnam and Feldstein, 2003: Savage, 2007). As epitomized in one of the union's organizing slogans, "You don't have to be anti-Harvard to be pro-union," the Harvard organizers refused to conduct an anti-boss, anti-employer campaign. Instead, they assumed that clerical workers cared about the enterprise in which they worked and about the quality of the service they delivered and so they emphasized open-ended concerns such as dignity, voice, and the recognition of the value of clerical services.

Once HUCTW secured recognition, it pushed hard on economic issues, including a long, drawn-out battle over winning raises and benefit parity for part-time employees. Yet the union also invested a lot of energy in meeting the nonmaterial needs of members as well. Union priorities included making work more interesting and rewarding, creating opportunities for learning and problem-solving, and improving the quality of relationships between employees at work and between employees and others with whom they interacted on a daily basis such as students, faculty, and administrators. When the Harvard administration offered "skills training" for clerical workers in how to handle "customer encounters" with irate and demanding students and faculty (the worst) with one lesson instructing the attendees to "think of yourself as a trash can" – a vessel that would simply fill up with everyone's ill humor throughout the day and then could be dumped after work – the union decided it needed an alternative. It insisted on its own training classes in "negotiating relationships." Their goal was to end the "customer is always right" rule and develop more humane norms for clerical-customer interactions.

In her 1983 book, *The Managed Heart*, Arlie Hochschild argued that many service jobs require "emotional labor" or the expenditure of energy to create an emotional state in the customer, client, patient, or passenger. She called for a new workplace movement that recognized workers' right to protect their emotions (their heart) and to establish their own "feeling rules" in much the same way as factory and other manual workers insisted a century ago on the right to protect their bodies from unwarranted abuse. Unions interested in representing service workers need to heed her call, whether it involves challenging the top-down scripting of Harvard secretaries, the "smile rules" for grocery store clerks instituted in 1999 by Safeway in Oakland, California, or the intensive personality remolding that was once required of flight attendants (Cobble, 1996; 2001).

The unions that represent teachers and nurses also are pioneering new models of representation. Before the spread of collective bargaining in the 1960s, the professional associations in this sector focused on what they defined as "professional concerns": status, control over workplace decisions affecting the worker-client relation, ability to set standards for competence, and the overall health of the enterprise or sector. Gradually, these organizations shifted their emphasis to more traditional union matters: salaries, benefits, seniority rights, and job protection. Yet, as Charles Kerchner and Douglas Mitchell (1988) observe for teacher unions, many are now moving toward a "third stage of unionism" in which they are concerned with the welfare of the overall educational system and with meeting the needs of their students as well as with protecting their own interests as employees (see also Kerchner et al., 1997).

Indeed, the most appealing organizations for professional service workers may be those that meld the best of both the professional association and collective bargaining traditions into a new organizational form. In her work on nurses, Pat Armstrong argues that, taken separately, neither the older model of professionalism nor the traditional collective bargaining unionism "neatly fits" the needs of nurses. In her view, a reconceived nurses' organization would concern itself with preserving the "ethic of care" as well as the status of the occupation. It would build on the best of the professional traditions – the concern for the patient and for expanding health care as a social right – without abandoning the union emphasis on "equity, collective rights, and improving conditions of work and pay" (Armstrong, 1993, p.320).

Macdonald and Merrill (2002) have made a similarly compelling argument for how child care unions should develop a strategy for upgrading or professionalizing child care work that retains a "vocabulary of virtue" and a notion of nurturance as skilled and worthy of recognition. The self-esteem and moral identities of the child care workers they studied were intimately bound up with being "altruistic carers" as well as being "good" at what they did. They wanted their "nurturing capacities" recognized through higher pay – a desire they legitimized as both good for them and for those they served. They also wanted "their willingness to make sacrifices for the benefit of care recipients" acknowledged and valued (Macdonald and Merrill, 2002: 68, 75).

Some would argue that for those stuck at the bottom of the income hierarchy, the union promise to raise wages is enough. We would say that wages are a good place to begin but not to end. Workers at every step of the ladder deserve and desire both monetary and social/subjective recognition (Macdonald and Merrill, 2002). Employers have been surprisingly successful in winning the loyalty and effort of non-supervisory workers by instituting what some have called a more modern form of "welfare capitalism." In this new "psychological contract," employees are not offered high wages or job security or even health or pension benefits. Rather, they are provided with skill training and other kinds of individual empowerment and cultural capital. In one study of young workers in "white-collar working-class jobs" involving a high degree of autonomy and work-flow management, Vicki Smith (1996) found that the communication classes the employer offered were seen as "real benefits" by the workers. The workers felt empowered in negotiations with customers over work specifications; they also believed they had gained valuable cultural capital that would help them move into management. Their personal relationships off the job improved as well.

Unions too should pay attention to the nonmaterial needs of workers. College-educated workers certainly have higher expectations about what the workplace should provide in the way of challenge and intellectual stimulation. But those stuck at the bottom also need "roses." Opportunities for learning and self-improvement, and a workplace that provides a sense of community and belonging are important to all workers and hence should be important to their unions as well.

## Beyond Collective Bargaining

Winning contracts with employers and increasing union density are crucial to improving the lives of service workers. Having a contract at work has often meant a lessening of employer autocracy and unfairness, opportunities for worker participation and leadership at the workplace, and greater economic and personal security. The economic benefits in terms of enhanced wages and benefits are sizeable. As Andy Stern, President of SEIU, puts it: "Unions are the best anti-poverty program America has invented."[10]

Yet it is important to emphasize that historically the labor movement has always relied on a range of strategies to improve the status of workers. It has lobbied for fair labor standards, including wage floors, hour limits, and health and safety controls; it has utilized law suits and public pressure to change employer practices. As we move into the twenty-first century, it is crucial that the new service worker unionism not forget this expansive history.

The NLRA may limit its coverage to "employees" and hence exclude independent contractors, the self-employed, and a range of others with "managerial" or "entrepreneurial" characteristics. But the labor movement need not draw its membership boundaries in the same way. A number of unions have experimented with organizing "independent contractors." This kind of big tent movement should be encouraged since a smaller and smaller proportion of the workforce are now technically "employees" in the old-fashioned sense of the term, which emphasizes lack of decision-making, dependence on a single employer, and income solely through wages or salary.

The labor movement must also define itself as about more than collective bargaining. As Janice Fine (2006) and Jennifer Gordon (2005a) have documented, new worker-run community-based organizations among immigrants, often referred to as worker centers, now exist in over a hundred cities across the country. Relying on litigation, negative publicity, and direct action organizing, some have had a substantial impact on low-wage service workers, chalking up impressive political and economic gains. Members of the Long Island Workplace Project, for example, lobbied the Unpaid Wages Prohibition Act past a Republican-dominated legislature and New York's Republican governor in 1997, requiring hefty penalties on employers who failed to pay for work and upgrading the enforcement of minimum wage and other labor laws (Gordon, 2005a). In 2003, the domestic worker center in New York won a municipal ordinance setting wage floors and other standards governing the lives of the army of nannies who now take care of the children of more elite New Yorkers and is making progress on state legislation (Fine, 2007).

Historically, self-help and fraternal organizations of workers existed prior to and alongside traditional contract unions. Today they are multiplying, with various websites facilitating the discussion of training, employment opportunities, and "tips of the trade," all activities long associated with professional development and advancement. One thriving and public-relations-savvy group, Working Today, founded in 1995, brings together freelancers and other "independent workers" for advocacy, health insurance, and professional services such as job referrals and negotiating techniques.[11]

New forms of cross-class solidarity are emerging as well with the flourishing of NGOs and other kinds of organizations whose members, primarily middle-class and professional, are dedicated to improving the conditions of workers. The involvement of middle-class allies has been crucial in instigating and sustaining movements across the globe that have drawn attention to the undervaluation and indignities of much service labor. The International Labor Organization's (ILO) campaign to make all work "decent work," for example, will disproportionately affect service workers, concentrated as they are at the bottom of the heap as well as initiatives to raise the global wage floor and convince more nations to honor the basic labor and human rights set forth by UN declarations and inscribed in various ILO and other international conventions and treaties. These developments are particularly important for the new migrant service workforce which often is not covered by either labor or discrimination laws in the countries in which they work (Ontiveros, 2007). Representing these workers will take a new service worker unionism. It will also take a transformation of labor law, government regulation, and public opinion.

## Intellectual Allies or Adversaries?

We think intellectuals have a role to play in this transformation. Theory does matter. Public opinion (as well as public policy) is influenced by the failure of economists and others, for example, to move beyond the older industrial paradigms that still dominate their accounts of labor productivity and value. Since at least the 1960s, economists have predicted that the transition to a service economy would lead to an inevitable slow-down in the rate of productivity growth; and, consequently, to the end of the continually improving living standards that have been the hallmark of the industrial age (Baumol, 1967; Fuchs, 1968). Services are, according to this line of thought, inherently resistant to the kinds of productivity gains that have marked goods-producing sectors since at least the industrial revolution, primarily because of the posited labor-intensive character of most service work. Productivity gains could be and have been realized in the goods-producing sector, so the argument goes, because most goods can be made by machines and with their assistance, a given hour of labor can be made to yield more goods, more cheaply. Machines cannot, however, reduce the labor content of most personal services. They cannot, for example, raise children, care for the sick or disabled, groom bodies, or flatter vanities as well as people can, and it seems unlikely that they will ever be able to do so. Because they cannot, it is held, service work is inherently resistant to traditional productivity gains; and, as a result, service employers will ever only be able to pay low wages.

How much can service sector employers pay? Will it ever be enough to provide service workers a decent standard of living? In the goods-producing sectors, the revenue required to pay workers well has come in part from raising productivity – i.e. increasing the number of items a given worker can make – and then selling this increased output at lower prices in order to expand the total revenue earned by the firm. It is now clear that in many service industries technical innovation can yield significant productivity gains.[12] Does anyone doubt that Wal-Mart could afford to raise employee pay as well as provide employees with better health care, education, and pension benefits? All that seems to be missing from the equation is what Charles Craypo (1986, p.28) has referred to as "the ability to make employers pay" – an organized presence in the industry that raises the bargaining leverage of its employees.

However, where caring and emotional labor are as important, if not more so, than information processing, productivity-enhancement will require a different strategy. In these cases, productivity gains depend less upon technical innovations than upon improvements in (perceived) quality and what economists call "demand elasticity." Head for head, turning a $5 barber into a successful $50 hair stylist raises their productivity ten-fold, even if it changes their work not at all. It all depends on whether customers are willing – and able – to pay ten times more for a hair cut. In other words, for the most labor-intensive service sectors, an increase in productivity is as much dependent on customers' perceptions of the service they are receiving as it is upon their effective willingness to pay more for it. Where the customers receive, or at least *believe* they receive, a different, more desirable service, they have shown themselves willing to pay the price.

To put the point differently: the productivity of most front-line service work is dependent upon the imputed value that the wider society places on the work and on those who do it. It is also dependent on the ability of those who want the service to pay more for it. The first of these issues is closely bound up with efforts to raise the social position of low-status work, especially personal service work, and of low-status workers, especially women and people of color. In these respects, the effort to organize service workers has been, and will remain, closely connected to feminist and other social movements seeking liberty and justice on an expanded scale. Similarly, winning intellectual support and thus legitimacy for efforts to raise service sector wages by recasting theories of productivity and value will need to be a broadly-based academic enterprise that draws on the now widespread literature challenging the devaluing of women and of historically female activities (see, for example, Devault, 1994).

On one level, this revaluation literature calls into question the usefulness of traditional notions of "productivity," which focus on physical outputs when measuring the relative contribution of jobs that require mental or emotional labor. Without a tangible product, the effort involved in service work often seems invisible. Moreover, even where "effort, skill, and responsibility" can be calculated, however imprecisely, ideology shapes the quantities measured. "Productivity" and "value" are deeply subjective, despite the quantitative apparatus involved. Mothering and other domains of female expertise, for example, are often thought instinctual and hence devalued. The perceived worth of the person affects the perceived worth of what they produce, whether it be tangible or not. A vicious cycle ensues in which those paid more are seen as being more worthy and hence more productive. And, conversely, those paid less are judged as less productive.

In this regard, many feminist scholars have zeroed in on the work of "caregiving" and its devaluation, arguing rightly that its underpayment in the market must be understood in the larger context of household exchange and the sexual division of labor (for example, England and Folbre, 1999). Raising the standards for service workers then is as much about gender hierarchies as it is about class inequalities. The debates among care work theorists over how to dismantle the former, particularly when care work is defined broadly to include the physically-demanding cleaning labor done predominantly by minority women (Duffy, 2005), have much to offer economists and others writing from within a more quantitative tradition in which gender is still largely absent as a category of analysis.

But service employers must not only be *willing* to pay more, they must also be *able* to pay more. If raising the productivity of service work in the most labor intensive occupations depends in part on raising the price of those services (as in the barber to hair stylist example above), the ability of customers to pay the higher costs must also be raised. In this sense, the improvement in the conditions of service workers is dependent upon the continuing betterment of the rest of society. Such is precisely the "historical tendency of capitalist accumulation," as described first by Marx (1863: 927–30), and then subsequently rediscovered by Clark (1940), Fuchs (1968), Bell (1973) and other mainstream economists and sociologists. With this difference: where Marx believed the end result of the historical tendency of capitalist accumulation was an increasing number of immiserated industrial proletarians and heightened class conflict, the mainstream economists and sociologists who came after him have generally been happy to celebrate the arrival of a new class of "knowledge workers," whose ambiguous class position they believed helped to explain the apparent softening of class conflict in the developed world.

It is certainly true that since the 1920s industrial capital in the developed countries has been "disaccumulating," to use Martin Sklar's term (Sklar, 1992: 143–96; see also Warsh, 2006), bringing with it the progressive disappearance of industrial workers and the continuing expansion in the number of service workers. But the drive to improve the economic and social conditions of service workers is directly dependent upon the continuing improvement in the economic well-being of society as a whole, and not, as in Marx, upon its "immiseration." The new service workforce will do well only if the rest of the society also does well along with it.

Of course, the distribution of income will need to flatten, with the bottom and the middle having more and the top having less. A flatter distribution of income would more accurately reflect the distribution of actual effort and productive contribution than it currently does, and would be an overall gain in fairness and efficiency wholly to the society's benefit. As things now stand, the large gains accruing to those at the top of our "winner-take-all" global economy, where a slight competitive edge yields disproportionate and continuing rewards, both economically and politically, have thrown the social structure seriously off center (Frank and Cook, 1996). The continued expansion of service unionism and the rise of a larger social justice movement will do much to expand the middle class and to ensure a more balanced distribution of social power, just as did the political and economic reform efforts of industrial workers two generations ago.

## Notes

1 The concept of the "imaginary," introduced into contemporary social theory by Cornelius Castoriadis (*The Imaginary Institution of Society* [1975: *trans.* 1987]), evokes the whole array of imaginative resources – metaphoric, theoretic, linguistic – with which people both constitute social reality and attempt to understand it.

2 The CTW federation consists of unions representing almost six million organized workers. These unions left the AFL-CIO at the July 2005 Convention and set up their own rival federation.

3 In the U.S., union density is a measure restricted to dues-paying employees in workplaces where employers have signed collective bargaining contracts.

4 For further information on the educational and political campaigns now underway, see American Rights at Work at www.americanrightsatwork.org.

5 New global union structures will be necessary as well but are beyond the scope of this chapter. For the problems of current global union institutions and a proposal for a new global unionism, see Lerner 2007.

6 Ritzer (for example, 2004) stresses the deskilling and rationalization of work in the service sector, positing the continuing spread of McDonald-like processes to an ever wider array of work settings. We agree, however, with Herzenberg, *et al.* (1998: 11–14, 42–43) that "tightly-constrained" rationalized work systems make up a small minority of all service environments. Even when employers favor rationalization, they are constrained in its implementation by

their dependence on the creativity and judgment of those providing the service (Benson 1988; Cobble 1991a; Leidner 1993; Korczynski 2002).

7 We part ways with scholars who emphasize inherent impediments to organizing service workers and assume that mass production workplaces are easier to organize and factory workers more amenable to "class" or collective consciousness. Before the advent of mass production unionism, construction, trucking, garment, restaurant and other workers scattered in dispersed worksites organized quite successfully in the U.S. (Cobble 1994). In addition, many service workers may not exhibit the same kind of "class consciousness" associated with mass production workers but that does not mean they are devoid of collective sentiment or of a sense of solidarity with those in similarly-exploited situations (see, for example, Korczynski 2003).

8 Here our emphasis differs from the now extensive literature which sees union revitalization as a matter of pursuing an "organizing or social movement unionism" as opposed to a "service or business unionism" (for example, Turner and Hurd 2001; Lopez 2004). Clearly, if unions are to organize workers, they will need to commit themselves to do so. At the same time, the most successful unions organizing in the U.S. today, including the majority of unions in the CTW federation, are former AFL "business unions," and they draw liberally on the occupationally-oriented approaches relied on in their past (Cobble 1991b; Milkman 2006).

9 Our analysis in this section underscores the conclusion of Heery (2002), Korczynski (2002), and others that researchers need to move beyond the either/ or debate over "adversarial unionism" versus "employer partnerships." Both strategies are necessary and the fastest-growing unions such as SEIU employ both effectively to advance worker interests and power. For further information on the Houston strategy, see http://www.seiu.org, accessed July 6, 2006. For an analysis of how SEIU and other U.S. unions use card check and neutrality agreements to lower employer hostility to unionizing, see Eaton and Kriesky (2001).

10 Stern Interview conducted by Leslie Stahl and aired on "60 Minutes." To view, www.ctw.org, accessed July 3, 2006.

11 Consult www.freelancersunion.org, accessed July 26, 2007, for more information. See also TECHSUNITE.org, sponsored by the Communications Workers of America, AFL-CIO.

12 See Gregory and Russo (2007) for a recent study documenting that the service sector is as productive as the goods sector, across a range of countries and over time, when measured on a product supply basis.

## References

Armstrong, P. (1993) "Professions, unions, or what? 'Learning from nurses'," in L. Briskin and P. McDermott (eds.), *Women Challenging Unions*, Toronto: University of Toronto Press, 304–21.

Baumol, W. J. (1967) "Macroeconomics of unbalanced growth: the anatomy of urban crisis," *The American Economic Review*, 57, 3 (June), 415–26.

Bell, D. (1973) *The Coming of Post-Industrial Society*, New York: Basic Books.

Benson, S.P. (1988) *Saleswomen, Managers, and Customers in American Department Stores, 1890–1940*, Urbana: University of Illinois Press.

Boris, E. and Klein, J. (2007) "We were the invisible workforce: unionizing home care," in D.S Cobble (ed.), *The Sex of Class: Women Transforming American Labor*, Ithaca: Cornell University Press, 177–93.

Clark, C. (1940) *The Conditions of Economic Progress*, London: Macmillan.

Cobble, D.S. (1991a) *Dishing It Out: Waitresses and Their Unions in the Twentieth Century*, Urbana: University of Illinois Press.

Cobble, D.S. (1991b) "Organizing the post-industrial work force: lessons from the history of waitress unionism," *Industrial and Labor Relations Review*, 44 (April), 419–36.

Cobble, D.S. (1994) "Making postindustrial unionism possible," in S. Friedman, R.W. Hurd, R.A. Oswald, and R.L. (eds.), Seeber *Restoring the Promise of American Labor Law*, Ithaca, NY: Cornell ILR Press, 285–302.

Cobble, D.S. (1996) "The prospects for unionism in a service society," in C. Macdonald and C. Sirianni (eds.), *Working in the Service Society*, Philadelphia: Temple University Press, 333–58.

Cobble, D.S. (1999) "A spontaneous loss of enthusiasm: workplace feminism and the transformation of women's service jobs in the 1970s," *International Labor and Working-Class History*, 56 (Fall), 23–44.

Cobble, D.S. (2001) "Lost ways of unionism: historical perspectives on reinventing the labor movement," in L. Turner, H.C. Katz, and R.W. Hurd (eds.), *Rekindling the Movement: Labor's Quest for Relevance in the 21ˢᵗ Century*, Ithaca, NY: Cornell University ILR Press, 82–96.

Cobble, D.S. (2005) "A 'tiger by the toenail': the 1970s origins of the new working-class majority," *Labor: Studies in Working-Class History of the Americas*, 2:3 (Fall), 103–14.

Cobble, D.S. and Merrill, M. (1994) "Collective bargaining in the hospitality industry," in P. Voos (ed.), *Contemporary Collective Bargaining in the Private Sector in the 1980s*, Ithaca, NY: Cornell University ILR Press, 447–89.

Compa, L. (2003) "Workers' freedom of association in the United States: the gap between ideals and practice," in J.A. Gross (ed.), *Workers' Rights as Human Rights*, Ithaca, NY: Cornell University Press, 23–52.

Craypo, C. (1986) *The Economics of Collective Bargaining*, Washington, DC: The Bureau of National Affairs, Inc.

Delp, L. and Quan, K. (2002) "Homecare worker organizing in California: an analysis of a successful strategy," *Labor Studies Journal*, 27, 1, 1–23.

Devault, M.L. (1994). *Feeding the Family: The Social Organization of Caring as Gendered Work*, Chicago: University of Chicago.

Dolvik, J.E. and Waddington, J. (2005) "Can trade unions meet the challenge? Unionisation in the marketised services," in G. Bosch and S. Lehndorff (eds.), *Working in the Service Sector: A Tale from Different Worlds*, London: Routledge, 316–41.

Duffy, M. (2005) "Reproducing labor inequalities: challenges for feminists conceptualizing care at the intersections of gender, race, and class," *Gender and Society*, 19, 1, 66–82.

Eaton, A. and Kriesky, J. (2001) "Union organizing under neutrality and card check agreements," *Industrial and Labor Relations Review*, 55, 1 (October), 42–59.

Eaton, S. (1996) "The customer is always interesting," in C. Macdonald and C. Sirianni (eds.), *Working in the Service Society*, Philadelphia: Temple University Press, 291–332.

England, P. and Folbre, N. (1999) "The cost of caring," *Annals* 561 (January), 39–51.

Fine, J. (2006) *Worker Centers: Organizing Communities at the Edge of the Dream*, Ithaca, NY: Cornell University Press.

Fine, J. (2007) "Worker centers and immigrant women," in D.S. Cobble (ed.), *The Sex of Class: Women Transforming American Labor*, Ithaca, NY: Cornell University Press, 211–30.

Frank, R. and Cook, P. (1996) *The Winner-Take-All Society: Why the Few at the Top Get So Much More Than the Rest of Us*, New York: Penguin.

Freeman, R.B. (2007) *America Works: Critical Thoughts on the Exceptional U.S. Labor Market*, New York: Russell Sage Foundation.

Fuchs, V.R. (1968) *The Service Economy*, New York: National Bureau of Economic Research, distributed by Columbia University Press.

Gordon, S. (2005a) *Suburban Sweatshops: The Fight for Immigrant Rights*. Cambridge, MA: Harvard University Press.

Gordon, S. (2005b) *Nursing Against the Odds: How Health Care Cost Cutting, Media*

*Stereotypes, and Medical Hubris Undermine Nurses and Patient Care*, Ithaca, NY: Cornell University ILR Press.

Gregory, M. and Russo, G. (2007) "Do demand differences cause the U.S.-European employment gap?" in Mary Gregory, W. Salverda and R. Schettkat (eds.), *Services and Employment: Explaining the U.S.-European Gap* (eds.), Princeton: Princeton University Press, 81–109.

Heery, E. (2002) "Partnership versus organising: alternative futures for British trade unionism," *Industrial Relations Journal*, 33, 1, 20–35.

Herzenberg, S., Alic, J. and Wial, H. (1998) *New Rules for a New Economy: Employment and Opportunity in Postindustrial America*, Ithaca, NY: Cornell University Press.

Hochschild, A. (1983) *The Managed Heart: The Commercialization of Human Feeling*, Berkeley, CA: University of California Press.

Howley, J. (1990) "Justice for janitors: the challenge of organizing in contract services," *Labor Research Review*, 15 (Spring), 61–72.

Kelleher, K. (1986) "Acorn organizing and Chicago homecare workers," *Labor Research Review*, 8 (Spring), 33–45.

Kelleher, K. (1994) Telephone interview with the head organizer, SEIU local 880, Chicago, conducted by J. Nagrod, October 17.

Kerchner, C. and Mitchell, D. (1988) *The Changing Idea of a Teachers' Union*, New York: The Falmer Press.

Kerchner, C., Koppich, J.E. and Weeres, J.G. (1997) *United Mind Workers: Unions and Teaching in the Knowledge Society*, San Francisco, CA: Jossey-Bass.

Kilborn, P.T. (1994) "Home health care is gaining appeal," *New York Times*, August 30, A14.

Korczynski, M. (2002) *Human Resource Management in Service Work*, Basingstoke: Macmillan Palgrave.

Korczynski, M. (2003) "Communities of coping: collective emotional labour in service work," *Organization*, 10, 1, 55–79.

Leidner, R. (1993) *Fast Food, Fast Talk: Service Work and the Routinization of Everyday Life*, Berkeley, CA: University of California Press.

Lerner, S. (1991) "Let's get moving: labor's survival depends on organizing industry-wide for justice and power," *Labor Research Review*, 18, 2, 1–16.

Lerner, S. (2007) "Global unions: a solution to labor's worldwide decline," *New Labor Forum*, 16,1 (Winter), 23–37.

Lopez, S. (2004) *Reorganizing the Rust Belt: An Inside Study of the American Labor Movement*, Berkeley, CA: University of California Press.

Macdonald, C.L. and Sirianni, C. (eds.) (1996) *Working in the Service Society*, Philadelphia: Temple University Press, 1–28.

Macdonald, C.L. and Merrill, D. (2002) "It shouldn't have to be a trade: recognition and redistribution in care work advocacy," *Hypatia*, 17, 2, 67–83.

Marx, K. (1863) *Capital: A Critique of Political Economy, Volume One*. Translated by B. Fowkes, Harmondsworth, Middlesex, England: Penguin Books, 1976.

Milkman, R. (2006) *L.A. Story: Immigrant Workers and the Future of the U.S. Labor Movement*, New York: Russell Sage Foundation.

Milkman, R. and Wong, K. (2001) "Organizing immigrant workers: case studies from Southern California," in L. Turner, H.C. Katz, and R.W. Hurd (eds.), *Rekindling the Movement: Labor's Quest for Relevance in the 21st Century*, Ithaca, NY: Cornell University ILR Press, 99–128.

Mills, C.W. (1951) *White-Collar: The American Middle-Classes*, New York: Oxford University Press.

Murphy, M. (1990) *Blackboard Unions: The AFT and the NEA, 1900–1980*, Ithaca, NY: Cornell University Press.

Ontiveros, M. (2007) "Female immigrant workers and the law: limits and opportunities," in D.S. Cobble (ed.), *The Sex of Class: Women Transforming American Labor*, Ithaca, NY: Cornell University Press, 235–52.

Pastreich, M. (1994) Telephone interview conducted by J. Nagrod, September 20 and October 4.

Putnam, R. and Feldstein, L.M. (with D. Cohen) (2003), *Better Together: Restoring the American Community*, New York: Simon and Schuster.

Ritzer, G. (2004) *The McDonaldization of Society, Revised New Century Edition*, Thousand Oaks, CA: Pine Forge Press.

Savage, L. (2007) "Changing work, changing people: a conversation with union organizers at Harvard University and the University of Massachusetts Memorial Medical Center," in D.S. Cobble (ed.), *The Sex of Class: Women Transforming American Labor*, Ithaca, NY: Cornell University ILR Press, 119–39.

Service Employees International Union. (2007a) "Child care providers win big for 60,000 children in Washington state." http://www.seiu.org/public/child_care/ccpwb.cfm, accessed July 14.

Service Employees International Union. (2007b) "Illinois child care victory," http://www.seiu.org/public/child_care/il_providers_unite.cfm, accessed July 14.

Service Employees International Union. (2007c) "Winning agreements in Illinois, Washington, and Oregon," http://www.seriu.org/public/child_care/put_kids_first.cfm, accessed July 14,

Service Employees International Union, Local 925. (2007d) *2007–2009 Collective Bargaining Agreement by and between State of Washington and SEIU 925, effective July 1, 2007 through June 20, 2009*. Seattle, Washington. SEIU925.

Simms, M. (2003) "Union organizing in a not-for-profit organization," in G. Gall (ed.), *Union Organizing: Campaigning for Trade Union Recognition*, London and New York: Routledge.

Simms, M., Stewart, P., Delbridge, R., Heery, E., Salmon, J. and Simpson, D. (2000) "Unionising call centre workers: the communication workers' union campaign at typetalk," Working Paper, Cardiff Business School, Cardiff, Wales.

Sklar, M. (1992) *The United States as a Developing Country: Studies in U.S. History in the Progressive Era and the 1920s*, Cambridge: Cambridge University Press.

Smith, P.R. (2004) "Caring for paid caregivers: linking quality child care with improved working conditions," *University of Cincinnati Law Review*, 73, 2 (Winter), 399–431.

Smith. V. (1996) "Employee involvement, involved employees," *Social Problems*, 43, 2 (May), 460–73.

Tannock, S. (2001). *Youth at Work: The Unionized Fast-Food and Grocery Workplace*, Philadelphia: Temple University Press.

Turner, L., Lowell. W., and Hurd, R. (2001) "Building social movement unionism: The transformation of the American labor movement," in L. Turner, H.C. Katz, and R.W Hurd (eds.), *Rekindling the Movement: Labor's Quest for Relevance in the 21ˢᵗ Century*, Ithaca, NY: Cornell University ILR Press, 9–26.

U.S. Department of Labor. Bureau of Labor Statistics. (2006) "Union members in 2005," Press release, January 20. Available at http://www.bls.gov/pub/news.release/union2.txt.

U.S. General Accounting Office. (2002) "Collective bargaining rights: Information on the number of workers with and without bargaining rights," GAO-02-835. September.

Walker, Harold (1994) Telephone interview with the lead organizer, Home Care Division, SEIU Local 250, San Francisco, conducted by J. Nagrod, November 3.

Warsh, D. (2006) *Knowledge and the Wealth of Nations: A Story of Economic Discovery*, New York and London: W.W. Norton & Company.

Whitebook, M. (2002) *Working for Worthy Wages: The Child Care Compensation Movement, 1970–2001*, Berkeley, CA: Institute of Industrial Relations, Center for the Study of Child Care Employment.

CHAPTER **10**

# Conclusion – Latte Capitalism and Late Capitalism

*Reflections on Fantasy and Care as Part of the Service Triangle*

YIANNIS GABRIEL

American tourists visiting cafés in Italy, the story goes, are advised not to ask for "latte," their favorite drink. They risk being given a glass of milk and incurring severely disapproving looks from the barista and other customers. Italian baristas are generally fast learners; they know perfectly well what American tourists are after and they usually oblige even if they fail to suppress a snigger; occasionally, however, they may decide to have a bit of fun and offer the unsuspecting tourist a glass of white milk.

The temptation to talk of "latte capitalism" as a preferable alternative to the social scientists' beloved "late capitalism" is strong. Charging a hefty mark-up for a cup of frothy milk with a shot of acqua sporca may seem to epitomize the rationale of value observed by several of the authors who have contributed to the admirable collection of chapters that make up this book. It lies at heart of merchandising, identified by Bryman as a crucial feature of Disneyization of society; it can be found behind the reinvention of the $5 barber into a $50 hair stylist noted by Cobble and Merrill; it can even be observed in Charlie Chaplin's magic transformation of a dull piece of mouse-trap cheese into illustrious Emmenthal by drilling some holes in it, as we are reminded by Sayers and Monin in their splendid commentary of the Red Moon Café scene in *Modern Times*. It captures, of course, the reasoning behind Ritzer's mischievous thesis of the globalization of nothing. What can be more vacuous than the froth that makes up a large part of the average glass of café-latte, or, for that matter, many of the global offerings of today's capitalism? It is after all the branding, the framing, the packaging where value is magically created rather than in the back-breaking labor of coffee producers who typically receive less that 3 percent of the price of the average cappuccino sold in Britain's cafés (The Fairtrade Foundation, 2002).

I am not seeking to imply that branding, framing, packaging, hyping and all the other activities necessary to create enchantment and luxury for the consumer are without value. Far from it, they depend vitally on an imaginary of resources that include language, pictures, sounds, textures and smells whose deployment requires, as several authors here remind us, work, whether it be called imagination, emotional labor, aesthetic labor or merely messing around with ideas. This may be back-harming work in a different way from that of coffee producers, as excitable employees brainstorm, trying to identify market gaps and dream up unique selling propositions.

This, however, is not the only type of service work socialized and commodified in late capitalism. Equally, as several of the contributors in this anthology remind us, a large part of service work is care work, most especially caring for the young, the old, the sick and the weak. Carmen's work (see contribution by Rhacel Salazar Parreñas, this volume) looking after the children of her Italian employer while her own children in the Philippines are cared for by a paid carer hardly qualifies as "nothing" in Ritzer's global trading. It is instead a continuation of two age-long phenomena associated with capitalism – the ever-expanding commodification of different aspects of social life and the vast dislocations of people to work across countries and continents. Much of this care work is unglamorous and unspectacular, yet profoundly emotional. Sayers and Monin again remind us of the caring aspect of feeding in several key scenes of *Modern Times*, as when Charlie feeds his supervisor or when he becomes the victim of mechanized feeding, feeding stripped of its caring dimensions and reduced to the logic of production and consumption. The mother's milk, rather than the commercial latte, is the prototype for this – care, positive or negative, is rooted in every human's early life experience of being cared for by somebody else. As an aspect of service work, care work has not received the attention that it merits – this is something that several of the authors who have contributed to this collection have sought to do and their contribution is to be welcomed.

My aim, in this concluding chapter, is to disentangle some of the emotional dynamics involved in the interaction between service worker and customer. In the past, much of this has been approached through the powerful but partial perspectives of labor process theory and theory of emotional labor. The dynamics of control, resistance and identity delineated for the industrial worker have been reconfigured for service work, through the realization that emotion is an important dimension of the service provided to the customer. Emotional labor involves the performance of different emotional scripts, dictated by different circumstances, specific to different jobs and the requirements of different employers. Thus the battle for control of emotional scripts and performances, resistance to exploitative emotional demands and other such phenomena have been sharply delineated (see, for example, several contributions in Sturdy *et al.*, 2001). In spite of the considerable strengths of this approach, it presents, in my opinion, only a partial view, one that tends to deny emotions any autonomy, subordinating them to cognition and the logic of capitalist controls. Emotions, according to this view, are socially constructed or even scripted to suit the logic of management and profit generation. If emotions are socially constructed along with every other social construction they follow the logic of power and privilege; they become capital ("emotional capital") to be deployed as legitimate basis to accumulate privilege, power and profit.

Now, I do not wish to deny the systematic commodification of emotions, aptly captured in the title and subtitle of Hochschild's (1983) path-opening book *The Managed Heart: Commercialization of Human Feeling*. This, however, is rather too narrow a conception, as an increasing number of scholars are now beginning to realize. Some, recent contributions to the emotional labor debate have noted that people at work often engage with others emotionally in ways that are not directly tied into the formal job requirements (most obviously, developing warm and supportive relationships with either co-workers or customers in the workplace out of personal choice) (see, for example, Bolton, 2005). Korczynski (2003), for his part, has referred to groups of employees forming warm and supportive emotional relationships as "communities of coping."

Emotions, I shall argue in this chapter flow from inner reality, much as they are channeled and controlled by outer reality. This is especially relevant to service interactions which may not follow rationalizing and controlling scripts – such interactions may entail flirtation (Guerrier and Adib, 2000; Hall, 1993), harassment (Folgero and Fjeldstad, 1995), emotional blackmail (Rosenthal *et al.*, 2001) or toxic exchanges (Stein, 2007). In this chapter, I will probe deeper into the emotional dynamics at the interface of the service worker and the customer to argue that they retain aspects that are unmanaged and unmanageable. Instead of looking at emotional performances as dictated solely by the logic of capital accumulation, I wish to examine them through a different prism. Emotional performances dictated by profit making cannot be considered independently of the feelings that are unleashed by the relation between service worker and customer.

Resistance as well as conformity to scripted performances can arise from feelings that are left out of emotional scripts. I shall argue that service worker and customer may arouse in each other feelings that are far more powerful, pervasive and potentially explosive than any script provided by management. I will then propose that these feelings are linked to the deeper symbolic processes evoked by the relationship between carer and cared for. Service worker and customer can then become fantasy objects for each other, arousing strong and ambivalent emotions noted by Korczynski (this volume) and others. Ambivalence, I will argue triggers off unconscious defenses of splitting – thus, the customer is liable to split into two distinct images in the eyes of the service worker; one is demanding, obnoxious and parasitical; the other is needy, human and deserving. Likewise, the service worker is liable to split into two distinct images in the eyes of the customer – one is helpful and caring, the other is indifferent and arrogant. These dynamics are linked to early life experiences of infantile dependency why each child is dependent on another for his/her sustenance and survival and cannot be fully domesticated within neatly pre-arranged emotional scripts. I will conclude by examining some of the implications of this line of thinking which highlights fantasy as a dimension of the service interface.

The rise of contemporary consumerism has forced a radical re-evaluation of a broad range of organizational and business phenomena. In the field of organizational studies there has been a wide-ranging recognition of the emergence of a triangle (Leidner, 1991) involving the worker, the manager and the customer, whose endlessly mutating dynamics form the basis of a wide range of organizational processes. Politics, identity, structure, culture and so forth can no longer be viewed from a perspective of the old fashioned tug-of-war of control, power, resistance and conflict between workers and bosses. Instead they must be viewed through a "lens" that acknowledges the triadic nature of contemporary work and organization. Triads, as Simmel (1950) recognized a long time ago, are radically different configurations from dyads. They are more unstable, they involve potentially shifting alliances and conflicts in which the third party can be the stakes or the beneficiary. The entry of the consumer as an important figure into the world of organizations has therefore not just complicated matters, by sometimes tipping the balance in unexpected and ambiguous ways. It has radically reshaped the nature of contemporary work, the more so as different parties of the triad are frequently found to swap masks and adopt each other's position. The worker is also employee as indeed is the manager. The manager becomes worker in her dealings with her superiors and customer in her relations with different departments within the same organization. The customer often re-enters an organization as manager or worker.

The rise of consumerism has prompted many theorists to explore the processes of value creation through innovation, branding, merchandizing and so forth. The cathedrals of consumption, like shopping malls, tourist destinations, theme parks and so forth, have been submitted to exhaustive scrutiny as have the immense varieties of images, spectacles and shows that seek to bewitch and bewilder consumers. Equally intensive have been the explorations of new work regimes designed to provide consumers with such experiences. What is less widely examined by theorists of organizations is the changing nature of care in a regime of consumerism. This is particularly interesting in the light of two significant developments, one historical and one theoretical. Historically, the rapidly aging population in the heartlands of consumerism calls for increased levels of care work. People in developed and developing countries live longer and are prepared to go to ever greater lengths to prolong their agonies of death. This translates into constantly increasing demands for caring for the elderly and for the infirm, a demand that may be met by relatives, by the state, by freelance workers (especially immigrants) or by a variety of voluntary and other organizations.

The second development is theoretical rather than historical. The last twenty years have seen a great deal of interest in the ethics of care among scholars such as moral philosophers and psychologists approaching ethics from feminist and environmental perspectives. Since the publication of Carol Gilligan's (1982) important and controversial book, caring for others has been increasingly recognized as a vital dimension of most human interactions and as the foundation of a particular type of morality, usually referred to as "ethics of care" (Held, 2006; Kittay and Feder, 2002; Ruddick, 1989; Tronto, 1993). In contrast to the "ethics of justice" that have long dominated the thinking of moral philosophers, ethics of care theorists argue for a different system of morality, one that does not rely on dubious claims of universality, absolute judgments of right and wrong, and perfect virtues. Instead, they advocate a morality that grows out of a recognition that all people are relations, being dependent on others for their survival and well-being and capable of supporting others in their moments of need and helplessness.

Care is attending to the needs of others to whom we feel close and for whom we are prepared or expected to take responsibility. It is not a scripted emotional performance but involves a wide range of actions, concerns, utterances and feelings that grow out of sensitivity and concern for the needs of those close to us. A fundamental aspect of the ethics of care is that those close to us and in direct contact with us are experienced as entitled to more care and attention than those distant and unknown.

Those who conscientiously care for others are not seeking primarily to further their own individual interests; their interests are intertwined with the persons they care for. Neither are they acting for the sake of all others or humanity in general; they seek instead to preserve or promote an actual human relation between themselves and particular others.

(Held, 2006, p12)

Interest in the ethics of care grew as a result of the argument, first put forward by Gilligan, that many girls follow a different path of moral development from boys, one that does not revolve around rights, rules and abstract principles of justice, but centers on compassion, care and the ability to sustain intimate relationships. Since then, a great deal of work on the nature of care has been done by psychologists and philosophers alike, leading to an increased recognition of the importance of care in all human relations.

While numerous debates are still unfolding on different dimensions of caring (most especially on its standing as an independent moral principle), there is a fair degree of agreement on the following:

1 Every child spends a prolonged period of dependence into the care of others – this leaves deep residues for later life; caring for others and being cared for are experiences that are liable to awaken powerful emotions from a person's earliest past and evoke reminiscences of infantile dependency and powerlessness (e.g. Ruddick, 1989).

2 Caring is relational and there are limits in the extent to which it can be depersonalized or mechanized; machines may facilitate care work but cannot replace the work of the carer (e.g. Sevenhuijsen, 1998).

3 Caring for another person is an individualized form of work – it relies on face-to-face interaction; in this sense, it resists bureaucratization and formalization (e.g. Bubeck, 1995).

4 Caring evokes complex emotions in both the carer and the cared for; these include gratitude, envy, fear and anxiety and are liable to entail ambivalence (e.g. Ruddick, 1989).

5 In spite of their importance, caring activities are systematically devalued, underpaid, and disproportionately occupied by the relatively powerless in society (e.g. Tronto, 1993).

6 Caring and being cared for are vitally important, if problematic, aspects of individuals' identities (e.g. Meyers, 2002).

Now, for all the attention that care has received by philosophers and psychologists, it seems to me to be seriously under-theorized by social and organizational theorists, especially as a feature of consumer capitalism. Yet, as several of the contributors to this volume remind us, care is a major aspect of much service work – indeed, Dorothy Sue Cobble and Michael Merrill argue that understanding workers' ethic of care can be a key point of departure for service work unionization. Care also defines the predominant character of many occupations (such as nursing, teaching, therapy, counseling, and so forth) including many of those working with the elderly, the sick and the young. Care work is heavily gendered both as domestic labor and across virtually all the so-called caring professions which are characterized by low status and low pay. In spite of the considerable aptitudes and talents it demands (not least hard emotional work), care work is widely viewed as low skill and low cost. Contrasted to the high value of latte, care work is decidedly low value. It therefore neatly conforms to the outsourcing and off-shoring logics of our times. Outsourcing and off-shoring are not only strategies of multinational corporations noted by Ritzer and Lair (this volume), but also of individuals and families as they seek to transfer responsibility of caring for elder relatives, younger children or needy dependents onto others as is argued by Parreñas (this volume).

In a culture that lionizes the sovereign consumer who spends her money as she pleases (the figure familiar to us from the service triangle) the individual dependent on the care of others cuts a distinctly dejected figure. Being cared for, whether by relatives, by the state or by other organizations, cannot shake off its associations with dependency, decay and failure. As Fraser and Gordon (1994) have demonstrated the concept of dependence has not only gradually narrowed down to represent a fault or failure of individuals, but it has been feminized and racialized to set it up as the "other" of independence, particularly as represented by the Anglo male wage-earner. The carer as well as the cared for are tarnished by this association with dependence. In a prototypical way, the caring mother as much as the cared for child are seen as enmeshed in dependency relations decidedly inferior to the myth of independent men going about their businesses as they please (Meyers, 2002). The mother's caring relationship to her child renders her dependent to a purportedly independent man who assumes a privileged position in this relationship. Caring for others thus creates a secondary or derivative dependency (Fineman, 1995; Kittay, 1999); it becomes a fetter, holding back careers, identities and achievements and, above all else, restricting freedom.

Yet, in spite of such negative associations, a caring orientation to work and to others retains elements of being a valued quality, even in our highly narcissistic and individualistic culture. A "caring person" may not be the commonest self-description seen in today's inflated résumés but remains the description of a valued and valuable person. Thus, inasmuch as caring is a feature of service work, a deep ambivalence, noted by Korczynski (this volume), becomes a central feature of such work, one in which the "customer" is seen both as a source of dissatisfaction, but also of satisfaction.

The customer generates now affectionate feelings of care and consideration, now resentful feelings of vengefulness and envy. What are we to make of this ambivalence, also noted by other eminent commentators of service work within contemporary consumerism (e.g. Sturdy, 1998)?

One revealing way in which the term "care" is used today are when it is said about a person, often a "leader," that "He does not care," habitually accompanied with "He only cares about himself." The affinity between servant and leader has been explored by Greenleaf (1977; 1978). Caring is one of the most powerful fantasies that followers project onto their leaders (Gabriel, 1997). Leaders who care are those who are willing to give generously their time, advice, recognition and support, who are genuinely concerned for the realization of a mission or a project and who are prepared to treat others with consideration and respect, rather than as pawns on a chessboard. By contrast, leaders who do not care are those who treat others as means to their own aggrandizement, are those who lack generosity and sensitivity. Although caring is often seen as a sign of altruistic orientation, caring leaders are by no means averse to conflict, hardness and resolution. On the contrary, the real test for caring leaders comes when they have to fight in order to defend those for whom they care, rather than opt for easy compromises and convenience. Far from being a soft and universally mild attitude, caring means taking responsibilities for others and being prepared to take personal risks in discharging such responsibilities. The same can be said about the caring attitude of service workers, whether they work in overtly caring occupations, such a nurses and social workers, or as employees in call centers or retail outlets. An employee who cares for the customer is one who is prepared to "go the extra mile" in order to offer a proper service and, by the same token, a company that cares for its customers is one that is prepared to face its responsibilities even if this has an adverse impact on bottom lines. This quality of "going the extra mile" or "going beyond the call of duty" seems to be a very important feature of care.

Another significant element of care that is frequently commented upon by "ethics of care" theorists is the personalized bond that links people (see, e.g. Held, 2006). Care seems to eschew the principle of equality in the most blatant manner. A mother will discriminate in favor of her child with modest concern for the implications of this for other mothers and other children. She will barge to the head of every queue in the interest of her child, she will bend every moral principle if the interest of the child demands it, since she views categorical imperatives and absolute norms as secondary to the pressing needs of her child. In the same manner, a caring employee who seeks to address the needs of the customer is standing in front of him, face-to-face, with scant regard for the implications of this for other customers. This creates a hierarchy among customers, most evident in the case of hospital queues.

I had ample opportunity to observe both of these aspects of care (i.e. "going the extra mile" and disregarding the principle of equality) during a recent round of interviews and focus groups with clinical staff in a London hospital aimed at identifying different ways in which "patient care" is socially constructed. Several of the staff interviewed identified "care" with the special attention given to specific patients, often at the expense of other patients. This is evident in the following comment by a junior doctor in a Gynaecology department:

A pregnant woman came in through A&E [Accident and Emergency]. She was having problems with her pregnancy. I asked the registrar what to do. They decided that the best thing to do was get the woman scanned to find the problem. However, being a night shift there were no porters to be seen and the scanning units were closed. I felt that the anxious woman could not stay in A&E surrounded by drunks and druggies as it was inappropriate. Instead of calling for porters, which would have taken time, I and the registrar moved the pregnant lady to the maternity ward ourselves where we opened up a scanning unit to find out what was wrong with the lady's pregnancy. I was proud of the leadership that I had received from my registrar; not every registrar would have done this but he solved the problem and delivered good patient care in the process. The problems were resolved within an hour with only skeletal night staff.

The contrast between the individualized care for the deserving patient expressed in this quote contrasts sharply with the indifference towards the plight of the anonymous "drunks and druggies" whose treatment was negatively affected by the preferential treatment offered to the pregnant woman. In his contribution to this anthology, Marek Korczynski observes the same ambivalence in many service employees between feelings of closeness to the needy and deserving customer and feelings of resentment towards the others. This ambivalence is linked to a split between two images of the customer in the minds of those who care for them. On the one hand, there is the deserving customer, the customer with a human face who is often a "regular"; this customer is invariably an individual with individualized tastes and needs, who evokes affection and sympathy. On the other hand, there is the hard "sovereign" customer, who is often seen as privileged, regal, pampered and parasitical, who provokes resentment and envy. At times the two images may merge into one, generating simultaneous affection and antipathy.

These two polar images of the customer can be viewed as social constructions – they recur in numerous contexts and, as Korczynski notes, they are familiar to most researchers who carry out field research on service work. But beyond being social constructions, the split images of the consumer as all-good and deserving and all-bad and undeserving are fantasies, which, I would like to propose grow out of early childhood experiences of helplessness and dependency. Freud (1926) noted that, compared to all other primates, the human child appears to be born prematurely, spending a prolonged period in a state of total dependency, when he/she can undertake no actions of his/her own and must rely on others for the satisfaction of every one of his/her needs. This has a favorable effect on the bonding process between the child and his/her parents, who appear omnipotent, but it creates, in the child, acute feelings of anxiety lest its needs should not be met. Even short periods of separation from the mother and the ensuing frustration can lead to acute rage on the part of the child. Subsequently, situations of extreme helplessness are liable to evoke feelings of anxiety and powerful fantasies similar those experienced in the earliest period of life.

Freud's theory of the consequences of infantile dependence was further developed by psychoanalyst Melanie Klein (1987) who identified the nature of the fantasies evoked by these situations. She argued that the key feature of these fantasies is a psychological splitting between good and bad. Splitting was viewed by Klein (1987) as the most primitive defense against anxiety, and in particular the anxiety created by ambivalence, i.e. the simultaneous experience of something as something as bad and good. Splitting first becomes manifested when a child desires the maternal breast and fails to find it. The breast is then imagined as two separate objects, a "good breast" that is always available and nourishing and a "bad breast" that is absent or withheld. Subsequently, the child projects the split onto the mother herself who at times is experienced as a "good mother," caring and available, and at times as "bad mother," cold and indifferent. The splitting of objects into good and bad "part objects" is later adopted as a way of coping with the anxiety provoked by objects that are both good and bad. Klein extended her theory to include other defense mechanisms but continued to view "splitting" as a fundamental process which is regularly deployed in later life.

It is now possible to argue that the caring dimension of the service relationship can reawaken in both care worker and cared for customer some of the fantasies first experienced by them in early life. They each become for the other objects of fantasy and desire, charged with extreme positive or negative qualities, rather than ordinary people caught up in a contractual relationship. The customer can then experience the service worker as generous, helpful and considerate or, conversely, as withholding, unhelpful and deliberately impudent. Equally, the service worker may experience the customer as a deserving and needy subject or, conversely, as a spoilt and undeserving. In each case, powerful emotions are generated, infusing the worker-customer relationship with some of the potentially explosive qualities we associate with family relationships.

That the relation between service worker and customer can become so charged with fantasy and emotion should not surprise us. The "servant" has long been a familiar character in myths, stories, parables, drama and literature. The character of Figaro who gives his name to a prominent French newspaper represents the servant who, without directly confronting his master, learns how to manage him, not least by reading and exploiting his master's emotions, reminding us that the control of emotions of other is not the sole prerogative of those in power. The master-servant relationship with its ambiguities and subtleties is explored in numerous works of art. Moxnes (1999) has argued that the servant represents an archetype, a highly charged symbolic image that springs from the collective symbolic heritage of humanity flowing through each and every human being (Jung, 1968). He argues that the servant exists in both positive and negative variants – as loyal, dedicated, caring and giving or, conversely, as malevolent, treacherous, devious and mendacious. Whether the servant should be included in the great archetypes of humanity may be disputed, but it seems to me that the something of the multifaceted quality of the relationship between master and servant is present in most service relationships, including those that are mediated by consumerist and capitalist structures. Servant and master are not fixed on a simple Marxist axis of exploitation and oppression. They are caught in a relationship that involves trust and mistrust, loyalty and resentment, identification and distancing, emotional manipulation and emotional neutralization. They know many of each other's secrets and therefore have a disproportionate ability to inflict damage on each other. It is a relationship which constantly has the potential of veering towards fantasy, and like all profound forms of human bonding invariably harbors unpredictable and potentially unmanageable possibilities.

What are the implications of looking at the relationship between service worker and customer through the prism of fantasy rather than through the now dominant theory of emotional labor? In the first instance, the ambivalence of emotions becomes immediately transparent, along with their disproportionate intensities and their ability to mutate into different and unpredictable ones. More importantly, however, once we acknowledge that the emotional lives of people in a service relation cannot be scripted in line with the expediencies of efficiency, control and profit, we are forced to recognize that the interface between service worker and customer entails unmanaged and unmanageable elements, including flirtation, tenderness, antipathy, jousting, repartee, gossip and so forth. Sometimes, this interface may blossom into passion and full scale romance (e.g. Mano and Gabriel, 2006), and in not a few cases it can lead to violence (e.g. Diamond, 1997; Pearson *et al.*, 2001).

Let us recapitulate. The arrival of consumerism and the service economy, as all contributors in this anthology recognize, has changed the nature of much contemporary work and the character of many organizations. Service work has introduced complexities and ambiguities that were not evident in traditional manufacturing industries; it has also introduced many complexities and ambiguities in the manner that people construct and sustain their identities as workers, managers and consumers. The tug of war between employees and employers has been reconfigured as a customer-worker-management triangle. A substantial body of theory has started to emerge emphasizing the emotional character of much service work and new modalities of management control that generate new forms of resistance. Along with several contributors to this volume, I argue that care work is an important dimension of many forms of service work. Care work cannot be reduced to the enactment of different emotional scripts or resistance to such scripts. Along with "ethics of care" theorists, I proposed that care can neither be mechanized nor bureaucratized the way that many other forms of work can. Instead, I proposed that care work unleashes certain emotional dynamics that stem from early life experiences that all humans have when, in a state of infantile dependency, must rely on others for their survival and well-being. This generates a deep ambivalence both for service workers and their customers, one that has been widely recognized by many of the scholars who have examined in detail the interface between customers and employees. Following the argument of Melanie Klein, I proposed that splitting emerges as one of the crucial defenses through which people seek to cope with such ambivalence. Splitting exacerbates positive and negative images and fantasies by keeping them apart. Fantasy comes to play a far greater role in the experiences of service workers than it does for manufacturing workers, leading to a degree of unpredictability and even unmanageability at the service interface. Attempts to theorize this interface must address this unpredictability and unmanageability.

We have only just started to address the implications of fantasy for the service triangle. Several scholars have looked at consumer fantasies and the way they support and feed contemporary consumerism (e.g. Bauman, 1997; Ritzer, 1999). Fantasy drives people to the "cathedrals of consumption" – tourist destinations, theme parks, shopping malls, museums, movie theaters, cruise ships, casinos and even fast food restaurants. There, many experience quasi-spiritual experiences where "dreams come true" and the world is purged of all that is dirty, ordinary and depressing. Campbell argues that, contrary to Weber's fears, late modernity did not lead to the disenchantment of the world. Many objects we use in our lives are essentially props for different fantasies. Fantasy is "the ability to treat sensory data 'as if' it were 'real' whilst knowing that it is indeed 'false'. . . . It is this 'as if' response which is at the heart of modern hedonism" (Campbell,

1989, p. 82). This hedonism is what Campbell calls the "Romantic ethic," the unending search for pleasure not in physical sensation but in exaggerated emotional excitations and the search for novel and stimulating experiences. A visit to Disneyworld may yield precisely such experiences, which are known to be fantastic but no less pleasurable for it.

Less attention has been paid to the fantasies of workers and those of managers (in short, employees) but it seems to me that they are no less significant. Several clusters of such fantasies can be discerned. One is the fantasy of freedom – that employees have the freedom to leave an organization when they have had enough, a fantasy that mirrors the consumers' fantasy of free choices in open marketplace. This is a fantasy that is especially common for those in professional and managerial jobs and it may be acted out in frequent job changes and the new patterns of career familiar from the work of scholars like Sennett (1998). A different set of fantasies derives from employees appropriating the perceived glamour and power of his or her organization and visualizing themselves as part of a winning team or brand. They may then construct their identities around idealized images of their employer, by internalizing what Schwartz (1987) has referred to as the "organizational ideal." In my own work I have tried to capture this set of fantasies through the metaphor of a glass palace that easily mutates into a glass cage (Gabriel, 2005). In place of Weber's foundational image of an iron cage which chokes individuality and passion, a glass enclosure is one that invites fantasy and display, emotional and aesthetic, reflecting the visual sensitivities of our times. The glass enclosure encourages people to imagine themselves as objects of beauty and display, as members of casts engaged in creative work, free from constraint.

The argument I developed in this paper on the emotional dynamics of care points at another set of fantasies that bring employees and customers together. These are most evident in the third type of service encounter noted by Leidner (1993) where the product being delivered is integral to the interaction between service worker and service recipient, for example, clinical staff and patients, teachers and students, as well as sex workers and other professionals and their clients. It is not accidental that these types of interaction feature regularly in every kind of contemporary narrative such as film, novel and so forth. Such interactions regularly unleash early life fantasies and desires of power, dependency, submission, vulnerability and many others. These fantasies are not absent, however, from service interactions of the more separable sort, such as those involving waiters, retail workers and call center employees. Such employees may sometimes imagine themselves as the champions of the customer frustrated by the exigencies of efficiency, as being under siege from unreasonable, parasitical or "irate" customers or as being asked to prostitute themselves for the sake of the customer. Fantasies may be directed at customers, at managers or at fellow workers about whom strong positive and negative images are constructed.

If we take the fantasy aspect of service work seriously, we will begin to understand why emotions in such jobs frequently and unexpectedly depart from the scripted set pieces, why they can be in contradiction or conflict with each other, and why they can lead to unexpected and unpredictable turns of events that lend such endless fascination. We will then begin to discern some of the unmanaged and unmanageable aspects of service organizations that at the moment we are rather too eager to disregard or to domesticate.

## References

Bauman, Z. (1997) *Postmodernity and Its Discontents*, Cambridge: Polity Press.

Bolton, S. (2005) *Emotion Management in the Workplace*, Houndsmills, Basingstoke: Palgrave.

Bubeck, D.E. (1995) *Care, Gender, and Justice*, Oxford: Oxford University Press.

Campbell, C. (1989) *The Romantic Ethic and the Spirit of Modern Consumerism*, Oxford: Macmillan.

Diamond, M.A. (1997) "Administrative assault: a contemporary psychoanalytic view of violence and aggression in the workplace," *American Review of Public Administration*, 27, 3, 228–47.

The Fairtrade Foundation. (2002) "Spilling the beans on the coffee trade" – http://www.fairtrade.org.uk/downloads/pdf/spilling.pdf, London.

Fineman, M. (1995) *The Neutered Mother, the Sexual Family, and Other Twentieth Century Tragedies*, New York: Routledge.

Folgero, I.S. and Fjeldstad, I.H. (1995) "On-duty off-guard: cultural norms and sexual harassment in-service organizations," *Organization Studies*, 16, 2, 299–13.

Fraser, N. and Gordon, L. (1994) "A genealogy of dependency – tracing a keyword of the United-States welfare state," *Signs*, 19, 2, 309–36.

Freud, S. (1926) *Inhibitions, Symptoms and Anxiety* (standard edn.), London: Hogarth Press.

Gabriel, Y. (1997) "Meeting God: when organizational members come face to face with the supreme leader," *Human Relations*, 50, 4, 315–42.

Gabriel, Y. (2005) "Glass cages and glass palaces: images of organizations in image-conscious times," *Organization*, 12, 1, 9–27.

Gilligan, C. (1982) *In a Different Voice: Psychological Theory and Women's Development*, Cambridge, MA: Harvard University Press.

Greenleaf, R.K. (1977) *Servant Leadership: A Journey into the Nature of Legitimate Power and Greatness*, New York: Paulist Press.

Greenleaf, R.K. (1978) *Servant, Leader and Follower*, New York: Paulist Press.

Guerrier, Y. and Adib, A.S. (2000) " 'No, we don't provide that service': The harassment of hotel employees by customers," *Work Employment and Society*, 14, 4, 689–705.

Hall, E.J. (1993). "Smiling, deferring, and flirting: doing gender by giving good service," *Work and Occupations*, 20, 4, 452–71.

Held, V. (2006) *The Ethics of Care: Personal, Political, and Global*, Oxford; New York: Oxford University Press.

Hochschild, A.R. (1983) *The Managed Heart: Commercialization of Human Feeling*, Berkeley, CA: University of California Press.

Jung, C.G. (1968) *The Archetypes and the Collective Unconscious*, London: Routledge.

Kittay, E.F. (1999) *Love's Labor: Essays on Women, Equality, and Dependency*, New York: Routledge.

Kittay, E.F. and Feder, E.K. (2002) *The Subject of Care: Feminist Perspectives on Dependency*, Lanham, MD: Rowan and Littlefield Publishers.

Klein, M. and Mitchell, J. (1987) *The Selected Melanie Klein* (1st American ed.), New York: Free Press.

Korczynski, M. 2003. "Communities of coping: collective emotional labor in service work," *Organization*, 10, 1, 55–79.

Leidner, R. (1991) "Serving hamburgers and selling insurance: gender, work and identity in interactive service jobs," *Gender and Society*, 5, 2, 154–77.

Leidner, R. (1993) *Fast Food, Fast Talk: Service Work and the Reutilization of Everyday Life*, Berkeley, CA: University of California Press.

Mano, R. and Gabriel, Y. (2006) "Workplace romances in cold and hot organizational climates: the experience of Israel and Taiwan," *Human Relations*, 59, 1, 7–37.

Meyers, D.T. (2002) *Gender in the Mirror: Cultural Imagery and Women's Agency*, Oxford; New York: Oxford University Press.

Moxnes, P. (1999) "Deep roles: Twelve primordial roles of mind and organization," *Human Relations*, 52, 11, 1427–44.

Pearson, C.M., Andersson, L.M. and Wegner, J.W. (2001) "When workers flout convention: a study of workplace incivility," *Human Relations*, 54, 11, 1387–419.

Ritzer, G. (1999) *Enchanting a Disenchanted World: Revolutionizing the Means of Consumption*, Thousand Oaks, CA: Pine Forge Press.

Rosenthal, P., Pecked, R. and Hill, S. (2001) "Academic discourse of the customer: 'Sovereign beings', 'management accomplices' of 'people like us'," in A. Sturdy, I. Grugulis, and H. Willmott (eds.), *Customer Service: Empowerment and Entrapment*, Basingstoke: Palgrave, 18–37.

Ruddick, S. (1989) *Maternal Thinking: Toward a Politics of Peace*, Boston: Beacon Press.

Schwartz, H.S. (1987) "Anti-social actions of committed organizational participants: An existential psychoanalytic perspective," *Organization Studies*, 8, 4, 327–40.

Sennett, R. (1998) *The Corrosion of Character: The Personal Consequences of Work in the New Capitalism*, New York: Norton.

Sevenhuijsen, S. (1998) *Citizenship and the Ethics of Care: Feminist Considerations on Justice, Morality, and Politics*, London: New York: Routledge.

Simmel, G. (1950) "The Triad" in W. Kurt, W. (ed.), *The Sociology of Georg Simmel*, Glencoe, IL: Free Press, 145–69.

Stein, M. (2007) "Toxicity and the unconscious experience of the body at the employee-customer interface," *Organization Studies*, 28, 8, 1223–41.

Sturdy, A. (1998) "Customer care in a consumer society: smiling and sometimes meaning it?" *Organization*, 5, 1, 27–53.

Sturdy, A., Grugulis, I. and Willmott, H. (eds.) (2001) *Customer Service: Empowerment and Entrapment*, Basingstoke: Palgrave.

Tronto, J.C. (1993) *Moral Boundaries: A Political Argument for an Ethic of Care*, New York: Routledge.

# Index

Learning Resources
Centre